Attack
Politics

PRAEGER SERIES IN POLITICAL COMMUNICATION

Robert E. Denton, Jr., General Editor

Playing the Game: The Presidential Rhetoric of Ronald Reagan
Mary E. Stuckey

Rhetorical Studies of National Political Debates: 1960–1988
Edited by Robert V. Friedenberg

Political Communication in America: Second Edition
Robert E. Denton, Jr., and Gary C. Woodward

Television Access and Political Power: The Networks, the Presidency, and the "Loyal Opposition"
Joe S. Foote

Listening for a President: A Citizen's Campaign Methodology
Ruth M. Gonchar Brennan and Dan F. Hahn

Attack Politics

Strategy and Defense

Michael Pfau
and Henry C. Kenski

Praeger Series in Political Communication

PRAEGER

New York
Westport, Connecticut
London

Copyright Acknowledgments

The author and publisher are grateful to the following for allowing the use of excerpts from:

Pfau, M. & Burgoon, M. (1988). Inoculation in political campaign communication. *Human Communication Research, 15*, 91–111, reprinted with permission.

Pfau, M. & Burgoon, M. (1990). Inoculation in political campaigns and gender. *Women's Studies in Communication*, reprinted with permission.

Pfau, M., Kenski, H. C., Nitz, M. & Sorenson, J. (1990). Efficacy of inoculation strategies in promoting resistance to political attack messages: Application to direct mail. *Communication Monographs, 57*, 1–12, reprinted with permission of the Speech Communication Association.

Library of Congress Cataloging-in-Publication Data

Pfau, Michael.
    Attack politics : strategy and defense / Michael Pfau and Henry C. Kenski.
      p. cm.—(Praeger series in political communication)
    Includes bibliographical references.
    ISBN 0–275–93375–X (alk. paper)
    1. Advertising, Political. 2. Advertising, Political—United
States. 3. Communication in politics. 4. Communication in
politics—United States. 5. Criticism, Personal. I. Kenski, Henry
C. II. Title. III. Series.
    JF2112.A4P33   1990
    659.1'932—dc20   89–29766

Library of Congress Catalog Card Number: 89–29766
ISBN: 0–275–93375–X

First published in 1990

Praeger Publishers, One Madison Avenue, New York, NY 10010
An imprint of Greenwood Publishing Group, Inc.

Printed in the United States of America

The paper used in this book complies with the
Permanent Paper Standard issued by the National
Information Standards Organization (Z39.48–1984).

10 9 8 7 6 5 4 3 2 1

To our wives:
Ginger Nelson Pfau and Margaret Corgan Kenski

Contents

Series Foreword by Robert E. Denton, Jr.   ix

Preface   xiii

1   Attack Messages in American Politics: An Overview   1

2   The Rapid Growth of Attack Politics: The Reagan Era   13

3   Attack Politics and the Election of 1988   39

4   Inadequacy of Present Defenses against Attack Messages   61

5   The Nature of Inoculation   73

6   Application of Inoculation to Political Campaigns   83

7   The Viability of the Inoculation Strategy   99

8   Inoculation and Political Party Disposition   125

9   Inoculation and Individual Differences   139

Conclusion   157

References   161

CONTENTS

Author Index   179

Subject Index   185

About the Authors   193

Series Foreword

Those of us from the discipline of communication studies have long believed that communication is prior to all other fields of inquiry. In several other forums I have argued that the essence of politics is "talk" or human interaction.[1] Such interaction may be formal or informal, verbal or nonverbal, public or private, but always persuasive—forcing us consciously or subconsciously to interpret, to evaluate, and to act. Communication is the vehicle for human action.

From this perspective, it is not surprising that Aristotle recognized the natural kinship of politics and communication in his writings of *Politics* and *Rhetoric*. In the former, he establishes that humans are "political beings" who "alone of the animals is furnished with the faculty of language."[2] And in the latter, he begins his systematic analysis of discourse by proclaiming that "rhetorical study, in its strict sense, is concerned with the modes of persuasion."[3] Thus, it was recognized over fifteen hundred years ago that politics and communication go hand in hand because they are essential parts of human nature.

Back in 1981, Dan Nimmo and Keith Sanders proclaimed that political communication was an emerging field.[4] Although its origin, as noted, dates back centuries, a "self-consciously cross-disciplinary" focus began in the late 1950s. Thousands of books and articles later, colleges and universities offer a variety of graduate and undergraduate coursework in the area in such diverse departments as communication, mass communication, journalism, political science, and sociology.[5] In Nimmo and Sanders' early assessment, the "key areas of inquiry" included rhetorical analysis, propaganda analysis, attitude change studies, voting studies, government and the news media, functional and systems analyses, technological changes, media technologies, campaign techniques, and research techniques.[6] In a survey of the state of the field in 1983 by the same authors and Lynda Kaid, they found additional, more specific areas of concerns such as the presidency, political polls, public opinion, debates, and advertising to name a few.[7] Since the first study, they also noted a shift away from the rather strict behavioral approach.

Then as now, the field of political communication continues to emerge. There is no precise definition, method, or disciplinary home of the area of inquiry. Its domain, quite simply, is the role, processes, and effects of communication within the context of politics.

In 1985, the editors of *Political Communication Yearbook: 1984* noted that "more things are happening in the study, teaching, and practice of political communication than can be captured within the space limitations of the relatively few publications available."[8] In addition, they argued that the backgrounds of "those involved in the field [are] so varied and pluralist in outlook and approach, . . . it [is] a mistake to adhere slavishly to any set format in shaping the content."[9]

In agreement with this assessment of the area, Praeger established the series entitled "Praeger Studies in Political Communication." The series is open to all qualitative and quantitative methodologies as well as contemporary and historical studies. The key to characterizing the studies in the series is the focus on communication variables or activities within a political context or dimension.

One of the most noted developments in political campaigns is the increasing use of negative or attack messages. This book provides a theoretical and empirical examination of the role and impact of attack messages in modern political campaigns. Although such messages have been with us since the founding of our nation, negative advertising has certainly become an intrinsic feature of recent campaigns. Without rendering judgment, this well-researched and informed study carefully reviews the social influence literature that reveals that attack messages work well, are more compelling, are remembered longer, and offer little risk of voter backlash. In addition, the book details the use of attack strategies in recent campaigns and the limitations of existing defenses against such tactics.

But perhaps the greatest contribution of the study is the identification and operationalization of the inoculation message strategy. It is a strategy, based on the work of William J. McGuire, designed to promote resistance to attitude changes when exposed to negative opponent messages.

This pioneering work is based on two large, experimental field studies. The results, carefully explained, indicate that an inoculation strategy deflects the persuasiveness of attack messages. The study further reveals the power of the strategy among all receiver groups, Democrats and Republicans, men and women, educated and uneducated, and young and old.

What makes this book especially valuable and important is the integration of theory and research with the experimental field study. Without question, this book is an important contribution to the field of political communication and of great interest to scholars and practitioners of contemporary campaign politics.

I am, without shame or modesty, a fan of the series. The joy of serving as its editor is in participating in the dialogue of the field of political communication and in reading the contributors' works. I invite you to join me.

Robert E. Denton, Jr.

NOTES

1. See, for example, Robert E. Denton, Jr., *The Symbolic Dimensions of the American Presidency* (Prospect Heights, Ill.: Waveland Press, 1981); Robert E. Denton, Jr., and Gary Woodward, *Political Communication in America* (New York: Praeger, 1985); and Robert E. Denton, Jr., and Dan Hahn, *Presidential Communication* (New York: Praeger, 1986).

2. Aristotle, *The Politics of Aristotle*, trans. Ernest Barker (New York: Oxford University Press, 1970), p. 5.

3. Aristotle, *Rhetoric*, trans. Rhys Roberts (New York: Modern Library, 1954), p. 22.

4. Dan Nimmo and Keith Sanders, "Introduction: The Emergence of Political Communication as a Field," *Handbook of Political Communication*, eds. Dan Nimmo and Keith Sanders (Beverly Hills, Calif.: Sage, 1981), pp. 12–15.

5. Nimmo and Sanders, "Introduction," p. 15.

6. Nimmo and Sanders, "Introduction," pp. 16–27.

7. Keith Sanders, Lynda Kaid, and Dan Nimmo, eds., *Political Communication Yearbook: 1984* (Carbondale, Ill.: Southern Illinois University Press, 1985), p. 284.

8. Sanders et al., *Political Communication*, p. xiv.

9. Sanders et al., *Political Communication*, p. xiv.

Preface

The political attack message, which stresses the negative aspects of an opponent, has grown more popular in contemporary political campaign advertising (Guskind & Hagstrom, 1988; Nyhan, 1988; Schneider, 1988; Taylor, 1986a). Research suggests that voters are quick to criticize attack messages, resulting in an initial backlash against sponsors (Garramone, 1984, 1985; Mann & Ornstein, 1983; Merritt, 1984; Stewart, 1975). However, our research confirms the position of most political professionals who argue that attack messages influence voters (Armstrong, 1988; Ehrenhalt, 1985; Hickey, 1986; Johnson-Cartee & Copeland, 1989; Louden, 1987; Mann & Ornstein, 1983; Martinez & DeLegal, 1988; Moyers, 1984a; Nugent, 1987; Pfau & Burgoon, 1989; Sabato, 1971, 1983; Schneider, 1988; Surlin & Gordon, 1977; Tarrance, 1980; Taylor, 1986a) because they are more compelling, hence more memorable (Ehrenhalt, 1985; Hagstrom & Guskind, 1988; Kern, 1988; Taylor, 1986a), and because in time voters disassociate the content of a message from its origins (Hagstrom & Guskind, 1986; Pfau, Kenski, Nitz & Sorenson, 1989b).

As a result, an important and timely question emerges from contemporary political campaign theory and practice: What can be done to combat the rising tide of attack messages? Short of restricting or banning attack messages, an improbable occurrence given the American judiciary's consistent support for unfettered political expression (Alexander & Haggerty, 1988; Broder, 1989; Neale, 1989), or the voluntary surrender of the attack option, an unlikely step given the widespread perception among political campaign professionals that the attack strategy is an important and effective option (Armstrong, 1988; Ehrenhalt, 1985; Guskind & Hagstrom, 1988; Louden, 1987; Sabato, 1981; Schneider, 1988; Taylor, 1986a), there are a limited number of strategic options available to candidates.

First, candidates can take the initiative and attack first, as employed success-fully by Alan Cranston in 1986 and Frank Lautenberg in 1988. This is a novel, but also high-risk, strategic response for candidates who anticipate attacks from their opponents during a campaign. Second, after an opponent attacks, candidates can and do counterattack. Instead of refuting the charge, candidates launch an assault on the attacker's positions and/or character. However, this is, at best, a damage containment option, since it permits the opponent to set the agenda initially for evaluation of candidates during the campaign.

Finally, candidates can employ a refutation strategy, which features a direct rebuttal to an opponent's attack. However, the refutation message, while an important, post-hoc response option, leaves much to be desired. The refutation option, like the counterattack, is a damage containment strategy, suffering the same limitations. It allows an opponent to seize the initiative in establishing the criteria for candidate evaluation. In addition, it is not clear whether refutation messages are very effective, especially over the long term, following the disas-sociation of the content of the attack and its origins. This problem is further compounded by the fact that refutation messages, by their very nature, call attention to the original attack at the same time they attempt to rebut it.

Finally, refutation messages are completely useless in response to an oppo-nent's attack that is launched in the last days in a close campaign, thus simply precluding a response. This is a particularly telling limitation in light of the growing tendency to hold back one or more particularly controversial political attacks until late in a campaign, as reported during the 1988 presidential primary contests (Colford, 1988a; Nyhan, 1988).

The most effective strategy is for candidates to preempt opponents' attacks prior to their use, thus militating their effectiveness. The preemptive strategy, in which candidates anticipate an opponent's attacks and respond in advance, is considered a new, but promising, option by some consultants (Frantzich, 1989; Salmore & Salmore, 1985; Taylor, 1986a).

Our research program has confirmed the effectiveness of a particular form of preemption, the inoculation message strategy. Inoculation seeks to strengthen the receiver's attitudes against change. It is a strategy designed to promote resistance against changes in attitudes and behaviors (Miller & Burgoon, 1973), thus minimizing the chance that political attacks might influence a potential voter's attitudes.

The strategy is based on William J. McGuire's work on the inoculation con-struct nearly thirty years ago (McGuire, 1961a, 1961b, 1962; McGuire & Pa-pageorgis, 1961, 1962; Papageorgis & McGuire, 1961). McGuire (1970, p. 37) uses a biological analogy to describe the inoculation process. "[W]e can develop disease resistance in a biologically overprotected man or animal; by exposing the person to a weak dose of the attacking material strong enough to stimulate his defenses but not strong enough to overwhelm him." Thus, the inoculation theory maintains that refutational pretreatments, in the presence of a supportive environment, threaten the individual, triggering the motivation to bolster arguments supporting attitudes, thereby conferring resistance to subsequent counter-persuasion.

McGuire and other scholars completed a number of important, experimental studies during the 1960s and 1970s, confirming the efficacy of inoculation in promoting resistance to subsequent persuasion. However, with the exception of our research program, it has been largely ignored by both political campaign scholars and practitioners.

We investigated the potential of the inoculation message strategy to confer resistance to political attack messages in two large, experimental field studies. The first study tested the general efficacy of the inoculation concept on potential voters during the 1986 Abdnor and Daschle Senate campaign in South Dakota. The second study examined the effectiveness of inoculation via direct mail during the 1988 Bush and Dukakis presidential campaign. More than 1,000 potential voters in the Sioux Falls, South Dakota, metropolitan area participated in the inoculation and/or attack phases of the two studies.

The results of the 1986 and 1988 studies clearly indicate that the inoculation strategy promotes resistance to attitude change, deflecting the persuasiveness of subsequent political attack messages which might be launched by an opponent during a campaign, thus reducing the likelihood that political attacks will influence receiver attitudes. Further, the results suggest important nuances that inform the use of the inoculation and refutation strategies using both traditional and direct mail channels in combating the influence of attack messages on voters who differ in political party disposition, gender, education, and age.

This book provides a theoretical and empirical examination of the role and impact of the attack message approach in modern political campaigns, and of inoculation as a strategy to promote resistance to the influence of political attacks. It integrates extant theory and research with the results of our experimental field research on political attack messages and on strategies of resistance to such attacks. As a result, the analysis and data should be of interest both to scholars and students in American politics and political communication, and to political campaign professionals.

We approach this task as scholars interested in the broad areas of social influence and American politics, respectively, who share a common fascination with the specialty of political campaign communication. We are indebted to Michael Burgoon, Professor and Head of the Department of Communication at the University of Arizona, who has done pioneering work in the area of resistance to persuasion, who inspires our own research in social influence, and who played an important role in the 1986 study of inoculation in the Abdnor and Daschle Senate race. We also thank John Sorenson, Professor of Sociology and Head of the Division of Social Sciences at Augustana College, for his polling work for the Center for the Study of Communication, and for his assistance with data analysis on the 1988 study; and Michael Nitz, a graduate student in the Department of Communication at the University of Arizona, for his valuable contributions to the design and implementation of the 1988 study.

Finally, we are grateful to a number of research assistants affiliated with the Center for the Study of Communication at Augustana College for their effort on behalf of the 1986 study (including Greg Abbott, Lisa Clausen, Jean Gilles, Jeff Grell, Geoff Henderson, Lisa Lucid, Jennifer Nelson, Mavis Fodness, Jeff Paulson, Kathy Poppe, Karla Reit, Martha Sichko, Darcy Valentine, Tamara Van Wyhe, and Phillip Voight) and the 1988 study (including Jill Arbogast, David Darr, Ann Jorgensen, Michael Laycock, Marcia Nelson, Michael Nitz, James Olson, William Ryan, Amy Schlotfelt, Kathryn Semmler, and Melanie Weber).

This book is a synthesis of our research program involving the influence of political attack messages. Some of the results of the 1986 and the 1988 studies that are reported in this book have appeared previously in other publications. The chapters that delineate the nature of, and the use of, the attack message strategy, and other results of the two studies that are reported in this book, are appearing for the first time.

We thank Praeger for its commitment to publish scholarship in political communication and for its support of this book. We are particularly grateful to Robert Denton, general editor of the Praeger Series in Political Communication, and to Alison Bricken, the Sociology/Communications editor, for their vision and support for this book from the outset. Finally, we thank Nina Neimark, project editor, and Rebecca Perry, copy editor, for their overall supervision and attention to detail during the editing and production phases of the book.

Attack
Politics

Chapter 1

Attack Messages in American Politics: An Overview

If you don't have something good to say about someone, come sit next to me.

—Alice Roosevelt Longworth
(Matthews, 1988, p. 117)

It's unfortunate, I hate it. But negative campaigns are the mode of the day. They're winning all over. People like them, the same way that they like wrestling and violence in the movies.

—Senator Frank R. Lautenberg
(May, 1988, November 4, p. A13)

The political campaigns of 1988, including the presidential contest, made extensive use of attack messages on television, on radio, and in print. Attack messages were so persuasive, and to many, so disturbing, that they became the object of extensive mass media coverage. One scholar (Jamieson, 1988), frequently interviewed during the 1988 campaign about the use and abuse of attack messages, maintained that, for televised mendacity, the 1988 election was the worst ever. Other analysts (Freund, 1988) argued that the use of attack messages during the 1988 campaign was typical of a well-established American political tradition. Although there are clearly different empirical and normative perspectives on attack politics, there is little doubt about a greater concern by political leaders, the media, and citizens about this phenomenon.

The growth of attack messages has occurred in a political campaign environmental context that has undergone revolutionary changes in strategies and tactics during the last forty years. This book will present an analysis of the problem involving the increased use of attack messages in political campaigns and then explain and demonstrate the viability of a promising strategy of resistance to political attacks, termed *the inoculation message strategy* (Pfau & Burgoon, 1988).

This chapter provides an overview of the problem. It begins by examining attack messages within the overall political message context. It then examines the use of attack messages in two historical periods: (1) Pre-New Deal (1789–1932) and (2) New Deal to Reagan (1932–1979).

TYPES OF POLITICAL MESSAGES

The messages that candidates transmit through paid media consist of four general types, categorized by Stephen Salmore and Barbara Salmore (1985, p. 150) as: "positive messages about themselves, negative messages about their opponents, comparisons of the candidates, and responses to charges by opponents. What type of message a candidate sends is affected by the stage of the campaign, the status of the candidate, and the competitiveness of the race."

Positive messages are designed to promote the positive attributes of a candidate's character, positions, and performance in public office. Most campaigns go through three and sometimes four distinct advertising phases. Positive messages occur most frequently in phase one and phase two of a campaign. "Phase one, early in the campaign employs advertising that stresses name identification. Phase two, with campaigning underway emphasizes advertising that establishes the candidate's position on key issues" (Young, 1987, p. 66).

Attack messages are negative in focus and designed to call attention to a candidate's weaknesses (character and/or issue positions). These messages are of two types. *Negative messages* concentrate entirely on the opponent, and only remind the voter of the alternative at the very end. *Comparative messages*, which some consultants feel are less distasteful to voters, move away from purely negative attacks on the opponent. They look instead at the record of the two candidates, to the advantage of one of them (Salmore & Salmore, 1985). Both negative and comparative messages traditionally have occurred in phase three, well into a campaign after name identification and issue positions have been established. They also have been employed during phase four of campaigns, when during the final days and hours "the campaign relies on saturation advertising over a short period of time to deliver a media blitz" (Young, 1987, p. 66). Conventional wisdom posits that attack messages be used primarily by challengers and not by incumbents, and not until late in the campaign.

Finally, there are *response messages* or rebuttals wherein a candidate responds to an opponent's attacks (Salmore & Salmore, 1985). These normally occur in the third phase when the campaign is well underway. If attack messages are used in campaigns that have a fourth phase, the late media blitz, the recipient of the attack has little or no time to respond.

The attack message strategy has been increasingly criticized in various quarters in recent years and has been termed in the popular press as "negative advertising" (Taylor, 1986a). Although some evidence suggests that strong attack messages can prove counterproductive and result in voter backlash (Garramone, 1984, 1985; Garramone & Smith, 1984; Guskind & Hagstrom, 1988; Mann & Ornstein, 1983; Merritt, 1984; Stewart, 1975), most political professionals and political commentators maintain that attack messages influence voters (Armstrong, 1988; Ehrenhalt, 1985; Guskind & Hagstrom, 1988; Hickey, 1986; Johnson-Cartee & Copeland, 1989; Louden, 1987; Mann & Ornstein, 1983; Moyers, 1984b; Nugent, 1987; Pfau & Burgoon, 1989; Sabato, 1981, 1983; Schneider, 1988; Surlin & Gordon, 1977; Tarrance, 1980; Taylor, 1986a, 1989). As Larry Sabato observes (1981, pp. 165–166), "Going on the offense, 'attack politics,' is becoming more popular because, while vicious, it has gained a reputation for effectiveness among professionals."

At the start of the 1980s, Sabato estimated (1981, p. 166) that nearly one-third of all political commercials were negative, and that the proportion was rising. Richard A. Joslyn (1986) content analyzed 506 televised political commercials over a number of years, offices, parties, and competitive conditions, concluding that 23% were negative or blame-placing. Will Feltus, head of the Washington office of Market Opinion Research, studied 175 Senate campaign ads for 1984, reporting that about half the messages were negative or comparative (cited in Taylor, 1986a). Michael Young observes that negative advertising is a growing proportion of all political advertising. "Experts estimate that today one of two political ads are negative; twenty years ago only about one in five were" (Young, 1987, p. 60). Young further observes that even these figures may understate the extent of negative advertising as some campaigns rely on it almost exclusively. Moreover, "so called independent expenditures—for example, money spent by PAC's without coordination with a candidate—are about 80% negative" (Young, 1987, p. 66).

In the 1986 Senate election, the use of attack messages was so pervasive that one analyst described the campaigns as "accentuating the negative" (Taylor, 1986a), while in the 1988 senatorial and gubernatorial contests the extensive role of attack politics prompted two prominent analysts to label the campaign ads as "In the Gutter" (Guskind & Hagstrom, 1988). One commentator described the 1988 presidential campaign as one of distortions and untruths (Peterson, 1988b); another (Taylor, 1989) described consultants as the new political bosses.

There has been considerable agreement among political practitioners and media analysts that attack messages work. In reviewing the use of attack message strategies for the *Congressional Quarterly Weekly Report*, Ehrenhalt concluded (1985, p. 2560) that, "[while] there is room for argument about whether negative ads will damage the political system in the long term, there is no argument about their short-term impact, they work and they win elections. Voters pay attention to them." Mark Mellman, a Democratic pollster, explains their success as follows: "One of the fundamental facts of psychology is that negative information is processed more deeply than positive information. People say they hate the stuff, but that's not the point. The point is, they absorb the information" (cited in Taylor, 1989, p. A14).

Senator Frank Lautenberg, who used negative advertising in his own 1988 reelection campaign, said: "It's unfortunate. I hate it. But negative campaigns are the mode of the day. They're winning all over. People like them, the same way that they like wrestling and violence in the movies" (May, 1988, p. A13). Eddie Mahe, a Washington-based Republican consultant agrees. "The bottom line is negative works. Most politicians would not say publicly what Lautenberg is saying, but they know it's true" (May, 1988, p. A13).

The attraction of negative advertising is due to several factors. As previously noted, recent research suggests that voters are more influenced by negatives. "Some studies have revealed that voters pay more attention to spots that attack or criticize, recall those spots more accurately, and remember them longer" (Young, 1987, p. 60). Moreover, negative advertising is particularly favored in certain types of campaigns. Candidates who are behind or find themselves slipping in the polls are quite inclined to go negative. The basic thinking here is that there is little to lose and much to gain by attacking an opponent who is pulling ahead. Also, negative messages are used heavily by challengers and those in low-budget campaigns. Negatives are viewed as a possible counterweight to the strong advantages of incumbency. "Low budget campaigns find negatives attractive because they are often cheaper to produce and they can be aired on low cost radio" (Young, 1987, p. 60).

More politicians, including incumbents, are inclined to use negative and comparative message strategies, partly because they know that some consultants can demonstrate which messages work and which don't, and partly because they know that their opponent has the same strategic opportunity and technology at his or her disposal. Democratic pollster Paul Maslin reports that he has moved from revulsion to grudging acceptance to something close to "an addiction." "It's like taking a shot . . . because you can see the way they move the numbers" (Taylor, 1989, p. A14). Moreover, "TV-age politics has created an environment more ripe than ever for 'negative' media, in which a candidate attacks an opponent with great effect. Time and again in recent years, campaigns have been won with negative commercials because the public is more disposed to believe the worst about politicians" (Axelrod, 1988, p. 92).

Attack messages are campaign options available to incumbents and challengers, but traditionally have been employed more by the latter. Most incumbents possess superior name recognition and political impression and job ratings, and frequently face weak challengers that lack electoral experience and adequate finance (Jacobson & Kernell, 1981; Kenski, 1987). In competitive races, both incumbents and challengers tend to employ a mix of message strategies. However, due to recent successes in 1986 and 1988 by candidates using attack strategies and the widespread perception of their efficacy among campaign practitioners, both negative and comparative messages will probably register continued increases compared to positive messages in the coming years. To better understand the various facets of political attack messages, this chapter examines two historical periods, beginning with 1789 to the New Deal.

PRE-NEW DEAL (1789–1932)

Although some commentators appeared overwhelmed by the negative advertising in 1988, its impact may have been due more to the use of television as a communication channel than to the content of the messages. Conventional wisdom posits that, since television is a cool medium, most hard-hitting negative attacks should be used within other more appropriate communication channels, mainly radio and direct mail (Sabato, 1981). Although some negative advertising appeared in television prior to 1986 and 1988, the bulk of it occurred on radio, in newspapers, and in direct mail.

If content were the main criterion of the nastiness or ugliness of political messages, then campaigns were certainly rougher during the era when print was the dominant channel of communication and there was a strong tradition of a partisan press compared to more objective, professional media. The latter really is a twentieth-century development.

In the pre-New Deal era, the message content in print was particularly vicious. Even the revered George Washington was attacked and embittered by stories that he was a dolt, a thief, and a philanderer who offered his beautiful slave women to Mount Vernon's visitors. Denounced from the nation's pulpits and in print as the Antichrist himself, Jefferson captured the White House but said that "I am the target of every man's dirt" (Freund, 1988).

At a time when image candidates became more popular, party organizers developed negative-image campaigns that targeted the opposition. In the election of 1828, for example, both Andrew Jackson and John Quincy Adams were the recipients of strong negative attack messages. "Jackson was hit with the accusation of being a would-be emperor, murderer, duelist, and adulterer," and Adams was attacked as a "monarchist, procurer, and an effete snob" (Melder, 1989a, p. 8).

Melder (1989a) argues that the first major media campaign was the election of 1840. A delightful but sordid tale, it pitted the Democrats against the Whigs in an election where substance was subsumed by style, major issues were avoided, negative attacks were rampant, and novel techniques reigned supreme. The incumbent, Democrat Martin Van Buren, lost to the Whig former military hero, William Henry Harrison.

A technological advancement was the development of a network of Whig newspapers, edited by Horace Greeley and led by his own weekly, named *The Log Cabin*. It reinforced all the campaign imagery depicted during rallies and processions and reached an estimated circulation of 100,000 a week. In it, Van Buren was attacked, among other things, for the profligate waste of public funds in decorating the White House. It was clearly one of the most offensive and effective of the Whig campaign attacks. The Democratic party tried to fight back with its own newspaper, the *Extra Globe*, but it lacked both the circulation and impact of the Whigs' *Log Cabin*. "Ultimately the Democrats had to admit they had been 'out-fought, out-drunk and out-sung'" (Melder, 1989b, p. 234).

The venerable Abraham Lincoln was attacked in his campaigns as an ape, and caricatured in political cartoons as a "clown" and "fiend." Grover Cleveland survived the 1884 election, despite vicious print attacks and political cartoons that claimed he had fathered an illegitimate child (Freund, 1988; Greenfield, 1988). In the 1928 campaign, pictures were disseminated of the Holland Tunnel connecting New York and New Jersey, alleging that there was a secret underground tunnel to the Vatican in Rome that the Democratic candidate Al Smith planned to use, if he were elected president (Greenfield, 1988). The 1928 election, of course, was the first presidential election in which both positive and negative messages were used on radio as well as in print. For pure negativity and viciousness, it would be hard for even the hard-hitting 1964 and 1988 presidential races in the modern era to top the negative content of some of the campaigns in the pre-New Deal period.

NEW DEAL TO REAGAN (1932–1979)

Attack messages remained a major factor in the campaign strategies during the period covering the New Deal to Reagan (1932–1979). What was different in this period, however, was that negative messages were now disseminated on radio and later on television along with the print media (Reinsch, 1988). Those new channels of communication were viewed as more potent vehicles for political persuasion and for transmitting both positive and negative messages. Due to the extraordinary importance of the presidency in the American system and the disproportionate share of all political advertising devoted to this office, our analysis will focus on it first, and then later on attack advertising in subpresidential contests (Senate, governor, House, and state and local offices).

Presidential Contests

The first use of positive and negative political messages on television occurred during the 1952 presidential election, primarily by the Eisenhower campaign. Rosser Reeves, a Madison Avenue marketing consultant, helped design numerous commercials for Eisenhower and the Republican party. His previous nonpolitical successes included the marketing of a hard-sell commercial for Anacin, a long-time headache remedy, and M&M milk chocolates. In an interview with Bill Moyers before his death, Reeves reflected back on this time period and stressed the incredible advertising potential of television to penetrate peoples' minds and thus to disseminate information. An important finding, he noted, was that the Anacin commercial was the most unpopular commercial on television at that time, and yet sales set new records and the product quickly moved off the shelves. Reeves observed that there was no correlation between a commercial's popularity and product sales. Although effects were difficult to explain, Reeves felt that advertising was but an instrument to disseminate information and to get people to remember the product. Television advertising, he suggested, had a similar potential in presidential politics (Moyers, 1984a). Although the early years of television featured few strong negative spots, the Eisenhower campaign aired one of the first—an antiwar masterpiece. "Two soldiers are pictured discussing the meaningless of war on a Korean battlefield, and when one is suddenly killed, the other futilely charges the enemy while an off-camera voice booms, 'Vote Republican!' " (Sabato, 1981, p. 169).

The Democrats resorted to television in 1956 and used both positive and negative messages. They really introduced the use of the negative spot as a major campaign tactic, with Stevenson and Kefauver appearing in ads that attacked the Eisenhower Administration as too tied to big business and industrialists and too unconcerned about the farmers and the little people (Diamond & Bates, 1988, Moyers, 1984a). The Democrats also used a series of ads entitled "How's That Again, General," which contrasted the 1952 footage of Eisenhower promises with charts and information that dramatized a different Eisenhower record (Beiler, 1987). Finally, the Democrats launched an attack on what they believed to be a major Eisenhower weakness—Vice-President Nixon—that asked viewers if they were nervous about Nixon (Moyers, 1984a). Due to Eisenhower's first-term heart attack, this tactic was the first to suggest that voters think of the presidential ticket as a team.

Negative advertisements, however, were still a rarity in 1960, since most consultants and politicians regarded them as potentially counterproductive. A major exception was a devastating television ad designed for John F. Kennedy that attacked experience, the central theme of Nixon's campaign (Beiler, 1987). The ad simply replayed President Eisenhower's response to a reporter's question at a press conference about the major decisions in which Vice-President Nixon had been influential. Eisenhower's direct words were: "If you give me a week, I might think of one" (Sabato, 1981, p. 169). Axelrod (1988, p. 88) suggests that the Kennedy campaign thus "gave birth to the first effective negative commercial."

Negative television became far more institutionalized in the election of 1964. It was the most comprehensive use of negative message dissemination to date (*Campaigns & Elections*, 1986a). It produced the most famous, and possibly the most effective, negative political commercial ever shown, a message that was so controversial that the Johnson campaign pulled it after one showing. The so-called "Daisy" spot, designed by Tony Schwartz, introduced the sights and sounds of spring surrounding a little girl picking flowers. It ends with a vivid nuclear explosion as President Johnson intones off camera about the stakes in the presidential election (Beiler, 1987; Sabato, 1981; Young, 1987).

Sabato (1981, p. 170) argues that "much of the rest of the Johnson (and Goldwater) advertising package was far more negative and vicious than the *Daisy Spot*, even though this one ad got the lion's share of press attention." Almost all of the Johnson spots played on the fear of what Goldwater would do as president, especially in the area of nuclear weapons. Johnson's negative campaign was far more intense than Goldwater's and included "Cone of Strontium

90,'' as a far more direct and inflammatory attack ad than "Daisy." In it a little blonde girl licks an ice cream cone, and a woman's voice (the first ever in a presidential spot) warns of dangers of dairy products contaminated by nuclear testing with Strontium 90 and Cesium 137 (Beiler, 1987). The spot ends with a contrast of Goldwater's support of nuclear testing and Johnson's opposition. "Merely Another Weapon?" was yet another ad to exploit Goldwater's opposition to the nuclear test ban treaty (Beiler, 1987).

Other Johnson campaign advertisements exploited Goldwater's contradictory statements about the United Nations, Medicare, and Social Security. Another devastating ad was one entitled "Sawed-off Seaboard," wherein the Atlantic seaboard is sawed off and is seen floating away. In it the announcer quotes Goldwater's words: "It might be a good idea to saw off the eastern seaboard and let it float out to sea" (Sabato, 1981, p. 171). Another facet of the Johnson negative attack strategy was to attract Republicans and Independents by depicting Goldwater as out of the mainstream. One ad entitled "Convention Litter" emphasized the opposition of Republican moderate governors like Rockefeller, Romney, and Scranton to Goldwater's nomination (Beiler, 1987). Another long, rambling ad features a confessional monologue by an actor playing the part of a nervous and upset young Republican, stressing that he had always been a Republican but that this man Goldwater scared him (Sabato, 1981).

Goldwater attempted to counterattack on the negative front with some commercials linking the Johnson Administration to "moral decay" with scenes of dope peddling, alcoholism, and juvenile delinquency appearing on the screen (Moyers, 1984a). Another spot attacked Johnson's character and was broadcast primarily in the Southwest. It was a heavy-handed endeavor to link Johnson to corrupt individuals like Bobby Baker and Billy Sol Estes and it criticized the president's acquisition of "a fourteen-million-dollar personal fortune gained on an average government salary of fourteen thousand dollars per year" (Sabato, 1981, pp. 171–172). By comparison, Goldwater's negative attacks were less frequent, less intense, heavy-handed, and amateurish. One ad had to be pulled due to an outcry over racial overtones and another was taken out of circulation voluntarily due to its ineffectiveness (Sabato, 1981).

The election of 1964 proved to be a radical departure in political message dissemination in many respects. The campaign was disproportionately negative in tone, and the incumbent rather than the challenger launched the most frequent and effective attacks. The attacks occurred on all communication channels (television, radio, and print), but the extensive use of negatives on television was another first. The Johnson campaign also pioneered *image transference*, wherein the same voice used in the television ad was used in the identical ad on radio. Doyle-Dane-Bernbach, then the nation's hottest advertising agency, which had recently attained stunning critical commercial successes with their campaigns for Volkswagen and Avis Rent-a-Car ("We're number two, we try harder"), did the Johnson campaign. This campaign was light-years beyond its predecessors in terms of sophistication and the use of negative advertising. Beiler (1987,

p. 35) observes: "Given the advances made in persuasion techniques over the past 22 years, it is astounding to note that this effort remains the popular choice as the most effective political media ever produced."

Negative messages were not used as extensively in the 1968 campaign. The most effective negative spot was designed by Tony Schwartz for the Democrats, a penetrating attack on Republican vice-presidential candidate Spiro Agnew. Both the television and radio versions of the message employed a sound track of tittering and laughing with a closing remark, "This would be funny, if it wasn't so serious"(Sabato, 1981, p. 173). The Humphrey campaign also used a clever weathervane ad, an advertisement focusing on Nixon's flip-flops on issues (Moyers, 1984a; Sabato, 1981). Nixon was so outraged that he called Humphrey personally and demanded that it be withdrawn. Humphrey complied. However, his outrage was short-lived. Four years later, the Nixon reelection campaign broadcast "a remarkably similar spot that had Democratic nominee George McGovern revolving in the shifting winds of his alleged position" (Sabato, 1981, p. 171).

In 1972 Nixon's campaign used a variety of negative spots against McGovern, including hard-hitting attacks on his defense cut proposal and welfare reform. They quoted McGovern's Democratic primary opponent Hubert Humphrey saying that the defense proposal would cut into the very fiber of our national defense and that the welfare reform proposal was costly and impractical (Moyers, 1984a). The 1976 race made extensive use of positive rather than negative messages. Kathleen Hall Jamieson (1984) contends that Carter's campaign effectively tapped a small but decisive portion of the electorate disturbed by Ford's pardon of Nixon. By not referring to the pardon directly in the advertising, Carter's character advantage of honesty and integrity was kept intact, while voters were indirectly reminded of the pardon. Meanwhile, Carter was helped by Nixon's untimely trip to China on the eve of the New Hampshire primary and the press's role in keeping the issue alive "by asking about the pardon in the first Carter-Ford debate and in the Mondale-Dole debate" (Jamieson, 1984, p. 376).

A key concern in presidential campaign advertising is to what extent it influences the vote. Mainline political science research in the 1950s and 1960s ignored the media influence variable because earlier research suggested limited media effects (Chaffee and Hernandez-Ramos, 1987). Popular works, like *The Selling of the President 1968* (McGinnis, 1969), on the other hand, grossly exaggerated the influence of media. In the first systematic and scientific effort to study the media during the 1972 campaign, Thomas Patterson and Robert McClure (1976) discovered that television advertisements contained five times as much issue content as campaign coverage in the evening news.

They ultimately concluded, however, that television spots, both positive and negative, did little to move voters. Patterson and McClure (1976) estimated that only 1% of the voting public was actually influenced by television ads and only 2% of the sample at the outside limit was in any way influenced by them. The article in Barber's election volume (1978) also suggests a limited effect for media. Although systematic and comprehensive research is lacking, the Kennedy 1960 Eisenhower Press Conference commercial, the Humphrey 1968 Anti-Agnew spot, and the multiple negative advertisements in the 1964 Johnson campaign are negative messages that probably had the greatest influence on voting.

Alternately, there is some survey evidence suggesting that President Ford's use of negative television messages against Ronald Reagan in the 1976 Republican primary in California were counterproductive. Decision Marketing Information's (DMI) Richard Wirthlin tracked a twelve-point boost in Reagan's vote "over a ten-day period, and he is convinced that backlash to Ford's negatives turned a close race into a landslide for Reagan" (Sabato, 1981, p. 168). Although negative attacks do not always create a backlash, they can do so on occasion, depending on the specific campaign circumstances.

In summary, the findings concerning the impact of attack messages in presidential campaigns prior to the 1980s are somewhat inconclusive. Specific negative commercials, as noted previously, have affected the vote in some races, most notably in 1960, 1964, and 1968.

A final lesson on negative attacks at the presidential level emerges from the election of 1944. Running for a fourth term, Franklin Roosevelt encountered an extremely aggressive opponent in Governor Thomas E. Dewey of New York. It was a race that was in his view the rottenest, dirtiest campaign in his then thirty-four years in politics. Republican negative attacks claimed Roosevelt had abused his office and that he had dispatched a destroyer to retrieve his dog, allegedly left behind on a tour of Alaska. Roosevelt used ridicule and humor to rebut the Republican charges. He delivered an effective dinner speech widely quoted in the media that suggested that "Republican leaders have not been content with attacks on me, or my wife, or my son. No, not content with that, they now include my little dog, Fala" (Matthews, 1988, p. 125).

Attacking Roosevelt, Republicans hoped to draw FDR out of the White House into a head-to-head contest with Dewey. The president's humorous rejoinder, widely known as the Fala Speech, stopped the Republican strategy in its tracks by making it look small-minded. Thus, ridicule and humor might be used in a response message or rebuttal and prove to be viable as a strategy of resistance to political attacks. However, other than the Roosevelt example, there is little evidence of other viable response strategies to political attack messages.

Subpresidential Contests

A sampling of subpresidential campaigns from 1932 to 1979 reveals some interesting facets of attack politics. Incumbents, of course, are hard to beat unless they pick up negative recognition. During this period, several factors have consistently emerged in successful challenger attack messages. All involve liabilities of the incumbent. "Incumbents may acquire negative reputations if they (1) are involved in personal scandal, (2) are thought to have handled salient issues incorrectly or incompetently, (3) are on the wrong side of the trends of the time"

(Salmore & Salmore, 1985, p. 75). An incumbent who takes no action to deflect these attacks is an officeholder skating on thin ice.

One of the most important lessons in attack politics is the necessity of responding to an attack quickly and persuasively. The 1950 Senate races underscore this point, as seven U.S. senators were defeated for reelection. None of the seven were in any way prepared for the savage attacks against their character and voting record. The most graphic case involved the late Claude Pepper and his 1950 Senate Democratic primary defeat in Florida. He was the first incumbent victim in 1950 and the one least prepared. Senator Pepper was challenged by his former protégé and campaign manager, George A. Smathers. Pepper had helped get Smathers an assistant U.S. attorney position and an early release from his service obligation in 1945 and had assisted Smathers' 1946 victory for the House of Representatives. Nevertheless, Smathers resorted to McCarthyism to attack his mentor in the infamous "Red Pepper campaign." Pepper was accused of being a traitor, a Bolshevik, and too liberal on the issues. A dirty-trick technique involved snapping a picture of Pepper shaking the hand of a black man, political suicide in then segregated Florida. The picture appeared in state newspapers. In a late campaign blitz, the Bolshevik charge was disseminated in tens of thousands of pamphlets passed out after church services on Sunday, three days before the primary. Pepper chose not to respond to any charges, noting that he never dreamed the attacks could be so persuasive (Matthews, 1988).

Looking back, Pepper felt that his campaign had made every mistake in the book. Particularly, he had only stressed the reasons why voters should reelect him and did not comment on his opponent. By failing to respond to charges or to attack the credibility of those making them, he left the voters with the idea that they might be true. In retrospect, Pepper noted that his best tactic would have been to start early and hit Smathers with everything he had. When Smathers leveled the "traitor" charge, Pepper said he should have called his former protégé a liar and an ingrate. Pepper claimed he should have said, "If he'll doublecross a friend, he'll doublecross you." Also, Pepper noted that Smathers' credibility would have been damaged if he had released the story of the superpatriot challenger's shameless efforts to get early release from the marines in order to get a head start in his political career (Matthews, 1988).

Richard Nixon, then an ambitious young congressman from California, studied the Smathers campaign and formulated a successful attack strategy of his own. He called his opponent, Representative Helen Gahagan Douglas, the "pink lady" and printed a campaign leaflet "pairing Douglas' voting record with that of a radical congressman, Vito Marcantonio of New York City." The document known as the "pink sheet" alienated the country's liberals, but launched Nixon's Senate career (Matthews, 1988).

Despite the potential strength of negative advertising, it must be used prudently since it does have a backlash-generating potential. A Republican-sponsored media study calls it "high-risk" advertising because "it must walk the fine line between making its point and turning off the voter" (Sabato, 1981, p. 166).

The performance of the Republican firm Bailey/Deardorff illustrates this point. In the 1978 Pennsylvania gubernatorial race, their candidate, Republican Richard L. Thornburgh, was trailing badly in the early October poll against his Democratic opponent, Pittsburgh Mayor Peter Flaherty. The Thornburgh campaign opted for a series of hard-hitting spots on Flaherty's performance as mayor. The announcer in these messages asked, "Can the man who drove Pittsburgh to its *knees* put Pennsylvania back on its *feet*?" Thornburgh came from behind to win. In the New York gubernatorial contest, however, the negative strategy backfired. Bailey and Deardorff's GOP candidate, Perry Duryea, unleashed a strong attack on Governor Hugh Carey during the closing weeks of the campaign. Duryea, who himself lacked a strong image, had been leading in the polls. After the negative attacks his support dropped substantially, although the negative strategy was only one of several reasons (Sabato, 1981). Doug Bailey (cited in Sabato, 1981, p. 166) stresses the art as well as the science in attack advertising in his observation that "the same commercial can be run by two different candidates and one would be seen as being fair and the other unfair."

An innovative mode of attack advertising emerged in the 1976 Wyoming Senate race, where consultant Robert Goodman's work for Republican challenger Malcolm Wallop played a key role in the defeat of three-term incumbent Democrat Gale McGee. Several messages were produced that attacked the generalized enemy—big, inefficient government. The advertisements combined scenery and extras (seventy-five horses and riders) with the accent, tone, and dramatic music of the old Marlboro commercials. One was called "The Wallop Senate Drive" and another, "Ride with Us, Wyoming." Two other negative messages focused on the inefficient delivery system of the "Post Office" (McGee being chairman of the Senate Post Office Committee) and excessive government regulation. The latter dealt with the "porta-potty" requirement for outdoor activity and focused on the strapping of a porta-potty to a donkey tied to a horse in order to go on a roundup. Wallop appears in the ad as angry and disgusted, with the announcer saying: "We need someone to tell 'em about Wyoming. Malcolm Wallop will" (Sabato, 1981, pp. 148–150). The Wallop ads utilized boosterism and state parochialism, opting not to attack the incumbent directly or personally. Having sampled the 1932–1979 period, we turn in the next chapter to the nature and rapid proliferation of attack politics in the 1980s.

Chapter 2

The Rapid Growth of Attack Politics: The Reagan Era

In my own campaigns I try to heed the wise old Navaho adage, "He who slings mud loses ground."
—Representative Morris K. Udall
(Udall, 1988, p. 148)

We are in an era where there are fewer solid voters on either side— the campaigns are more contested so the ads are more contested.
—Robert Squier, Democratic Consultant
(cited in Berke 1986, p. A18)

The 1980s experienced an explosive growth in attack politics. A harbinger of a few of the new trends appeared in the 1978 election. In that contest, for example, the modern genesis of the generic spot first appeared. Under the leadership of new Republican Party Chairman Bill Brock, the National Republican Congressional Committee used carefully applied technology and modestly applied generic spots with much perceived success (Beiler, 1987). Moreover, the 1978 race witnessed more extensive involvement of well-organized single-issue groups in political campaigns. The attack strategies of pro-life groups, according to many commentators, made a difference in the unexpected defeat of three Democratic senatorial incumbents, Dick Clark of Iowa, Tom McIntyre of New Hampshire, and Floyd Haskell of Colorado. "The three incumbents should not have lost, according to the polls, but they *did* lose" (Hershey, 1984, p. 215). Generic spots, as well as independent advertising—both innovative in 1978—became permanent features in the attack politics of the 1980s.

Due to the diverse circumstances surrounding the four elections in the Reagan era, as well as the need to separate presidential from nonpresidential or subpresidential campaigns, this chapter will focus on attack politics in each election separately.

THE ELECTION OF 1980

The political decade began with Ronald Reagan's defeat of incumbent President Jimmy Carter, along with the Republican capture of the U.S. Senate. All things considered, attack advertising did *not* play a decisive role in the presidential nomination politics of 1980 (Robinson, 1981). Although considerable amounts of money were spent by candidates in both political parties for both positive and negative advertising in the 1980 primaries, social science evidence indicates that the television ads were "artistic successes, but political duds." Working with viewers of campaign ads in Iowa, New Hampshire, Massachusetts, New York, and Connecticut, MIT's Edwin Diamond "found little evidence that [the ads] influenced the votes of anyone" (cited in Robinson, 1981, p. 183). Robinson argues that paid political advertising, both positive and negative, had an even weaker impact in the 1980 general election.

Both Reagan and Carter used a mix of positive and negative messages in their advertising campaigns, although the incumbent's were clearly more negative as the campaign came down the home stretch. A concerted effort was made to associate Reagan with warmongering and racial strife (Pomper, 1981). In September Carter used a *comparative message* that claimed the country had a choice between two futures, a choice that would "determine the kind of life you and your family will have, whether this nation will make progress or go backward, and *whether* we have war or peace" (Hunt, 1981, p. 155). In early October, his comparative message was that the election would determine if "America will be unified or, if I lose the election, whether Americans might be separated, black from white, Jew from Christian, North from South, rural from urban" (Hunt, 1981, p. 155).

Some Carter campaign strategists like Pat Caddell insisted that polling data showed that the attacks on Reagan were working and causing negative feelings about Reagan's competency, leadership, and qualifications. Others had doubts. Vice-President Mondale, for example, privately voiced concern in early October about the attack strategy. Greg Schneiders, another Carter adviser, admitted later that the attacks raised a meanness issue that took an unexpected toll on the perception of Carter's character in the polls. "The continuous charges of meanness and pettiness had an effect; people vote on character, and that was supposed to be our issue" (Hunt, 1981, p. 156).

While not denying that negative attacks can be effective, political analyst Albert Hunt suggests the need for a balanced and prudent mix of positive and negative messages. Carter's failure, he argues, was attacking constantly and failing to provide the voters with a positive basis for support. "Almost the entire thrust of the Carter messages was anti-Reagan; from both calculation and necessity, the president offered little vision of where he would like to lead the country or how a second Carter Administration would differ from the first and perhaps avoid some of its problems" (Hunt, 1981, p. 164). In 1980, a disproportionately negative message strategy for the incumbent president ultimately proved to be a substantial political liability.

At the nonpresidential level, attack politics proved more effective. One mode of attack involved an *extensive generic advertising campaign* by the Republican National Committee, a series of well-designed ads emphasizing that the Democrats had controlled Congress for a long time and blaming them for inflation, energy shortages, and unemployment. The tag line was "Vote Republican, for a change." Private research by Republican pollster Robert Teeter confirmed the effectiveness of the ads which were run initially in three cities in the Midwest where response was measured both before and after their showing. A second round of evaluations was also conducted in these same test cities in April and June of 1980. Teeter's results were stunning, showing a substantial drop in the percentage of respondents planning to vote Democratic in the congressional elections (Robinson, 1981).

One of the more popular generic advertisements was entitled "Democrats Out of Gas." The theme focused on an unresponsive and irresponsible Democratic Congress. The scapegoat used was House Speaker Tip O'Neill, the quintessential good-old-boy-in-the-back-room politician, portrayed in the ads by a look-alike actor. O'Neill is cautioned that his car needs gas, but he proceeds to drive and drive. Disregarding his staff member's plea to look at the gauge, the car finally stalls. The ad ends by proclaiming humorously that the Democrats are out of gas, urging viewers to "Vote Republican, for a change" (Beiler, 1987; *Campaigns & Elections*, 1986a).

Robinson concludes that Republican generic advertising in 1980 demonstrated two truths. "First, once ad campaigns move below the rarefied atmosphere of presidential politics, they can work relative wonders. Second, when ad campaigns are not challenged by the other side—especially at the congressional level—they have considerably greater chance of success" (Robinson, 1981, p. 186).

Another prominent feature in the attack messages of 1980 was their *extensive use by independent groups* who formed political action committees (PACs) and spent considerable sums of money for their dissemination. The largest and best known was the National Conservative PAC (NCPAC, or "nickpack" to campaign aficionados and the media). NCPAC spent $1.4 million in 1980, with the major goal being the defeat of six liberal Democrats seeking reelection to the Senate (Hershey, 1984). The five largest conservative PACs also spent a little under $2 million on anti-Carter messages, primarily in the South. It was the coming of age of PAC television, for "nothing nearly as expensive, as visible, or as negative as this had ever happened before on television" (Robinson, 1981, p. 187).

The NCPAC attack strategy was to start early and disseminate messages in the fall of 1979 and spring of 1980 in order to neutralize some of the traditional political advantages of incumbents by lowering their job performance and general popularity ratings. Marjorie Randon Hershey (1984) notes that "the aim was to define the Senate races to voters as a kind of referendum on the Democratic incumbent. Any opponents, NCPAC figures, would have their own liabilities and weak points; thus, once an opponent began to be featured in the media, voters would see a fallible incumbent facing an also-fallible challenger" (Hershey, 1984, p. 9). This strategy utilized third parties to initiate basic attacks, damaging an incumbent, after which the third parties stepped back and the race got seriously on its way. This enabled challengers to begin the campaign on the high road because the attacks had already occurred, and because they were initiated independently.

Scholars and political practitioners are still divided on whether the NCPAC attack strategy helped or hurt. The targeted senators fought back and attacked NCPAC for carpetbagging and hatemongering. NCPAC's own professional evaluation of the impact of their advertising in four states—Iowa, South Dakota, Idaho, and Missouri—showed mixed results. Using a private pollster, NCPAC measured public attitudes both before and after its radio and television blitz. The NCPAC generic slogan was: "The closer you look at (Senator X's) record, the less you like what you see." In Missouri, for example, NCPAC data showed considerable damage to Senator Tom Eagleton, but it was not sufficient to prevent his reelection. In South Dakota, on the other hand, George McGovern was defeated, but the NCPAC data indicated that a clear majority of voters who said that the ads were influential were moved in the direction of the liberal target. Thus by November, among those seeing the ads, "twice as many voters were *more* likely than were less likely to vote for McGovern because of the ads. Even so, NCPAC directors believe the ads helped the conservative candidates more than they hurt, because the ads put liberal incumbents on the defensive and set the agenda of the campaign" (Robinson, 1981, pp. 188–189). Moreover, both political practitioners and scholars were struck by the fact that, "whether because of NCPAC's independent spending or in spite of it, four of the six NCPAC targets lost their races for reelection in 1980" (Hershey, 1984, p. 10).

The successful attack messages of 1980 were primarily *issue oriented* and used issue content in both the public rhetoric and voting record of incumbents to create the perception that they were too tied to Washington and thus out of touch with their constituents. The effective assault on twelve Democratic senatorial incumbents is illustrative. Although other factors always play a role in campaign outcomes, the unprecedented, unexpected defeat of these senators, including Birch Bayh, Frank Church, Herman Talmadge, George McGovern, Warren Magnuson, and Gaylord Nelson, was in part due to the accusation that these powerful committee chairmen had forgotten the folks back home.

Although Thomas E. Mann and Norman J. Ornstein caution against overly simple, ideological explanations, they concede that the 1980 electorate opted for a much more conservative Senate than it had in past elections. "With the exception of John Culver, most liberal Democratic incumbent senators were on the defensive throughout the 1980 campaign, tempering their viewpoints and downplaying their voting records. Conservative challengers were clearly on the offensive, proclaiming proudly their ideological points of view'' (Mann & Ornstein, 1981, p. 294).

Issue attacks were also used successfully at the *nomination level*, as Alaska Democrat Mike Gravel was hurt by his failure to deliver on the Alaska lands bill, and Florida Democrat Richard Stone was attacked on issues from both the Right and the Left, including his support for the Panama Canal Treaty, an intense issue for conservatives. On the Republican side, Alphonse D'Amato defeated incumbent Jacob Javits in New York with a successful negative campaign that portrayed him as an old-line liberal out of step with his party (Mann & Ornstein, 1981).

Similar issue attack strategies also worked in House races and were disseminated through television, radio, and direct mail. The effectiveness of the attack messages depended in part on other factors necessary for a vigorous challenge, such as ''the strength of the opposition party, the popularity of the incumbent, the availability of money and other campaign resources, and so on'' (Mann & Ornstein, 1981, p. 283). In the end, the political casualties included seven congressmen, among them Al Ullman (Oregon), John Brademas (Indiana), Harold ''Bizz'' Johnson (California), Jim Corman (California), and Lud Ashley (Ohio).

Although most successful attack messages were issue based, some 1980 *character attack messages* proved successful as well. In Senate races, Herman Talmadge of Georgia was hurt by a highly publicized scandal involving a broken marriage, alcoholism, and most significantly, an alleged impropriety involving misuse of office funds. Since most of the details had been disseminated in the free media, the relative unknown Republican challenger, Mack Mattingly, had only to use generalized character themes to reinforce the point (Mann & Ornstein, 1981). In Washington, the six-term, seventy-five-year-old Warren Magnuson was attacked indirectly as too old and lethargic for the job by political ads for Slade Gorton that showed his zest for mountain climbing and bicycle racing (Jacob, 1981).

In the House contests, six incumbents lost in large part to successful attacks that they were tainted with scandal. Three Democrats (John Jenrette, South Carolina; John Murphy, New York; and Frank Thompson, New Jersey) were hurt by their implication in the FBI's Abscam operation. Republican Robert Bauman of Maryland was charged with sex solicitation from a sixteen-year-old boy, while Louisiana Democrat ''Buddy'' Leach was attacked for violating the federal election law in his 1978 victory. Missouri Democrat Bill Burlison was accused of using his office to provide special treatment for a fired postal worker in his district (Mann & Ornstein, 1981). Another successful character assault was on New York Democrat Lester Wolff for the irresponsible use of his office, underscored by a ''late media blitz criticizing Wolff's frequent trips around the world'' (Mann & Ornstein, 1981, p. 297).

The election of 1980 was also characterized by extensive use of *response messages*, or rebuttals. Much of this is a function of the unprecedented number of attack messages that mushroomed across the 1980 political landscape. Hershey (1984) studied a number of the highly contested 1980 Senate campaigns from a social-learning theory perspective and pointed out the constraints facing the incumbents as they faced both NCPAC, single-issue groups, and highly competitive challengers.

First, the campaigners' previous experience did not always prepare them well; there were enough differences between their earlier encounters with single-issue groups and the current pro-life targeting to make any generalizations hazardous. Second, adapting that prior experience required good information about the targeting and its likely effects, and that information was often in short supply. Third, the result was a very uncertain, trial-and-error learning process, one that put these Senate campaigns at a real disadvantage in trying to cope effectively with the pro-life challenge. (Hershey, 1984, p. 237)

Many of the campaigns did fight back and rebut the charges. Both the Bayh and Church campaigns were attacked in leaflets in November and held press conferences to denounce the tactic and its sponsors. Often being leafletted in his primary, McGovern chose to send out an "Open Letter to My Fellow South Dakotans" to the state newspapers and members of the clergy. Culver in Iowa planned a radio blitz for the week before the general election to warn voters to prepare for last-minute attacks on the senator by extremist groups. This campaign made an initial decision not to counterleaflet. An unexpected event happened to change this decision. On the weekend before election day, Culver was again hit with another pro-life leaflet, and his campaign decided to rebut it with a counterleaflet. Some 50,000 fliers were printed and disseminated before election day in the areas of the state where the pro-life leaflet appeared. The various poll data available show that negative advertising hurt these incumbents, but their response or rebuttal messages helped cut the gap in the polls. Culver, McGovern, and Church all gained in the polls by hitting back at their attackers (Hershey, 1984). In some cases the result was victory (Eagleton) or a close loss (Church), and in other cases it simply cut the margin of their defeat.

In generalizing about attack strategies in the 1980 election, Robinson (1981, p. 190) concludes: "paid media work well when public images of the candidate are vague, when the opponents let the paid media go unanswered, and when the incumbent is clearly on the 'wrong' side of the issues." In assessing the defeat of so many Democrats in 1980, the Democratic Congressional Campaign Committee advised their campaigners in 1982 to develop a forceful response strategy to the attacks. More specifically it suggested:

Anticipate what the New Right targeters are going to use against you and hit back quickly. Don't let the candidate respond personally to the attack; find someone else—a staff member, a friendly group leader, or an elected official—to do it for you. Keep the targeters on the defensive; expose their tactics, question their credibility, denounce their motives. (Hershey, 1984, p. 248)

THE ELECTION OF 1982

The political environment in the 1982 midterm election was dramatically different from the presidential election year of 1980. Whereas economic conditions favored the Republicans in 1980, an economic recession in 1982 enhanced the political strength of the Democrats, as many weak party partisans who defected in 1980 came home in 1982. Mann and Ornstein (1983, p. 144) contend that "the message is that in times of economic adversity and policy uncertainty, more voters than usual are loyal to their own political party, particularly those who identify with the party out of power." The overall image/issue theme for Republicans was a message "to stay the course," while Democrats opted for an indirect assault on Reagan by calling for a "mid-course correction." Unemployment and Social Security were salient issues that enhanced the impact of the equity theme in the attack messages used by Democrats.

In 1982, both parties utilized *generic advertising*. The Republicans used it effectively in 1980 with a $9.5 million series of commercials that attacked the Democratic Congress and ended with a tag line, "Vote Republican, for a change." In 1982, the Republican National Committee continued to build on this advertising mode, with a $2.3 million advertising package and the theme of "Republican: leadership that works, for a change." The "stay the course theme" was used in other commercials. In an effort to neutralize anticipated Democratic attacks, Republicans also crafted *preemptive commercials* with themes like "Republicans are beginning to make things better" and "give the guy a chance." In what many political consultants regard as one of the best commercials of 1982, a white-haired mailman was seen delivering Social Security checks with the automatic 7.4% cost of living increase. The mailman said: "I'm probably one of the most popular people in town . . . [Reagan] promised that raise, and he kept his promise in spite of the stick-in-the-mud who tried to keep him from doing what we elected him to do . . . For gosh sake, let's give the guy a chance" (Sabato, 1983, p. 78).

Republican research confirmed the persuasive appeal of this ad, which helped mitigate the sting in strong Democratic Social Security attack messages. Not all Republicans, however, were as enthused about the generic ads, which worked at cross-purposes with the efforts of some GOP candidates. Sabato observes that it may be true that generic ads are better suited for the party out of presidential power (Sabato, 1983, pp. 78–79).

Mann and Ornstein (1983) contend that many of the generic commercials that focused on a party message were unsuccessful. Few Republican candidates emphasized party in their campaign advertising. In fact, most Republicans ran the more traditional, individualistic campaigns, emphasizing their own personalities, their own service to the constituents, their own independence (Mann & Ornstein, 1983, p. 148). This was particularly true of moderate Republican House members, the so-called "Gypsy Moths," who sought to keep their distance from both the party and the president.

Stung by their 1980 losses and their failure to respond to generic ads, the Democrats in 1982 opted for their own carefully crafted generic spots. Some of the television attack spots were especially creative. One of them featured "Dixie," a Republican elephant rumbling through a china shop and smashing items labeled "Social Security," "jobs," etc. The announcer says: "Two years ago, we trusted the Republicans to mind the store in Washington. They promised us they'd bring prosperity and respect to America's heritage of fairness and compassion. The Republicans have made a mess of things" (Sabato, 1983, p. 85). Other generic ads used the tag line, "It isn't fair. It's Republican." These included one in which a Social Security card was being clipped by scissors while another showed a 1982 unemployment line (Sabato, 1983, p. 85).

A very clever attack message was a trickle-down Reaganomics advertisement in which a champagne of tax benefits gushed into sparkling crystal glasses for the rich, while only a few drops fell into tin cups for the average person. "Firmly rooted in the populist tradition of the Democratic party, this spot effectively exploited the elitist reputation of the opposition while harkening the disparate components of the New Deal coalition back into the fold" (Beiler, 1987, p. 41). James A. Willders, an unemployed Baltimore blue-collar worker, was featured in a 1980 Republican generic ad that had him say: "If the Democrats are so good for working people, then how come so many people aren't working?" In 1982 he appeared in a Democratic generic ad that stressed his Democratic homecoming. It ends with Willders saying: "I'm a Democrat but I voted Republican once—and it's a mistake I'll never make again. And I didn't get paid to do this" (Sabato, 1983, p. 85). Despite financial constraints, the Democratic overall use of well-conceived generic ads matched Republican creativity.

A number of lessons about attack politics emerged from the 1982 campaign. One lesson involved the *importance of credible or believable attacks*. If the attack is not believable, it will be counterproductive and tarnish the political reputation of the attacker. Two examples illustrate the point. In a California open seat Senate race, Democrat Jerry Brown ran a pro-nuclear freeze ad that suggested that a vote for Pete Wilson might be a vote to blow up the world. In Tennessee, Republican Robin Beard accused incumbent Democrat Jim Sasser of "murder" because of his position on an abortion issue, and in another ad with a Fidel Castro look-alike, the Cuban dictator thanks "Señor Sasser" for supporting foreign aid. Hunt (1983, pp. 32–33) underscores that "Brown and Beard were decisively defeated, and their negative commercials hurt them."

Another lesson concerned the *difficulty of trying to defeat an incumbent with only positive messages*, as illustrated by the Connecticut gubernatorial election. Republican challenger Lewis Rome tried to stick to a positive campaign that stressed his own competence and integrity in a contest against Democrat incumbent William O'Neill. He did not advance much in the polls, however, until he opted for a negative television advertisement in the campaign's final days that stressed detailed rising taxes, a state budget deficit, and indictments of administration officials. The voice-over said, "What does Bill O'Neill have to say?

He has no comment.'' The attack came too late to overcome a large incumbent advantage, but it did close the gap. Salmore and Salmore (1985, p. 135) note that ''a campaign that drew the comparison between challenger and incumbent earlier might well have succeeded for Rome.''

By contrast, Republican gubernatorial challenger in nearby New Hampshire, John Sununu, used negative advertising to *give voters a reason to reject the incumbent*. After painting a picture of himself as an intelligent and smart businessman, Sununu attacked the incumbent, Hugh Gallen, for the budget deficit, high taxes, and the suggestion that Gallen might push for a sales or income tax. His successful attack led to a narrow victory, the only Republican to defeat an incumbent Democratic governor in 1982 (Salmore & Salmore, 1985, p. 135).

A third lesson learned was that, when faced with a strong negative attack, the *incumbent needs to respond quickly and persuasively*. In Missouri Democratic challenger Harriet Woods used hard-hitting ads to tarnish incumbent Senator John Danforth's voting record and question his compassion for victims of the economic recession. The messages even used material from Danforth's own ads against him, a technique used twenty-six years earlier by Stevenson against Eisenhower, and one spot in particular, called ''What Are the Facts?'' is widely credited for closing a forty-point gap in the polls (Beiler, 1987). Still, Danforth was reluctant to counterattack, preferring the traditional incumbent-type, very soft, good-guy campaign. Approximately two-and-a-half weeks before the election, Danforth's pollster told him the contest was dead even and that he would lose without a vigorous response. Danforth finally approved new spots that attacked Woods's liberal positions, and Danforth won a 51–49% squeaker (Broder, 1989, Jan. 19). Although the candidate did not respond personally, his campaign organization and not a third-party source was used for the reply. In 1989 Danforth, still troubled by negative advertising, nevertheless took a more pragmatic view. Specifically he said, ''Campaigns are so volatile now, someone who isn't prepared to respond very, very quickly is likely to lose. You see massive shifts in the polls as the [negative] ads hit'' (Broder, 1989, p. A22).

The election of 1982 also demonstrated the efficacy of both *prevention and response strategies*. The prevention endeavor proved successful against NCPAC, who turned out to be a financial success but an electoral failure in 1982. Where NCPAC assisted in the defeat of four of six liberal Democratic senators it targeted in 1980, it defeated only one of twenty senators it targeted in 1982 and lost its three top House targets as well. Democratic Senator Daniel Moynihan helped organize a legal challenge to NCPAC ads, informing television and radio stations that they were not immune from libel action for misrepresentation in NCPAC ads. In New York, not a single station would broadcast NCPAC ads. NCPAC Chairman John T. ''Terry'' Dolan claimed that NCPAC was sabotaged in some areas by television and radio stations who refused to carry their negative ads. Moynihan's prevention strategy was effective.

One of the most effective response messages or rebuttals of 1982 was a ''Talking Cows'' ad produced for Montana Democrat John Melcher. He was a prime NCPAC target, and the conservative group spent $228,000 (a large sum by Montana standards) to run ads in which constituents expressed their disapproval of Melcher's voting record. Like Republican incumbent Danforth in Missouri, Melcher chose to use his own campaign ad, as opposed to a third-party source, for the rebuttal. In one creative and humorous response commercial, "talking cows" warn voters about outsiders who have come to Montana to badmouth Doc Melcher and point out that the cow pasture was full of material like NCPAC's (Beiler, 1987). In another Melcher response ad, sleazy-type characters get off a plane with dark glasses and NCPAC briefcases. The announcer intones: "For more than a year now a pack of East Coast politicos have been scurrying into Montana with briefcases full of money, trying to convince us that our John Melcher is out of step with Montana. Montana isn't buying it, especially those who know bull when they hear it" (Sabato, 1983, p. 101).

In 1980, NCPAC had the advantage of surprise and was an unknown with respect to source credibility. Incumbents were unsure of the quickest and most effective response to its attacks. In 1982, in a more favorable Democratic environment, successful efforts were made either to preempt NCPAC's messages or to rebut them with efficacy and dispatch.

THE ELECTION OF 1984

Political advertising, both positive and negative, had only a marginal impact on the outcome of the presidential nomination battle. Reagan was unopposed on the Republican side, and the Democratic clash ultimately pitted a traditional liberal, Walter Mondale, against a new style/future-oriented liberal, Gary Hart. After reviewing the available data, Gary Orren (1985, p. 54) posited that "political advertising, the form of media exposure most under the control of candidates, was apparently not crucial in influencing votes during the 1980 nomination season, and it probably was not a major force in 1984."

Although political advertising may not have been overly influential, the nomination process witnessed the return of *concept or production spots*. Concept or production spots are those ads "in which the candidate was unseen, unheard, and hence—the strategists hoped—unblamed for the ad" (Jamieson, 1986, pp. 17–18). These spots allow candidates to attack without appearing unpresidential. In analyzing the 1984 nomination fight, Jamieson (1986, p. 19) notes that "in the bloody Democratic primaries Mondale attacked Hart in ads whose central characters included a red phone and a handgun. An ad for Hart countered with a burning fuse and the hyperbolic charges that Mondale favored using our boys as 'bodyguards for dictators' and as 'trading chips.' "

At the presidential level, an improved economy compared to 1982 and a relatively peaceful international environment led the Republicans to largely *positive and credit-claiming messages*. A political ad called "Morning Again" used superb visuals and light music and was a credit-claiming endeavor for the economic and social improvement that had occurred. It was the quintessential statement of the Reagan reelection campaign. The ad was subtle and reflected a golden glow, and President Reagan wasn't even mentioned. Instead, the commentator reminded people how well things were going for the country, especially compared to "four short years ago" (Beiler, 1987, p. 17).

Faced with an impossible situation, Mondale used *multiple-issue attack messages* on the budget, arms control, education, Jerry Falwell and the Moral Majority, health, and other issues, via all communication channels (television, radio, and print), but to no avail (Light & Lake, 1985; Pomper, 1985). The red phone was used for a nuclear weapons commercial, and a roller coaster ad was used "to dramatize the impending collapse of the Reagan recovery" (Jamieson, 1986, p. 19). In a high-risk effort at the campaign's end, one Democratic spot featured children "juxtaposed with missiles, as the tune, 'Teach Your Children Well,' was sung, and Mondale phrased oblique indictments of Reagan" (Jamieson, 1986, pp. 19–20). Although the Reagan ads were primarily positive, a few were negative. One comparative message ad "reduced Mondale's plan for the future to raising taxes and Reagan's to growth, trimming waste and adding jobs" (Jamieson, 1986, p. 20). A sophisticated but subtle scare tactic ad called the "Bear" commanded viewer attention with a bear roaming through the forest. The bear is symbolic of the Soviet Union, and the ad asks that shouldn't we be ready for the bear, if there is a bear? The tag line stresses Reagan for a strong defense for America (Aristotle Industries, 1985).

The nonpresidential campaigns were carried out against the backdrop of a lopsided presidential contest. Although the public preferred Reagan for president, it generally endorsed the status quo elsewhere. The Republicans lost two seats in the Senate and gained only fourteen seats in the House, even though Reagan recorded a landslide presidential victory. As Jacobson (1985) put it, it was a landslide without coattails. A similar outcome occurred in the gubernatorial races as the Republicans picked up but one governorship (Watson, 1984). It was not the kind of electoral year in which attack politics nourish and thrive.

Given the shift from 1982 in the economy and in the political environment to the Republicans' political advantage in 1984, there was a corresponding *decline in the use of negative generic advertising*. As noted previously, generic advertising is most effective when it uses negative messages and is potentially more potent for the party out of presidential power. Due to its political context advantages, many 1984 GOP generics touted the record of the Reagan Administration (Beiler, 1987). The Democrats also took a lower profile on generic ads, with the Republican advantage in the issue context (peace and prosperity) and the inclination of entrenched and well-funded incumbents to minimize party in favor of more traditional, individualistic campaigns that stressed personality, seniority and clout, constituency service, and their own independence.

Political advertising by independent groups like NCPAC was given less media publicity, and such groups adopted a more targeted orientation by spending more money on fewer races. Money and independent attack advertising were concentrated in expensive and hotly contested Senate races in North Carolina, Texas,

West Virginia, Illinois, and Minnesota (Jacob, 1985). Some of the most strident negative advertising in the 1980s occurred in North Carolina (Salmore & Salmore, 1985) on behalf of both of the candidates, Jesse Helms and Jim Hunt.

The 1984 election once again illustrated that *issue and character attack messages, if done realistically and correctly, do work.* Iowa Democratic challenger, Tom Harkin, upset incumbent Roger Jepsen with a combination of issue and character attack messages. Actually, the free media had prepared the way by simply reporting on Jepsen's inconsistent and controversial behavior. In the end, Jepsen was defeated because of flip-flops on issues, rhetorical blunders, and an inability to explain his application for membership in a club that was subsequently closed for prostitution (Jacob, 1985).

A very effective television attack spot was used by liberal Austin state senator Lloyd Doggett in a frontal assault on his favored opponent, conservative U.S. Congressman Kent Hance, in a 1984 Texas Democratic run-off primary. Hance was a Boll Weevil Democrat who coauthored Reagan's 1981 tax bill. Doggett's ad was called "The Butler," and it used lighting, settings, and chamber music to portray Hance as a servant of the rich, for coauthoring what Doggett contended was an elite-oriented tax policy. The attack proved effective, and after losing by a small fraction of a percentage point, Hance switched his registration to Republican the following year (Beiler, 1987). In the general election for Senate in Texas, Republican Phil Gramm went on the offensive against Doggett, with a comparative message ad linking Doggett to Mondale and himself to Reagan. The ad also emphasized their differing positions on a constitutional amendment to balance the budget (Aristotle Industries, 1985).

At the House level, one of the authors (Henry Kenski) was involved as a pollster in Republican Jim Kolbe's upset victory of popular Democratic incumbent Jim McNulty in Arizona's Fifth Congressional District. Two-thirds of the district was in urban Tucson, and another third in six rural counties. The district had a 10% Democratic registration advantage, or a 32,000–plus plurality. A year before the election, the challenger trailed by 25%, despite the fact that he had only lost in 1982 by less than 2%.

A concerted direct mail effort was used to promote voter information and positive impressions of Kolbe. The survey data showed that while personally popular, the incumbent had differing views from his constituents on a variety of policy issues, including the budget, taxes, and capital punishment. His policy views were considerably more liberal than those of a sizable number of rural Democrats. The challenger made no effort to criticize the country lawyer, strong "friends and neighbors" appeal of the incumbent. Instead, Kolbe opted for a strong issue attack in September and October on McNulty's voting record, through television, radio, and direct mail. One attack television spot was called "The Two McNultys," and it contrasted the way he appeared in the district to his voting record in Washington (Kenski, 1987).

Instead of defending McNulty's record or rebuffing Kolbe's charges, the incumbent's campaign opted for a strategy to discredit Kolbe, claiming the challenger distorted McNulty's voting record. A Pinocchio television ad was used to accuse Kolbe of telling untruths. Both local newspapers covered the exchange, expressing greater sympathy for McNulty's view. Kolbe repeated the attacks, using the distance theme that McNulty was out of touch and too liberal and anti-Reagan for the district. The attack messages appeared on television, on radio, and in print, with specific vote citations from the *Congressional Record*. A comparative message linked Kolbe with Reagan and McNulty with Mondale. The attacks proved effective, more so in the rural counties than in the Tucson area, and Kolbe won a 51–48% upset, with a 6,223 plurality (Kenski, 1987).

The 1984 election also underscored that *incumbents, as well as challengers, could adopt a strong issue attack strategy*. Michigan's Democratic Senator, Carl Levin, who was thought to be politically vulnerable, was challenged by a well-financed and attractive candidate, former astronaut Jack Lousma. The liberal Levin pulled out a five-point victory through an aggressive attack strategy and a "Toyota Hall" television spot. Beiler (1987, p. 21) says that "if ever a single campaign spot made a difference in an election's outcome, this one would top the list." The spot included video and audio material from Lousma praising Toyota while visiting Japan. To many Michigan voters, living in a state with many financially pressed American automobile manufacturers, Lousma's Toyota Hall address was incriminating. It turned the electoral tide in Levin's favor.

One of the most successful attack messages involved voting attendance, and it resulted in Republican Mitch McConnell's upset Senate victory over Kentucky Democratic incumbent Walter Dee Huddleston. At the start of the campaign, Huddleston's approval rating was 68% and McConnell's prospects were limited. Moreover, McConnell trailed by 50% in a trial ballot. McConnell's media adviser, Roger Ailes, designed a humorous attack spot using a rural-type character actor and some hound dogs. Although Huddleston's overall attendance record was better than average, he missed some votes while earning honorariums in exotic locales. The "Hound Dogs" advertisement depicts hounds searching for the missing Huddleston. The message called attention to McConnell's campaign and put it on a competitive track. Still down by seventeen points with two weeks to go, "Hounds II" appeared. This time the dogs catch sight of the globe-trotting senator, played by a Shakespearean actor look-alike from New York, and they try to chase him down, hoping to confront him with what the ad called a "sorry record." References were made to votes on the Panama Canal, school prayer issue, etc. By election day, the humorous attack ads had taken their toll, and McConnell won by 3,000 votes out of 1.3 million cast (Beiler, 1987). A critical factor in this race was Huddleston's underestimation of his opponent, and his *failure to respond* to these humorous but deceptive attacks.

Finally, the election of 1984 marked the birth of some very *effective and creative response messages*. Although the Social Security issue had subsided considerably since 1982, it was still an emotive issue, and some Democrats sought to exploit it one more time. In the Texas Senate open seat race, Democrat Lloyd Doggett hit Republican Phil Gramm hard on the issue. Gramm's response was called the "Mamma Ad." In a talking head spot, Phil Gramm displays a Social Security check to the audience. He announces that his mamma worked hard to earn it by cleaning bedpans and that he would not let anyone take this check away from his mamma. Gramm further includes veterans, railway retirement workers, and others in governmental service and says they earned their benefits and he won't let anybody take them away from them (Aristotle Industries, 1985). The ad identifies Gramm with Social Security and other earned governmental pensions and is offered as a refutation to claims he is opposed to them.

New Hampshire Republican incumbent Senator Gordon Humphrey was attacked strongly by his Democratic challenger for being hostile to Social Security. In a spot called "Mildred Ingram," one of Humphrey's constituents—an older woman—tells us that she is on Social Security, Humphrey's parents are, as are many friends and neighbors. She conveys a sincere faith in Humphrey and accuses the Democratic challenger, Norman D'Amours, of upsetting and scaring old people. The spot ends with a very effective line, "Shame on you, Mr. D'Amours" (Beiler, 1987, *Campaigns & Elections*, 1986a). Both the Humphrey and Gramm responses did the job, as they won seats to the U.S. Senate.

The 1984 election also witnessed increasing use of what is termed *neutralization* or *preemption*—messages that are designed to reduce the effectiveness of potential issue and/or character attacks. A few examples will be cited to illustrate the point.

Salmore and Salmore (1985) maintain that incumbents can neutralize an attack in a variety of ways. One is to incorporate a potential weakness into the basic theme of the campaign in a positive way. A second method is to turn a negative into a positive, and a third is to educate voters about the validity of an unpopular policy. Examples of *incorporating a potential weakness into a positive campaign theme* appear in the reelection campaigns of Democratic Senator Max Baucus and California House Democrat Leon Panetta, as well as the reelection endeavors of Boston Mayor Kevin White (Aristotle Industries, 1985).

Anticipating attacks on his liberalism, Baucus preempted them with an advertisement that identifies him with Montana's lifestyle, fighting the Japanese on trade, and championing both agriculture and the elderly. In the commercial, Baucus is seen talking to Montanans and saying he does not believe in political labels like liberal–conservative, left–right, but only believes in going forward for Montana.

Also anticipating big-spender, too-liberal assaults, House Democrat Leon Panetta appears in a soft ad working on a farm, with music and animals. The ad notes he voted to balance the budget eight times and is a friend you can count on. Mayor Kevin White was traditionally vulnerable to character attacks that he is too arrogant and not a good listener. His ad preempts against this charge by suggesting that he is a loner and a complicated man in love with Boston. Much of the ad humanizes him with scenes in which he interacts with and listens to Bostonians and displays both concern for problems and a sense of humor. In all three cases the preemptive strategy worked and the incumbents won.

Another neutralization strategy is to turn the tables by *taking a vulnerability and turning it into an asset* (Bart & Pfau, 1989). In 1984, a key example of the effective use of this strategy was Phil Gramm's race as a Republican for the Senate in Texas. A year earlier Gramm had switched parties from Democrat to Republican. Party switchers traditionally are hurt by charges of instability and opportunism. Gramm addressed this liability head-on, turning it into an asset. His ad included coverage of the press conference of the day he switched and the reasons for it, describing it as an act of political courage, with Gramm saying it was the only honorable thing to do. He emphasized that he had to make a choice between Tip O'Neill and the people of the congressional district he represented, and he chose the people. He resigned to run as a Republican in a special election. This 1984 advertisement has been termed "a preemptive masterpiece" (Aristotle Industries, 1985).

A more difficult neutralization strategy is for an incumbent to *educate the voters about the validity of an apparently unpopular policy*. Republican Senator William Cohen of Maine did so on the nuclear freeze issue. Cohen opposed the popular freeze position and instead supported the Reagan Administration's "build-down" proposal, which he explained in a commercial. His message stressed his argument of responsible leadership on arms control with a reminder of his strong record on constituency service, captured in his slogan, "A senator for Maine and America." However, due to the difficulties of educating the public and the time constraints in campaigns, educating voters about the validity of an apparently unpopular position is a neutralization strategy least likely to be used.

The political fulcrum would swing again in 1986. It would be a midterm election, with the expected drop in voter turnout. Although a basic satisfaction prevailed throughout much of the country, some sections like the Farm Belt and the South were suffering economically. In certain states and districts, the political climate was ripe for an acceleration of attack politics.

THE ELECTION OF 1986

The election of 1984 was conducted against the positive backdrop of good economic news ("Morning in America") and patriotism ("America Is Back"). However, a dominant positive background was lacking in 1986, and many campaigns accentuated the negative. Three weeks before the election, one political journalist (Taylor, 1986a, p. 6) observed that "in state after state, television ad after television ad, the electronic debate of 1986 has deteriorated into a wail of name-calling, distortion, accusations, and high dudgeon, all staples of the negative campaign style that has become the hallmark of American media politics in the mid-1980s." Such negative campaigning was not new, he observed, but what was distinctive from past elections was that the name-calling started earlier and was more pervasive, more often than not packaged in thirty-second television spots (Taylor, 1986a). Some analysts went so far as to call 1986 "The Year of the Mudslinger" (*Campaigns & Elections*, 1986b).

Numerous commentators stressed the absence of dominant issues in 1986 (Bonafede, 1986; Cohen, 1986b; Ehrenhalt, 1986). As a result, Senate and House incumbents preferred to run individualistic campaigns, stressing personalities, service, independence, and legislative accomplishments. The political advertising was similar in using a combination of messages to inform voters about a candidate's personality, background, accomplishments, etc. Although negative commercials were only a small fraction of all messages disseminated, they were more pervasive than in the past. Democrats especially preferred to focus on state and local issues and offered no national party theme. Robert Hagstrom and Jerry Guskind (1986) screened 375 political television ads in fourteen key Senate and gubernatorial races and found only one Democrat making an open appeal to party.

Attack messages, in the view of political practitioners, were increasingly used because they worked, with advantages like the clarity of the message (compared to positive ads) and memory recall. Karl Struble, media consultant to South Dakota Democrat Tom Daschle, repeated an increasingly widespread perception of political consultants. ''People hate negative ads, but they remember them'' (cited in Hagstrom & Guskind, 1986, p. 2621). Moreover, those attacked almost always have to respond. As Republican consultant Robert Goodman noted, ''Silence is perceived as guilt, but undoing a negative is difficult'' (cited in Hagstrom & Guskind, 1986, p. 2621).

Generic commercials were not used extensively by Senate candidates in either party, but the Democratic Congressional Campaign Committee arranged for eleven formula ads, positive and negative, that were used in sixty-six congressional districts. The formula used a hypothetical candidate, Pat Michaels. Two of the best generic advertisements contained attack messages. One of them focused on farms in decline and stressed the need to save the family farm and help farm families from the consequences of Reagan's agricultural policy. It ended with the message, ''Vote Democratic.'' Another generic ad emphasized toxic waste, saying the Reagan Administration was doing nothing to stop it. It ended with the theme that to stop it, ''Send X to Congress'' (*Campaigns & Elections*, 1986b).

Independent spending occurred again in 1986, but independent television, radio, and direct mail messages were not singled out for coverage by the media. There was no dominant NCPAC effort to be a visible presence in independent television media, as there was in 1980, 1982, and 1984. Instead, the more prominent campaign trend involved more extensive use of neutralization and preemptive strategies by incumbents.

Multiple factors influence the outcome of a competitive campaign. When the outcome is close, candidates, consultants, and political analysts frequently single out one or two factors as being decisive, when in reality other factors can be cited as well. In a close contest, everything counts. Conversely, if a candidate loses, a particular advertising strategy may be cited to blame, when in reality it may have kept a losing campaign in contention. In short, we cannot say definitively that a preemptive or neutralization strategy was the major cause of a victory or defeat, but only that candidates or their consultants perceived them to be a factor and that they were associated with a winning or losing effort.

A *preemptive or neutralization strategy* can focus on issues or character and attempt to incorporate a potential weakness in the candidate's campaign themes, turn a potential liability into a positive, or educate voters about the validity of an unpopular policy. Most preemptive efforts use the incorporation tactic, and only a rare few attempt to educate voters. Some do attempt to convert a negative into a positive.

There are numerous examples of candidates opting for the incorporation approach in 1986. Some Democrats anticipated a liberal, big-spender attack, for example, and sought to minimize it using advertising that underscored their commitment to balance the budget. In Senate races for the Democratic side, South Dakota Democrat Tom Daschle used an ad showing him driving his old Pontiac in Washington, D.C. and stressing his commitment to traditional economic values like budget balancing. Nevada Democrat Harry Reid ran an ad with a credit card machine going haywire and noting his own awareness of the deficit and his commitment to a balanced budget. A similar tactic was used by Vermont incumbent Patrick Leahy, who sought a visual association with Reagan. President Reagan was apparently popular enough in Vermont "that Senator Leahy, a liberal Democrat who scarcely even votes with the president, shows himself sitting with Mr. Reagan in the Oval Office in three of his own ads" (Mayer, 1986).

On the Republican side in the Senate, many incumbents from agricultural states attempted to distance themselves from an unpopular Reagan farm policy by underscoring their concerns and commitment to agricultural support programs. In Oklahoma the incumbent, Don Nickles, managed to avoid being associated with agricultural hard times, the worst since the Depression, with advertising that stressed concern and commitment, including a proposal to require banks to consider loan restructuring before foreclosing on farms and businesses ("Oklahoma," *Congressional Quarterly Weekly Report*, 1986, pp. 2473–2474). North Dakota incumbent Mark Andrews and South Dakota incumbent James Abdnor pursued a similar strategy ("North Dakota" and "South Dakota," *Congressional Quarterly Weekly Report*, 1986, pp. 2469, 2488–2487) that helped them wage competitive races which they lost in the end. In more urban-oriented Pennsylvania, Arlen Specter sought to distance himself from the Reagan Administration by ignoring it and stressing independence and performance for Pennsylvania. His ads stressed saving jobs, obtaining relief for farmers, and aiding the parents of missing children, with the slogan "Out Front, Fighting for Pennsylvania" (Cohen, 1986a, p. 2425).

Similar issue preemptive strategies by candidates in both parties were also used in House races. One very creative and humorous effort occurred in an Oregon House contest, where Democrat Les AuCoin preempted a big-spender attack in an ad featuring his son Kelly washing the car and talking about how cheap his father is. "When my dad pulls into a gas station for free air, he asks for an extra five pounds," the son says. He also adds that the congressman takes his own popcorn to ball games and chews "discount" gum (Houston, 1986, p. 17).

If some Republican senators in farm states came up short politically, the same was not true of Midwestern Republican governors. All of them successfully distanced themselves from the unpopular Reagan farm policy. Typical of these efforts was incumbent Terry Brandstad's campaign in Iowa. His advertising separated himself from the Administration and blasted President Reagan for a lack of "empathy" for the extent of the farm crisis. Alternately, he emphasized his own actions to address farm woes. "He has championed a limited moratorium on farm foreclosures that he initially resisted, traveled to Moscow and the Far East in a bid to open up agricultural markets, and just joined a lawsuit filed by farmers against the federal Farm Credit System" (Solomon, 1986, p. 2573).

Others successfully preempted potential attack messages based on their vulnerabilities. An example of a successful preemption at the Democratic gubernatorial level is provided by Michigan's Jim Blanchard. Opposed by William Lucas, a black Republican, Blanchard preempted potential attack issues early and publicized his positions and performance on tax relief, law-and-order initiatives, and the promotion of business expansion ((Kirschten, 1986). Politically vulnerable only a few years previously, Blanchard skillfully used his office to make himself virtually unbeatable by denying his opponent any critical issue attack openings.

Neutralization or preemption, however, is not confined to issues, but extends to *character* as well. Colorado's Republican senatorial candidate, Ken Kramer, came from behind to create a very competitive race with the eventual winner, Democrat Tim Wirth. A key factor in his comeback was his advertising effort to solve his image problem as a belligerent, excitable, and conservative ideologue. His preemptive effort consisted of various ads to portray himself as a likable sort of person and just "plain folks." He appeared in some of the ads himself and assured viewers that he would work hard to represent them. Matched against the more polished and telegenic Wirth, Kramer's first round of ads proclaimed, "I'm not slick. Just good" ("Colorado," *Congressional Quarterly Weekly Report*, 1986, p. 2410). Idaho's Steve Symms, on the other hand, undertook a summer travel and advertising offensive to convince voters that he was not a flaky maverick. He used a series of television ads with testimonials from constituents citing his efforts to bring in money for projects around the state and touting his work for farmers and lumbermen ("Idaho," *Congressional Quarterly Weekly Report*, 1986, pp. 2420–2421). In the end, Symms narrowly prevailed.

Overall, however, the attack strategy was pervasive and effective in 1986. Indeed, one of the new features of attack politics in 1986 was the *willingness of incumbents not only to attack, but to attack much earlier in the campaign*. California Democratic incumbent, Senator Alan Cranston, began his attacks on

Republican challenger Ed Zschau the day after the June California primary and some five months before the general election. Faced with anticipated challenger attacks that he was too old and too liberal, Cranston launched an offensive that utilized a series of flip-flop ads to portray Zschau as indecisive (Madison, 1986). Having an incumbent exhibit challenger-type attack behavior so early and so relentlessly caught the Zschau campaign off guard. "Cranston's attacks put Zschau off balance, forcing him to explain his positions and reassure his supporters. They also undercut the challenger's credibility at the time he needed it most—when he was trying to get voters familiar with him and lay groundwork for his campaign" ("California," *Congressional Quarterly Weekly Report*, 1986, p. 2405). By his early attack strategy, Cranston sought to define Zschau before he had a chance to define himself for voters. As Zschau put it, "People don't know very much about me, and he set out to say I had no substance" (Shribman, 1986, p. 28).

Zschau began to make some political headway beginning in September when he launched his own attacks on Cranston's voting record on drugs, terrorism, and capital punishment ("California," *Congressional Quarterly Weekly Report*, 1986). Cranston struck back with an offensive strategy, calling the Zschau attacks the big lie technique and comparing Zschau's tactics to those of Richard Nixon (Secter, 1986). The attacks and counterattacks proliferated at an accelerated pace until early November, when both campaigns shifted gears to more positive messages (Balzar & Love, 1986). Before this point, however, this was a textbook election on the use of negative advertising. Cranston's campaign excelled at *flip-flop ads*, running flip-flop updates featuring two photos of Zschau with the words "Zschau vs. Zschau" superimposed, contending that Zschau voted two different ways on arms sales to the Middle East, on South African divestment, on nuclear test bans, and on toxic waste (Hagstrom & Guskind, 1986). Zschau's campaign, on the other hand, used *compare and contrast* messages on the voting record of the two candidates to proclaim Zschau's support of the death penalty and his strong stand against terrorism and drugs. Cranston was portrayed as opposing the death penalty and being "soft" on terrorists and drug dealers (Hagstrom & Guskind, 1986).

The *Los Angeles Times* California exit poll asked voters which issues were most important to them in voting for senator. The top issues included government spending, the vote to reconfirm Rose Bird as chief justice of the California Supreme Court, the death penalty for terrorists, and whether the candidate represented the past or the future. All four of these issues worked to Zschau's advantage. "The only issue that worked to Cranston's advantage was a statewide initiative on toxic wastes. Otherwise, Cranston's supporters were more concerned with negative campaign commercials and candidate flip-flops on the issues" (Schneider, 1986, p. 2710). Cranston's vote was largely a personal and partisan one. His strategy of attacking the challenger early, however, put Zschau on the defensive, requiring damage repair before Zschau could mount his own attacks.

What the California Senate race illustrates is that the conventional wisdom of incumbents not attacking challengers or waiting to counterattack until the later stages of a campaign no longer prevails. Ironically, it was Bob Beckel, a Democratic strategist who orchestrated Mondale's negative attacks on Hart in 1984, who had argued for the efficacy of early incumbent attacks in 1983 when he said:

There used to be an old adage in politics that you don't mention your opponent's name because he's somebody who isn't known. But the ridiculous thing about it is by election day, a good challenger is going to be known by most everybody who goes to the polls. Our theory is that on the way up, when name recognition increases, you try to associate some negative notions with that name. (Salmore & Salmore, 1985, pp. 150–151)

Both issue and character attack messages were rampant in the electoral battle of 1986, but issue attacks were more prevalent. A sampling from Senate contests illustrates what transpired (*National Journal*, 1986, pp. 2682–2683).

In Washington, former Democratic Congressman Brock Adams defeated Slade Gorton with effective issue attacks on Gorton's failure to overturn the Energy Department's decision to include the state's Hanford site as a potential nuclear waste dump and the incumbent's crucial switch to support the judicial nomination of Daniel A. Manion in exchange for a Reagan Administration agreement to nominate Gorton's selection for another judgeship. In North Dakota, Kent Conrad used a hard-hitting attack on the state's farm problem, as did Tom Daschle in South Dakota to oust their respective Republican incumbents, Andrews and Abdnor. Economic issues generally, and the state's economy specifically, were issues emphasized by Terry Sanford as he defeated the recently appointed North Carolina incumbent, James T. Broyhill. In doing so, he successfully turned back Broyhill's efforts to label him as a high-tax liberal. In Alabama Richard Shelby ousted Jeremiah Denton by exploiting Denton's votes on Social Security, while Wyche Fowler came from behind to defeat Mack Mattingly in Georgia by pressing an attack on his ineffectiveness as incumbent. Robert Graham, a popular two-term governor, won in part by contending that incumbent Paula Hawkins spent too much time on a few issues (drug abuse and missing children) and was an ineffective lawmaker. The content of successful issue attacks appeared to focus on the economy—especially the farm problem—the environment, Social Security, and incumbent ineffectiveness.

In the open Senate seat (*National Journal*, 1986, pp. 2682–2683) John Breaux, the Democratic candidate, won in Louisiana by stressing anti-Republican economic attack positions, while Colorado Tim Wirth succeeded by projecting a moderate image and avoiding Ken Kramer's efforts to tag him as a traditional liberal. Republican Kit Bond won Missouri's Senate seat in a contest marked by voter resentment of excessive negative advertising on both sides by an attack message that Democrat Harriet Woods was too liberal for a centrist state. In a bitter race in Maryland, Democrat Barbara Mikulski won easily over Republican

Linda Chavez by emphasizing economic concerns, her Baltimore roots, and her experience in the House of Representatives. Mikulski basically ignored Chavez's strong personal attacks that she was "anti-male" and a "San Francisco Democrat." Republican John McCain retained Goldwater's seat for the party in Arizona by projecting himself as a moderate conservative and Democrat Richard Kimball as too liberal. In neighboring Nevada, in a race characterized by extensive attacks and counterattacks, Democrat Harry Reid triumphed over Republican Jim Santini. He "benefited from clever campaign advertising portraying him as David against Goliath and from his criticism that outsiders were trying to impose a Senator on Nevada" (*National Journal*, 1986, p. 2683).

Strong issue attacks also occurred at the gubernatorial level. In California Democratic challenger Tom Bradley ran hard-hitting radio ads that focused on Governor George Deukmejian's "receipt of campaign contributions from the hazardous waste industry and his veto of 21 bills that would have aided toxic cleanup," with Deukmejian calling the ads "dirty politics" (Paddock, 1986, p. 32). Deukmejian later employed commercials focusing attention on Bradley's decision to remain neutral on the reconfirmation of Chief Justice Rose Bird, his environmental record, his city's fiscal performance, and even the city's failure to stop its pollution of Santa Monica (Boyarsky, 1986, p. 3). In the end, Deukmejian prevailed easily.

Texas experienced a Western-style shoot-out involving the Democratic Governor Mark White and the former Republican governor Bill Clements. Both candidates had high percentages of negative ratings in the polls. Clements attacked White for the state's poor economic performance and higher taxes. White hit Clements repeatedly as a politician of the past and poked fun at Clements's never-revealed "secret plan" to cut the Texas $3.5 billion budget deficit. Another White scare ad underscored the devastating cuts in programs that would occur if Clements won (Hagstrom & Guskind, 1986). Political analyst Ronald Brownstein (1986, p. 2713) contends that in this venomous race between two unpopular candidates, "White's intense negative advertising against Clements was unable to overcome his own weakness, brutally exposed in a Democratic primary last May that saw him poll only 54% of the vote against five nondescript opponents."

In a very bitter gubernatorial contest in Pennsylvania, Democrat Robert Casey attacked Republican William Scranton III for limited accomplishments in office, absenteeism on the job, early drug use, and involvement with transcendental meditation. Scranton countered with a generational theme that claimed that Casey was a representative of the "Walter Mondale industrial-age politics which was born of heavy manufacturing and views that declare the end of their world as a party" (Cohen, 1986a, p. 2427). Casey referred to Scranton's tenure as lieutenant governor as irresponsible in an ad that proclaimed, "They gave him the job because of his father's name. The least he could do is show up for work." Scranton's campaign manager conceded that Casey's negative advertising hurt, and Scranton's 12% lead in the polls dwindled to a near dead heat (Taylor,

1986b, p. A3). In late October Scranton dropped his negative advertising and took the high road. Casey labeled the tactic a political ploy and continued to run his own attack messages.

Political journalists like Tom Wicker of the *New York Times* called Scranton's action a welcome move in a year of negative campaigning (Wicker, 1986), while an editorial across the country in the *Los Angeles Times* said that the road back to reasonable campaigning "may have started in Pennsylvania, where Republican gubernatorial candidate William P. Scranton III announced he was canceling all his negative radio and television advertising. Just another gimmick? Maybe. But we'll be watching the Pennsylvania returns on November 4 to see if it seemed to do Scranton any good" ("Television Bashing," *Los Angeles Times*, 1986, p. 4). It did not. Casey's attacks continued through the election, and he emerged the victor.

The Florida Senate race was distinctive in that the Democratic challenger, Bob Graham, shifted to an unusual strategy of attacking the Republican incumbent, Paula Hawkins, who was trailing him. What was equally surprising was that his issue attacks focused on the drug issue, thought to be Hawkins turf. Graham ran a television advertisement that cited her vote on a transportation bill that reduced funds for the Coast Guard, thereby damaging efforts to curtail drug smuggling. Hawkins retorted that Graham was a liar, but Graham's campaign consultants believed the angry response set in motion an exchange of arguments and comparison of records that worked to Graham's advantage ("Florida," *Congressional Quarterly Weekly Report*, 1986, p. 2415). Hawkins was also hurt by the media's role as an independent arbiter. The Florida press discovered that the Hawkins claim about a meeting she had with Chinese leader Deng Xiaoping "to agree to stop the manufacture and shipment" of quaaludes was false and that the meeting had never taken place. This gave Graham an opening to use new headlines critical of the Hawkins's spot with his own ad with an announcer saying, "We have learned that two of Hawkins's own aides admit on the record that the meeting never took place and that she never discussed the drug issue with the Chinese leader. If the people who work for Paula Hawkins now say they don't believe her, how can we?" (Hagstrom & Guskind, 1986, p. 2625). This race illustrates how *the handling of an issue attack can spill over into a character attack.*

Response messages or rebuttals were quite numerous in 1986, due to extensive negative advertising. A superb response message was Louisiana Democrat John Breaux's reply to Republican Henson Moore's attack on his voting record. Encouraged by Mitch McConnell's 1984 upset of Democratic incumbent Dee Huddleston with attack messages on voting absenteeism and honoraria, some 1986 attack strategies opted to use the voting attendance issue. Henson Moore is a case in point, and one Moore ad asked people in the street what the number 1,083 meant, with the final answer being the total number of votes Breaux missed while serving in the House. Breaux responded with a matching ad that also asked people what the number 1,083 represented, only the answer was the number of jobs lost in Louisiana every ten working days due to Republican economic policies. The ad tied Henson Moore to these policies and then ended with a comparative message on legislative effectiveness that said eighteen pieces of legislation were passed by John Breaux and zero for Henson Moore. Breaux clearly won this exchange, as the Moore campaign pulled their original attack ad (*Campaigns & Elections*, 1986b).

Breaux also responded cleverly to a direct mail attack by Moore that called the Democrat a "politician's politician." One of Breaux's television ads displayed the Moore mailer and accused Moore of running "a petulant, mean-spirited campaign" at the direction of national Republican strategists. Breaux employed the outsider theme and "made an issue of the national GOP's involvement in the contest, commenting to audiences that outsiders are trying to tell Louisianians how to vote" ("Louisiana," *Congressional Quarterly Weekly Report*, 1986, pp. 2434–2435).

A very negative Senate race was also waged in Wisconsin, with Democratic challenger Ed Garvey attacking Republican incumbent Robert Kasten's character based on a drunk-driving conviction, Kasten's associates being convicted for securities fraud, and the incumbent's failure to file federal income tax a few years earlier. Unfortunately for Garvey, it became public knowledge that he had hired a private investigator. Kasten's response ads claimed it was "a return to Watergate politics" and later leveled his own attack that $750,000 had disappeared from a union treasury while Garvey was in charge (Germond & Witcover, 1986). Kasten's response messages turned back Garvey's attacks, and he was reelected.

A response message gem was Vermont Senator Pat Leahy's reply to challenger Dick Snelling's "big-spender attack." The Leahy rebuttal was a television commercial that cost somewhere between $2,500 and $3,000, and it was appropriately entitled "Cheap." In the spot, the narrator states that Leahy "voted for smaller budgets than even President Reagan asked for." The commercial ends with a shot of Leahy in a diner with a cup of coffee before him. The commentator says, "Big spender? C'mon. The man is *cheap*." Leahy's campaign felt the ad blunted Snelling's big-spender attack ("Attack and Counterattack," 1986, p. 63).

CBS said that Colorado Republican gubernatorial challenger Ted Strickland had the most effective negative ad of the year, a piece called "Hats" that attacked Democrat Roy Romer for shiftiness, poor use of state money while state treasurer, and a claim that he would raise taxes. Despite the CBS kudos, Romer won decisively 59–41% and used effective response messages. One response ad explained why as state treasurer he had investment money placed in Colorado and not New York and ended with his own testimonial quip that identifies him with Colorado's economic interest. He stressed that he preferred Main Street to Wall Street and said, "Sorry New York. I happen to love Colorado" (*Campaigns & Elections*, 1986b).

One very interesting Senate race involving response messages pitted Democrat Tom Daschle against incumbent Jim Abdnor in South Dakota. Daschle offered a strong contrast in style and substance to the incumbent and fought to make the election a referendum on Reagan's farm policy. Abdnor tried to distance himself from the Reagan Administration on farm issues. Daschle sought to hang Abdnor with his own words, using a television ad with coverage of Abdnor speaking at a June forum, when he said that farmers might have to "sell below cost" in order to be competitive. Daschle's ad contended that farmers deserve a fair price. The attack put Abdnor on the defensive, and he claimed his remarks were misinterpreted. Regardless of the merits of the dispute, it forced Abdnor to use valuable campaign time to defuse it ("South Dakota," *Congressional Quarterly Weekly Report*, 1986, p. 2486).

Saddled with a weak rebuttal in the "sell below cost" versus "fair price" dispute, Abdnor shifted to a counterattack response that pinned Daschle with an outsider label and pictured him as weak, ineffective, and a captive of California and New York liberals. One ad criticized Daschle and tied him to actress Jane Fonda, who, Abdnor's ad contended, was invited instead of a South Dakotan to testify before the House Agricultural Committee. Another ad read, "Money Girl Streisand Sings for Daschle, Five Other Democrats." The announcer asks, "Does Tom Daschle really think the way South Dakotans do? Or is he the liberal all his Hollywood and New York supporters say he is?" Daschle's creative response was a negative ad showing a smoke-filled room filled with consultants chomping on cigars. "We'll distort the farm thing, confuse 'em with Fonda, all the usual liberal stuff," says one consultant as he blows a cloud of cigar smoke. "When we're finished, Daschle's mother won't vote for him," laughed another. "Let's go tell Jim," he says excitedly, as the commercial ends (Hagstrom & Guskind, 1986, pp. 2623–2624).

Abdnor's Jane Fonda ad appeared to revive his political standing and pulled him even or slightly ahead until late October. However, a final Daschle attack advertisement depicted an eighty-three-year-old woman looking for her Social Security check in the mailbox. The ad asserts that Abdnor had voted thirty times to cut Social Security and Medicare. Roger Ailes, Abdnor's media adviser, claims that this ad finished his candidate. This might be somewhat exaggerated, as the CBS exit poll suggests that the issues voters cared most about were the state's sagging economy and the failed Reagan farm policy, issues more advantageous for the challenger and his attack strategy (Fialka, 1986, p. 6).

Confronted by strong attack messages, a candidate must respond or increase the risk of defeat. The one exception would be attacks by a weak candidate (low name recognition, no prior electoral experience, inadequate funding) or a discredited third-party source. Democrat Barbara Mikulski's victory in Maryland while ignoring issue and character attacks constitutes such a case.

It is also important to respond quickly, persuasively, and frequently to continuous attack messages. In 1986, some response messages were helpful, but a little late. California Senator Alan Cranston's early attack on his opponent, Representative Ed Zschau, began in June, and the latter was thrown off guard and did not use counterattack messages until September. It resulted in Cranston's narrow victory. "Sometimes the negative commercial will be all the public knows about the challenger, so the challenger must spend valuable time trying to repair the damage" (Dillin, 1986, p. 5). That is what happened to Zschau.

Another race where strong response messages came late was Alabama's Senate contest. Republican incumbent Jeremiah Denton was hit hard for being too aloof and more interested in national issues than in Alabama problems and for several Senate votes against cost-of-living adjustments in Social Security. Denton's response messages included press releases, radio, and television emphasizing his pleasure at visiting voters, wearing more informal dress, ads calling him Jerry, and one television ad that features his elderly mother defending him as a supporter of Social Security ("Alabama," *Congressional Quarterly Weekly Report*, 1986, p. 2400). Denton lost narrowly, and Shelby's Social Security attack had definitely been damaging.

In other cases candidates respond, but with insufficient frequency. Early in the Senate race in Georgia, Republican incumbent Mack Mattlingly contained Democrat Wyche Fowler with a mix of largely positive and a few negative messages. One strong negative was his attack on Fowler's voting absenteeism, with a tag line, "Absent for Georgia" ("Georgia," *Congressional Quarterly Weekly Report*, 1986, p. 2416). Mattingly did not follow through, however, and Robert Teeter, a leading Republican strategist and pollster observed, "One apparent reason for the loss was that Senator Mattingly failed to run enough negative ads" (cited in Dillin, 1986, p. 5). A similar situation existed in North Dakota. Republican incumbent Mark Andrews faced a strong attack from Kent Conrad on the state's economy and farm issues. "Andrews's commercials have relied heavily on dramatic testimonials underscoring his commitment to the state and opposition to Reagan farm policy. Attacks on Conrad have been rare" (Hagstrom & Guskind, 1986, p. 2624). Andrews lost narrowly.

Another variant of the insufficient attack response is the unique case of a vigorous negative campaign that abandons the attack messages coming down the stretch. As noted previously, this is what Republican William Scranton III did in his bitter race with Bob Casey in Pennsylvania. He received praise in the media for taking the high road, but Casey won the governorship. Scranton appeared to be leading narrowly in a close race that was approaching a standoff when he withdrew his negative ads in the latter half of October. Brownstein (1986, p. 2717) contends "that Casey didn't, and this apparently hurt Scranton, with final weekend ads associating him with transcendental meditation, a form of Eastern mysticism."

One of Alabama Jeremiah Denton's response messages was a thirty-second television spot where Denton himself looks into the camera and proclaims, "Some politicians will say anything and do anything to get themselves elected. The Senate campaign here in Alabama shows what my opponent [Rep. Richard C. Shelby] will do, and it's not very pretty. Already my opponent has distorted my record on Social Security . . . " (Taylor, 1986a, p. 7). Denton's response underscores how strategic campaign thinking has changed. Since the advent of political advertising, conventional wisdom has posited that the best mode of attack is with surrogates. The candidate's hands were always to be kept clean. "In 1980, the ads of the National Conservative Political Action Committee (NCPAC) against liberal senators were deemed effective because they were third-party attacks, sparing the conservative challenger accountability" (Taylor, 1986a, p. 7).

By 1986 NCPAC was largely quiescent, but its attack tactics have been adopted by the campaigns themselves. Some campaigns, like Denton's, were even willing to put the candidate in front of the camera to make the attack personally. Ironically, Feltus (cited in Taylor, 1986a, p. 7) of Market Opinion Research says, "No candidate wants to get on TV and be negative, but when they do, the research shows it is highly effective." Moreover, a study of viewer reaction to 175 ads in 1984 found that if the candidate goes on camera "the credibility of the attack goes way up" (Taylor, 1986a, p. 7).

After the 1986 election ended, many articles were written criticizing negative advertising and expressing the hope that the extensive use of attack messages would not characterize the election of 1988. In November of 1986, Republican campaign strategist and pollster Robert Teeter suggested that this was wishful thinking and predicted that negative political ads would be back in 1988. The reason: "Negative ads work." In 1986 they played a major role in the electoral outcome in a number of states, particularly California, Georgia, and Missouri. Moreover, a major lesson of 1986 is that negative ads work against both incumbents and challengers, but the strategy is different in each case (Dillin, 1986, p. 5). Teeter's prescience is evident, as analysis of the 1988 election will demonstrate.

Chapter 3

Attack Politics and the Election of 1988

It's clear that a negative message in a volatile environment where the support for your candidate is soft can have a decidedly big impact on the voter's decision.

—Richard Wirthlin, Republican Pollster
(Grove, 1988, p. A10)

Unless you are a prohibitive front-runner, an unanswered smear is believed.

—Richard Moe, Campaign Adviser
(Taylor & Broder, 1988, p. 15)

It's gonna be a long and bloody autumn.

—Anticipating the use of attack politics in the Fall presidential campaign ("GOP Ads May Signal High Noon in America," *Advertising Age*, 1988, p. 50)

Republican pollster Robert Teeter's November 1986 prediction was right on target. Negative political ads did come back in 1988, and the scope and intensity of attack politics were phenomenal. The election of 1986 was not an aberration, but a precursor of what was to come. What appeared distinctive in 1988 was the extensive use of attack politics within both political parties in the presidential nomination contests and the early and widespread use of negative messages in the presidential race as well. Attack politics at the nonpresidential level proliferated and picked up where the 1986 contests had left off. This chapter will examine the presidential nomination contests, the presidential election, and the nonpresidential races.

PRESIDENTIAL NOMINATION CONTESTS IN 1988

Attack politics played a key role in the race for the presidential nomination in both political parties. Up until 1988 the judgment of political scholars was that political advertising was artistic but relatively noninfluential in presidential nomination outcomes. Robinson (1981) and others had taken this position while acknowledging that the potential impact of political advertising was greater in intraparty nomination contests where party identification meant less and image more. The coming of age of political advertising, particularly attack politics, surfaced in 1988.

On the Republican side a number of candidates used attack messages. The first event of the campaign season, the low-turnout Iowa caucuses, was relatively free of attack messages on the Republican side, with Kansan Bob Dole coming in first in this neighboring farm state with 37%, Pat Robertson second with 25%, and Bush an anemic third with 19% (Nyhan, 1988). Robertson's success was surprising but would prove short-lived, while Bush was sufficiently tarnished to make the New Hampshire primary a do-or-die situation for his candidacy.

The first Republican candidate to resort to attack politics in New Hampshire was Jack Kemp. Kemp's earlier positive spots were soft and emphasized character and broad optimism. They did not result in much movement in the polls, and so in late 1987 and early 1988 his campaign turned to sharp comparative ads to draw distinctions between Kemp and the two front-runners, Bush and Dole. His attack messages on oil prices, taxes, and Social Security resulted in advances in his poll ranking. They prompted a response ad from Bush claiming his positions were being distorted and that he was opposed to both raising taxes and an oil import fee. Although choosing not to respond with paid media, Dole, too, denounced Kemp's ads as distortions in various speeches (Gigot, 1988). Kemp's advancement in the polls was slowed down considerably.

Building on his Iowa caucus victory, the polls showed Dole overtaking Bush in New Hampshire as the race approached the weekend before the February 16 primary, with Dole having a 5% lead in Richard Wirthlin's poll (Goldman, 1988a) and an 8% lead in the Gallup poll (Obermayer, 1989). To offset the Dole surge, the Bush campaign opted for a two-pronged attack. One was a massive effort to get free media coverage for George Bush performing a number of jobs like working a forklift and driving an eighteen-wheeler. It worked as "the visuals of Bush playing at work made all the newscasts and began a five-day run in which he dominated every broadcast medium from drive-time radio to network TV'' (Goldman, 1988a, p. 94). The second, more devastating endeavor, was a late TV blitz ad called "Straddle,'' that attacked Dole for waffling on defense, oil import fees, and raising taxes. Bush was reluctant to approve the ad's airing, but his campaign strategists, particularly Lee Atwater, Roger Ailes, and New Hampshire Governor John Sununu, insisted that, if he did not use it, he would lose. Bush won the primary with 37.6% to Dole's 28.4% and went on to win the nomination (Pomper, 1989a).

Voter preferences in nomination caucuses and primaries, where party identification does not play a major role, are subject to both considerable indecision and last-minute changes. CBS exit polls, for example, estimated that one of three Republican voters had decided in the last three days of the New Hampshire primary (Nyhan, 1988). Pollsters acknowledged their major errors, failing to poll up to election day and giving insufficient weight to the large number of voters not strongly committed to Dole. Gallup's memo to its clients read, "The lesson learned is that even if a front-runner's lead appears stable, it remains vulnerable to last-minute change if support is soft" (Obermayer, 1989, p. 48). Dole's pollster, Richard Wirthlin, stressed the importance of attack messages on voter preferences when he said, "It's clear that a negative message in a volatile environment where the support for your candidate is soft can have a decidedly big impact on the voter's decision" (Grove, 1988, p. A10).

Dole's failure to rebut the Bush attack commerical on straddling proved to be politically fatal (Colford, 1988a). What is ironic is that Dole began to catch up to Bush in New Hampshire even a week before his victory in the Iowa caucuses when he used an attack commercial known as the "Doonesbury Spot," "in which Bush's face slowly faded away as an announcer claimed Bush had nothing to do with a list of Reagan Administration accomplishments" (Grove, 1988, p. A10). After his victory in Iowa, Dole shifted the focus of his advertising from an attack mode to one of running positive ads stressing his leadership and experience. In one, Dole spoke in presidential tones about the need to negotiate from a position of strength (Rosenthal, 1988a). The advertising shift proved to be a miscalculation, as attack politics carried the day.

Afterwards Richard Wirthlin said, "If you ask people how they respond to negative advertising, and they are answering in a rational, reasonable fashion, voters say they don't like them. But from an emotional, visceral point of view, [negative commercials] do seem to change perception, which is what campaigning is all about" (Grove, 1988, p. A10). Wirthlin noted further that the impact of negative advertising is less important in races where the vote commitment is more crystallized, but that the 1988 New Hampshire primary was not such a contest. If he had to do New Hampshire over again, "we would clearly have put a much more negative cast to our advertising" in the final days before the primary (Grove, 1988, p. A10).

Dole learned his lesson too late. He returned to attack messages in comparative ads contrasting his position to Bush on taxes, textiles, the INF Treaty, and the arms-for-hostages trade with Iran (Aristotle Industries, 1988a) in the March 8 "Super Tuesday" showdown when sixteen states held a primary and one a caucus. Bush's organization, money, Reagan association, and message strategy advantages were too formidable, and the vice-president emerged with sixteen state primary victories, "a rout that left only the Washington state caucuses for Robertson and nothing at all for Dole" (Goldman, 1988a, p. 96). For all practical purposes, Bush had clinched the Republican nomination.

On the Democratic side, attack politics was also salient. Missouri Democratic

Representative Richard Gephardt pulled into a narrow lead in the polls in January of 1988 in Iowa, largely because of television advertising. His seven spots hammered home his basic campaign themes: support for family farmers and for the elderly, and a need for tougher trade legislation to increase American exports and save American jobs (Rasky, 1988). One of the most creative spots was an issue attack on U.S. trade policy that sought to show that Gephardt's position emphasized fairness and not protectionism. It stressed that a Chrysler K-car would cost $48,000 in South Korea if the United States used the same trade practices as the Koreans. Gephardt's ad stressed that America would always keep its defense commitment to South Korea because of the kind of country we are, but that he would allocate six months time as president to try to negotiate a fair trade settlement. If one could not be reached, then South Korea would find out how many Americans would pay $48,000 for a Hyundai (Aristotle Industries, 1988a; Mathews, 1988). It proved to be a powerful message, tapping economic discontent (Rosenthal, 1988b). Illinois Senator Paul Simon tried to overtake Gephardt and win Iowa himself by a mixed media strategy of positive and negative advertising. He was the only Democratic candidate to use attack politics on an opponent in Iowa, as he aired a radio attack on Gephardt's voting record, particularly his votes in favor of an embargo on grain sales to the Soviet Union, President Reagan's 1981 tax cut, the MX missile, B–1 bomber, chemical weapons and the neutron bomb, and a vote on freezing the cost-of-living increases for Social Security recipients in 1985. The ad was a comparative message that contrasted Gephardt's votes to more favorable ones by Simon. Gephardt responded and called on his most prominent Iowa supporters to denounce Simon's tactic as negative campaigning. Simon replied through a surrogate, his top adviser Paul Maslin, who said that "for them to suggest that running ads on Dick Gephardt's record is negative suggests that they're not very confident about Dick Gephardt's record" (Dionne, 1988, p. 9). Gephardt survived the attack and eked out a 3,000 vote victory over Simon in Iowa (Mathews, 1988).

The attacks sharpened in the New Hampshire primary. Presidential candidates aired more negative advertising than ever before and did it earlier in the campaign. Following his second place finish in Iowa, Simon resumed his attacks on Gephardt in New Hampshire, claiming that Gephardt flip-flopped on nuclear energy and weapons programs. Gephardt responded with an ad accusing Simon of distorting his record, but also attacked Dukakis as "one of the biggest tax-raisers in Massachusetts history." Dukakis, by contrast, stuck to positive advertising, except for a commercial containing an oblique reference to Gephardt's trade policies (Rosenthal, 1988a, p. 11). Dukakis advisers unanimously urged him to attack Gephardt and Simon. He rejected their advice, "saying he'd rather lose than start throwing mud. He'd answer press queries with barbs at these two, but he wouldn't air negative TV spots" (Nyhan, 1988, p. 97). The Dukakis philosophy was to stick with who you are and not to emphasize what's wrong with the other candidates. In neighboring New Hampshire with a strong organization and adequate funding, the Massachusetts governor prevailed with 37% of the vote, compared to 20% for Gephardt and 18% for the third place finisher Simon. Jackson, Gore, Babbitt, and Hart all received less than 10% of the Democratic party vote (Nyhan, 1988).

On February 23, Dukakis looked forward to finishing off Simon in Minnesota and trouncing Gephardt in South Dakota (Mathews, 1988). He succeeded in the former, as he picked up 33% of the vote to Simon's 18% and Gephardt's 7%. Jesse Jackson came in second in Minnesota with 20%. In South Dakota, however, Dukakis was overtaken and defeated by Gephardt 43.5–31.2% (Pomper, 1989a). A late-breaking Gephardt attack, four days before the voting, overcame an 11% Dukakis South Dakota lead. Although Gephardt had a powerful message ("It's your fight, too") and an important endorsement commercial from popular South Dakota Senator Tom Daschle, both sides agreed the attack played a key role in Gephardt's victory in this agricultural state (Grove, 1988). The attack ad (Aristotle Industries, 1988a) called Dukakis a tax-raiser who told Iowa farmers to solve their problems by growing Belgian endive. It ended with a voice saying quizzically, "Belgian endive?" Before the ad, 65% of the voters who leaned toward one candidate but were not strongly committed favored Dukakis. After the ad, only 23% of these leaners favored Dukakis (Mathews, 1988). Dukakis chose not to run a response ad, but stuck to the themes of economic recovery and Central American peace. His failure to answer the negative commercial was clearly a factor in his loss. Dukakis vowed that he had learned his lesson and promised to take appropriate measures in the Super Tuesday battle, only two weeks away (Grove, 1988).

Dukakis began by calling Gephardt a "flip-flopper" and a "prince of darkness" on the campaign trail in Florida (Peterson & Broder, 1988). Short on money and organization, Gephardt kicked off his Super Tuesday effort by strengthening his attacks on both Dukakis and regional contender, Tennessee Senator Al Gore. Gephardt called Dukakis "the candidate with the most money [and] the least message," while stating that Gore's claim for the presidency seems to rest primarily on an accident of geography. "He appears more interested in discussing where he comes from than where he stands" (Peterson, 1988a, p. A10).

Gephardt used the "Endive" commercial again but was overwhelmed by attack messages from both Dukakis and Gore. The Dukakis ads were particularly devastating. One ad was a flip-flop commercial on Gephardt's voting record. To attack Gephardt, the Dukakis organization found a high school coach, sprayed his hair red like Gephardt's, and filmed him doing forward and back flips. Another attack message was called "List," and it attacked Gephardt's populist message ("It's your fight, too") by listing numerous political action committees from whom Gephardt accepted money. It underscored the inherent conflict in Gephardt, a consummate congressional leadership insider playing the political outsider by capitalizing on the economic discontent of the farmers, blue collar workers, and the elderly. The ad ended by questioning whose side Dick Gephardt is really on (Aristotle Industries, 1988a; Mathews, 1988). After Super Tuesday on March 8, the clear loser was Gephardt, who won only his home state of Missouri. In the balloting covering sixteen state primaries and one state caucus, Dukakis, Jesse Jackson, and Gore split almost equally (Pomper, 1989a).

After Super Tuesday, Dukakis used attack politics only sparingly and relied on organization, money, and a well-conceived strategy to capture the Democratic nomination. Gore received the endorsement of volatile New York City Mayor Ed Koch for the April 19 New York primary, and Koch's counterproductive assaults on Jackson hurt Gore, who received only 10% of the vote, thus assuring a primary victory and the nomination for Dukakis (Stengel, 1988). The outcome underscored that attack politics are not always successful and can result in a boomerang effect.

Dukakis sparred with Jackson the rest of the way on his road to a convincing nomination victory. In late April/early May in Ohio, Jackson unleashed his first negative ad, a comparative message that lumped Dukakis with Vice-President Bush as an aspiring caretaker for Reagan economic policies. Bush, the ad said, would "stay the course" while Dukakis would "manage the damage." It ended by saying only one candidate—Jesse Jackson—would change the course of the country and save jobs, protect neighborhoods from drugs, and keep families together (Schwartz, Kurtz & Grove, 1988). It was too little and too late. Dukakis won eleven of the last twelve primaries, losing only in the heavily black District of Columbia.

Despite his strong finish, doubts remained about how strong a vote-getter Dukakis really was. He concluded the primaries with 42% of the nationwide Democratic primary vote, less than Bush's 68% share on the Republican side. It appeared he did not inspire passionate support, even among those who voted for him. He ran poorly among blacks, Southern whites, and young voters, with his strongest support among fellow suburbanites and ethnics (Cook, 1989).

Dukakis was reluctant to use attack politics in a year in which attack politics would prove critical. Hershey notes that "he did not believe in attack politics. Even when he seemed to be losing the nomination race in Illinois and Michigan, he resisted making changes in his campaign. He would not adopt a style with which he was uncomfortable" (1989, p. 78). Dukakis was capable of communicating attack messages, however, as his negative spots against Gephardt on Super Tuesday demonstrated. It is ironic that his Republican opponent, George Bush, was also reluctant to use attack politics but did so in a devastating fashion to defeat Senator Robert Dole in New Hampshire. Despite the discomfort of both with attack politics, Bush was the more willing of the two to put personal feelings aside and adopt an attack strategy both during the summer and in the general election.

THE PRESIDENTIAL ELECTION OF 1988

Attack politics would play a prominent role in the making of the president in 1988. In late May on the Thursday before Memorial Day weekend, five of

Bush's senior campaign aides traveled to Paramus, New Jersey for an important strategy session on what to do. The latest Gallup Poll had Bush sixteen points behind Dukakis on the trial heat question. "And the horse race numbers weren't the worst of it. The same survey found that, although roughly an equal number of voters liked Bush as disliked him, a staggering five voters liked Dukakis for every one who didn't" (Taylor & Broder, 1988, p. 14).

Bush's negative ratings were extraordinarily high, while Dukakis's ratings were excellent. Bush's strategists were aware, however, that voters knew very little about Dukakis (Taylor & Broder, 1988), so that the Dukakis image benefited from comparison to his remaining Democratic opponent, Jesse Jackson (Hershey, 1989). Still, the political situation could not be allowed to drift, and a course of action had to be taken.

Bush campaign manager Lee Atwater was a strong believer in attack politics. In a 1985 interview he said, "When I first got into [politics], I just stumbled across the fact that candidates who went into action with negatives higher than 30 or 40 points inevitably lost" (Edsall, 1988, p. 26). It was this discovery early in his career running South Carolina campaigns when the Southern Democratic party was under siege by the GOP, that resulted in his specialty: driving up the opposition's negatives. So-called wedge issues were needed to draw a contrast between Bush and Dukakis that would boost the popularity of the former and pull down the ratings of the latter.

The May pre-Memorial Day Bush strategy group explored the possibilities. They arranged for two groups of fifteen voters, all of them 1984 Reagan Democrats, to assemble in Paramus for a market test of potential campaign material. Before the tests, all thirty had been Dukakis supporters. After exposure to the focus group material, fifteen were inclined to switch. The attitudinal movement in these groups suggested the potency of such issues as the Massachusetts prisoner furlough program, Dukakis's veto of legislation requiring teachers to lead their classes in the Pledge of Allegiance, pollution in the Boston Harbor, and other issues later used in the Bush campaign (Taylor & Broder, 1988). There was little doubt that the campaign found its wedge issues. Although Bush was initially reluctant about both the use of these attack issues and when to use them, he was ultimately convinced. The focus group screening had its desired effect. Bush himself concluded, "They don't know this guy's record. They don't know enough about him" (Goldman, 1988a, p. 100).

The attack strategy adopted by the Bush presidential campaign was unique in several respects. First, George Bush, the candidate, would play a prominent role in it. The conventional wisdom and much past research (Garramone, 1985; Merritt, 1984; Roddy & Garramone, 1988; Shapiro & Rieger, 1989; Stewart, 1975) taught that attack messages are best delivered by third parties or campaign surrogates. Bush's advisers felt, however, that he was in a unique position to lead the attack. "Not only would such a strategy call attention to Bush's definition of Dukakis, it would also help erase the image, prevalent in media coverage, that Bush was a wimp, a lap dog, a weak man in Reagan's shadow" (Hershey,

1989, pp. 82–83). Second, the attack would begin immediately. ABC TV's "Nightline" political reporter Jeff Greenfield observed in late October, "The Bush campaign this year launched their negative ads very early, compared to the historic pattern of first using ads to establish your candidate's positives. This is the first time that negatives came so early, and it shocked people" (cited in Colford, 1988c, p. 4).

The initial assault, however, relied more on Bush's public appearances than attack ads, and the strategy did not seem to work as well as Bush's strategists had hoped in June and July. "Nevertheless, some change was taking place. By July, some polls were measuring a decrease in favorable opinions of Dukakis and an increase in unfavorable opinions" (Hershey, 1989, p. 83). After the Republican convention in mid-August, however, a well-synchronized campaign attack and extensive television advertising helped Bush to set the campaign agenda and campaign on his issues. The strategy allowed Bush "to define Dukakis to the voters before he was able, or willing, to define himself" (Hershey, 1989, p. 82). Among the issues used successfully were the prison furlough, Pledge of Allegiance, capital punishment, Boston Harbor pollution, defense policy, and tax increases (Goldman, 1988b). As Bush's advisers saw it, the vice-president had unusually high negative ratings and trying to advertise these negatives away would take longer than the remaining time in the campaign. The other route, attacking the opponent, was the logical alternative (Colford, 1988b).

The overall Bush strategy, often neglected by the popular press, was a mixed one. Roger Stone, a senior Bush adviser, said, "We are running a campaign that is designed for network TV. That means only one message a day, and getting it out early enough to get on the networks and major media markets that night. It means not allowing anything unpleasant [to happen]" (Perry & Langley, 1988, p. A24). All TV ads were tested in front of "focus groups" and carefully scrutinized by a senior advertising staff. For every message there was almost always one positive and one negative commercial. Special messages focusing on regional or local concerns were also used (Perry & Langley, 1988).

There was little doubt that the strategy worked, and Bush took the lead in the polls for the first time after the Republican convention in mid-August and never lost it. In mid-September the *Washington Post* staff reviewed extensive survey and focus group data and made the following conclusion:

One of the strongest findings from the interviews and focus groups across the country is that Dukakis begins the last two months of the presidential campaign in a dangerous position: Many voters either have no clear image of him, or their views have been influenced by a combination of Bush's negative portrayal of and hostility toward the Democratic party. (Broder, Edsall, Ifill, Taylor & Rhoney, 1988, p. 9)

Hershey suggests that one reason Bush continued to attack was that he was not considered a strong enough candidate to win on his own with positive messages, and another reason was that the negative campaign kept working.

By late October, even Jesse Jackson's approval ratings were higher than Dukakis's. Even more significantly, the proportion of respondents saying that George Bush was "tough enough" on crime and criminals rose from 23% in July to a full 61% in late October, while the proportion saying Dukakis was not tough enough rose from 36% to 49%. It would be hard to find more convincing proof of the efficacy of attack politics. (Hershey, 1989, pp. 95–96)

Barbara Farah and Ethel Klein (1989) analyzed the *New York Times*–CBS polls over the entire campaign and noted numerous instances where the Bush attack messages proved persuasive. They conclude, for example, that the "Bush campaign was effective in its use of ideology as a campaign issue; it was able to label the candidate who said the campaign would not be about labels" (p. 111). Bush shored up his support among self-identified conservatives, while Dukakis lost his edge among self-identified moderates, and this group split its support equally among the two candidates on election day. "By championing the pledge, Bush helped his candidacy gain momentum as he benefited from a 17% advantage among nearly a third of the electorate who felt it was an important issue" (Farah & Klein, 1989, p. 114). Moreover, "national security became increasingly important in shaping the voters' perspective as the campaign progressed" (p. 115). Overall, these issues "served as symbols of patriotism and national and personal security. They allowed the Republican campaign to portray Bush as closer to people's values" (Farah & Klein, 1989, p. 118).

Farah and Klein (1989) further contend that a key factor in the electoral outcome was a missed message, economic vulnerability. Early campaign polls showed Bush as weak on this issue and susceptible to a gender gap disadvantage, due to the greater economic vulnerability of women. The Bush attack strategy, however, shifted the spring and summer focus of voters on economic vulnerability to one of personal security by the fall. Specifically, they (Farah & Klein, 1989, p. 120) say, "After the Labor Day kickoff, the economy was eclipsed by discussions of national security, patriotism, and crime. The Republicans were setting the agenda, and they wanted to keep the focus off the economy." In the end, Lee Atwater's philosophy of raising your opponent's negatives worked. Farah and Klein (1989, p. 127) conclude that "by the beginning of October, the Republicans' verbal assaults on Dukakis had hit their mark: Dukakis's negative ratings slipped to an 8% deficit, while Bush held on to a 10% advantage in his favorable–unfavorable ratings."

The Bush attack strategy succeeded in defining Dukakis before he could define himself. Confronting a Republican ticket that had the advantage on the key issues of peace and prosperity, the Dukakis campaign sought a pervasive theme that tapped the notion of change. Pomper (1989b) notes that Dukakis shifted his focus at least three different times in order to find the most convincing theme. At the Democratic convention, Dukakis contended that the campaign was about competence, not ideology. By the end of September and the first presidential debate, he focused on the future under the slogan, "The best America is yet to come.'' Finally, by mid-October he discussed economic populism and argued that Republican policies were unfair to the middle class. Pomper (1989b, p. 139) contends that ''as the challenging party, the Democrats needed to argue for change, but failed in three efforts to establish a convincing theme.''

In addition to the absence of a consistent overall message or theme, the single biggest factor in the successful Bush attack strategy may have been the long delay before Dukakis responded. Dukakis could neither reveal himself or define his candidacy and was reluctant to respond to the attacks. ''Bush's imagists had an empty screen for their slides of the governor as a wet and dangerous liberal'' (Goldman, 1988b, p. 112). Many of the attacks that were made may have been surprising in that they came early and were used repeatedly, but there is sufficient evidence that the Dukakis campaign had to expect them. On the very day of the Dukakis July acceptance speech at the Democratic convention, the *Washington Post* ran a story that Bush would use a prison furlough attack. It said that a black man named Willie Horton, who escaped to Maryland while on a weekend pass and brutalized a white man and raped his fiancée, would serve as a symbol that Dukakis was not tough enough on crime (Hershey, 1989).

Once the attacks started, the Dukakis campaign was not blind to their impact. Pollster Stanley Greenberg had been hired to do focus group research in California and Texas and found the furlough issue to be quite damaging. He said (cited in Taylor & Broder, 1988, p. 15):

I argued in a memo in August that the furlough issue had become a very serious blockage to people wanting to find out more about Dukakis. They had a lurid vision of Dukakis because of this issue, and they needed to be able to rationalize it before they were willing to find out more about him. I pressed them to do this. There were lots of conference phone calls. Nothing happened.

In an article at the close of the campaign, Shribman and Perry described the Dukakis endeavor as a series of lost opportunities. They felt that as a candidate, Dukakis had little understanding of the voters or the election and offered no compelling message or rationale for his campaign. Moreover, confronted by the potent attack politics of his Republican counterpart, Dukakis:

—Resisted every effort to get him to leave the relative security of his State House office in August to campaign outside of Massachusetts at a time when the Republicans were on the offensive.

—Sternly lectured his aides that he would not engage in negative campaigning, even as his lead was seeping away, and rejected response after response to Mr. Bush's attacks.

—Delayed for months the important defense speeches that might have inoculated the candidate from charges that he wasn't fit to be a commander and chief.

—And failed to resolve a struggle among powerful aides that paralyzed the campaign at crucial moments. (Shribman & Perry, 1988, November 8, p. A1)

The outcome, they (Shribman & Perry, 1988, p. A1) further observe, was "a campaign that never understood the demands of a general-election battle, that underestimated Mr. Bush and the ferocity of the campaign he would wage, and that seriously miscalculated the effect of sustained negative attacks." Sources in the Dukakis campaign say that Dukakis was making all the strategic decisions, and he didn't want to respond. He wanted to campaign on his issues. The nonresponse orientation violated the basic role of attack politics: "Unless you are a prohibitive front-runner," says campaign adviser Richard Moe, "an un-answered smear is believed" (cited in Taylor & Broder, 1988, p. 15). Robert Squier, a Democratic media consultant who was used sparingly in the Dukakis campaign, expressed similar sentiments. "With the Boston Harbor and furlough commercials, they [the Bush strategists] took the campaign straight at Dukakis, and the charges went unanswered for more than a month. It is a truism in politics: An attack unanswered eventually becomes an attack agreed to" (cited in Perry & Langley, 1988, p. A24).

Although it is clear that Dukakis was slow to respond to the Bush attacks, the popular account that he did not use negative campaigning is somewhat overdrawn. Quirk (1989) points out that Dukakis did a great deal of negative campaigning or attack politics himself, but chose to focus on different issues. Quirk (1989, p. 76) notes:

He frequently attacked Bush on the Iran-Contra scandal and the Noriega connection; he pronounced Bush a failure at keeping drugs out of the country and chastised him for refusing to promise that he would cut off foreign aid to countries that tolerate the drug trade; he asserted that Bush lacked the necessary skill to conduct foreign policy; and he attempted to link Bush with ethics scandals in the Administration and even on Wall Street. What Dukakis was unable to do was conduct his negative campaign in the focused and compelling manner of the Bush organization.

The Dukakis campaign finally did respond. A major series of Dukakis ad-vertisements in October depicting the "packaging" of Bush by a cynical group of handlers proved obscure and ineffective. Elshtain (1989, p. 122) says they failed because they suggested that voters were being manipulated, making them appear gullible and easily duped. As she puts it, "Voters cannot be manipulated unless something real is there to be tapped" (Elshtain, 1989, p. 122). Moreover, she stresses that no handy criteria exist to allow either the voter or the political analyst to separate real from so-called symbolic or rhetorical issues. Issues like abortion, handgun control, crime, and Pledge of Allegiance, etc., should be viewed as real as well as symbolic issues (Elshtain, 1989).

Unlike the elections of 1980, 1982, 1984, and 1986, economic issues were not as salient in 1988. Republican pollster Richard Wirthlin contrasted his 1988 findings with the 1984 election data. When voters were asked in 1984 to name the most important problem facing the country, some 77% listed an economic or foreign policy issue. In 1988, Wirthlin found that only 35% did so, and of that, only 8% was foreign policy, an all-time low in his presidential polling. By contrast, Wirthlin found that drugs and crime were foremost in the voters' minds in mid-October, as both were listed by 20% of the voters, compared to only 2% in 1984 (cited in Taylor & Broder, 1988). It should not be surprising then that the Bush attack strategy using social issues proved effective.

Finally, our review of a video documentary (Aristotle Industries, 1988b) of the campaign commercials used by both Bush and Dukakis campaigns shows attack ads being used by both sides. It is not true that Dukakis made no response at all to the Bush attacks. Response commercials addressing the key attack issues were produced, but unfortunately, many of them were not produced and aired until the end of the campaign. Dukakis, of course, did pick up votes at the end after acknowledging his liberalism and stressing a populist theme: "I'm on your side" (Quirk, 1989). The thematic shift was coterminous with his long-awaited response ads and rebuttals. As Farah and Klein (1989, p. 127) assess it:

Michael Dukakis did not find his voice to counter the charges made against him until very late in the campaign. The damage had already been done. The American public had decided they liked Bush, or at least what he stood for, and they did not like Dukakis, at least not for president.

NONPRESIDENTIAL ELECTIONS IN 1988

The 1988 elections marked several changes in the nature of attack politics. First, negative messages or comparative ads dominated message dissemination in Senate and gubernatorial races. In 1986, negative ads were more prominent than in previous elections but still only a fraction of a candidate's overall messages to voters. By contrast, a 1988 *National Journal* screening of more than 250 commercials from twenty-two statewide races indicated that in state after state attack politics predominated, with a take-no-prisoner tenor in Senate and gubernatorial campaigns. Some analysts felt that the tone of the election had been set by the presidential campaign and that the attack politics that worked for Bush could work for others, too. Second, whereas in previous years attack politics was used primarily by challengers and appeared late in the campaign, it was now equally popular with incumbents and challengers alike. Moreover, it was as likely to occur at the beginning as at the end of a campaign. The 1986 "Cranston strategy" of an incumbent going negative early inspired similar efforts in 1988. Finally, the attacks were shrill, personal, and often delivered by candidates with distinguished reputations rather than surrogates or third-party sources (Guskind & Hagstrom, 1988).

Viewed overall, the 1988 ads suggest the end of the Reagan era and the emergence of a new political age. Guskind and Hagstrom (1988, pp. 2783–2784) contend that "the anti-government themes that prevailed from the late 1970s through the early 1980s are largely gone, replaced in both parties by ads that dramatize programs and make vague pleas for more action on the environment, education, and child care.'' Weaknesses of opponents on these issues are frequently a centerpiece for attack messages. The epic efforts/vague plans focus was especially noticeable in 1988, as campaigns searched for persuasive messages in a political environment characterized by relative peace and relative prosperity.

Despite the scope and intensity of attack politics, the status quo emerged as the big winner in the 1988 election with the trend of divided government continuing. In the Senate, some seven seats changed party hands, with the Democrats winning four Republican seats and the GOP capturing three from the Democrats. In the House, the Democrats gained three seats, giving them an eighty-five-seat advantage (260–175). It was ''the first time in twenty-eight years, however, that the party winning the presidency failed to gain seats in Congress'' (Baker, 1989, p. 157). Although competence-over-ideology was not a persuasive theme at the presidential level, it was a winner in the gubernatorial arena. There were only twelve gubernatorial races in the presidential election year. Of the nine involving incumbents, eight won stressing managerial skill. The only incumbent to lose was West Virginia Republican Arch Moore. Two of three open seats changed hands, with the Democrats winning Indiana and the Republicans Montana.

In the 1988 political environment, with so many campaigns using attack politics extensively, both political parties used broader strokes in their *generic advertising*. The Republicans sought to capture the spirit of its 1984 ''Morning in America'' message with two predominantly positive ads, a spot called ''Little Girl'' and another entitled ''Going to Work.'' Both underscored economic and social improvements. In the most negative of the three generic ads, ''I Remember You,'' there is an ''Empty'' sign in front of a gas station, a magazine cover with a shark crunching the word inflation, and finally a picture of Jimmy Carter as the words ''You're the one who made me so blue'' are heard. All three commercials end with the same tag line: ''Seven years of jobs, peace, and economic growth, brought to you by the Republicans'' (Schwartz & Grove, 1988a, p. A8). Democratic generic efforts later challenged the Republican claim of creating general prosperity and touted the Democrats' ability to ''Bring Prosperity Home'' (Schwartz & Grove, 1988b).

Given the growing evidence of the efficacy of attack politics, more candidates attempted to mitigate potential political damage by issue or character attacks by *preemptive efforts*. In the Senate race in Washington, both a moderate Republican and a liberal Democrat used a preemptive strategy that incorporated potential weaknesses into their campaign themes. Republican Slade Gorton had lost his Senate seat to Brock Adams in 1986, but decided to seek the seat of retiring Senate Republican Daniel Evans. Gorton addressed the anticipated criticisms that he was aloof and uncaring. His television commercials used the slogan, ''Life's experiences make us grow'' (Yang, 1988a, p. 54) . He donned stylish new glasses and campaigned more informally. His ads stressed that ''I need to listen more. But my parents taught me that you could lose and come back from a loss and be even stronger.'' In one ad, he appears feeding his granddaughter and says, ''This is Betsy's election'' (Guskind & Hagstrom, 1988, p. 2787). Gorton also sought to neutralize anticipated attacks on issues by publicly stating he was arrogant, out of touch, and wrong in 1986 on tax increases, Social Security cost-of-living adjustments, the environment, and the homeless (Partlow, 1989).

Gorton's opponent, liberal Congressman Mike Lowry, shaved his beard and donned Brooks Brothers suits to alter his old bearded and rumpled look, and aired ads with warm images, low-key rhetoric, and pledges to ''work hard'' (Guskind & Hagstrom, 1988; Partlow, 1989). He attempted to neutralize potential attacks on his liberalism by applying a different spin to it, making statements such as ''we need to reinvest in education and the environment'' (Partlow, 1989, p. 4). In the final weeks of the campaign, both Gorton and Lowry went negative. Gorton's negative ads used a respected third-party source, retiring Senator Daniel Evans, to hammer Lowry for his vote against one version of last year's anti-drug legislation and to charge Lowry with favoring legalizing marijuana, citing a nine-year-old newspaper story. Lowry's attack ads said, ''Slade had his chance'' and used it to vote against the environment, education, and the handicapped. He originally planned to use a strategy similar to Gorton's by using Democratic Senator Brock Adams as a respected third-party source for the attacks. Adams was hit with allegations of sexual misconduct about a month before the election, and Lowry decided not to use him and had to go it alone. In the end, Gorton prevailed narrowly and won by roughly 20,000 votes out of two million cast (Partlow, 1989).

Republican senatorial candidates were sensitive to possible attacks that they were insensitive to socio-economic needs of their constituents and neglectful of the environment. California Republican Senator Pete Wilson ran a number of preemptive ads on the environment (fighting federal bureaucrats to protect California rivers and offshore water, etc.), the elderly, and abused children (Aristotle Industries, 1989). Republican Senator Chic Hecht of Nevada emphasized his support of health care (Aristotle Industries, 1989). One of the best preemptive efforts, however, was put forth by successful Mississippi Republican Trent Lott, who moved up from the House to the Senate. Although a strong Reagan Republican, Lott moderated his image through a series of messages that stressed Lott's support of select issues like Social Security, college loans, and the environment (Aristotle Industries, 1989). His Democratic opponent, Wayne Dowdy, ''pointed out that messages in the ads were often at odds with Lott's voting record, but he never succeeded in countering them effectively'' (Copseky, 1989, p. 23).

The North Dakota Senate race featured eighty-year-old Democratic incumbent Quentin Burdick and a classic preemptive strike on the age issue. He went on television a year and a half before the election, with advertisements that portrayed him as vigorous and wielding considerable influence on Capitol Hill. The clout and vigor theme proved effective. Burdick's opponent, Earl Strinder, tried to counter with ads that poked at the age question, with unflattering Burdick photos, criticism for ducking debates, and a claim that "this isn't the Quentin Burdick we used to know." Strinder even called in Ronald Reagan who appears in an ad and says: "It's been twenty-two years since I started running for office. Frankly, I'm looking forward to giving a younger man a chance" (Guskind & Hagstrom, 1988, p. 2785). In the end, Burdick prevailed by a three-to-two margin (60–40%).

One of the most remarkable Senate victories of the year was that of liberal Ohio Democrat Howard Metzenbaum. His voting record regularly received 100% ratings from the liberal Americans for Democratic Action, and his style was viewed widely as brusque and temperamental. Many analysts identified him as one of the most vulnerable incumbents at the start of the 1987–88 campaign cycle (Lane, 1989). He preempted the character criticism via television advertising that projected benevolence and warmth. Baker (1989, p. 163) observes:

Republicans were openly envious of Metzenbaum's campaign spots; they gave the irascible and temperamental Metzenbaum a personality face lift by showing him holding small children on his lap and discussing major social issues. Metzenbaum, moreover, could point to projects and jobs that had come to Ohio, for which he could take credit.

Anticipating attacks on his liberalism, Metzenbaum defined himself and the issues he wanted to address early in the campaign and put forth a populist interpretation of liberalism. His ads generally included constituents, while depicting him as a fighter for the workers, senior citizens, and a young girl with a rare disease. One powerful ad "which ran repeatedly in the home stretch showed a blue-collar worker emptying his locker and trudging off with the shoulders lowered, only to turn for one last look at his closed-down factory" (Lane, 1989, p. 22). Whereas Dukakis allowed Bush to focus on the social issues of contemporary liberalism (criminal justice policies, opposition to capital punishment, etc.) and to associate those issues with him, Metzenbaum captured the populist and economic policy dimension and defined liberalism as a kind of benevolence and warmth. It made for one of the best-run campaigns of 1988.

Another neutralization technique, noted previously, is to turn a potential liability into a political asset. In a Wisconsin Senate race, Democrat Herbert Kohl, whose campaign spent nearly $9 million, mostly from his private fortune (Guskind & Hagstrom, 1988), sought to deflect resentment against his wealth into a positive by stressing it made him independent and too rich to be influenced by special-interests or campaign contributions. For months his television advertisements proclaimed he'd be "nobody's senator but yours" (Shribman, 1988, p. A16). His Republican opponent, Susan Engeleiter, used ads to attack his wealth and privileged background indirectly with such themes as: "She wasn't born into a world of privilege. Yet she was raised with a wealth of determination. It's the Wisconsin way." Her tag line read: "Experience, energy, and ideas that money can't buy'' (Guskind & Hagstrom, 1988, p. 2790). In the end, Kohl won a close contest.

Another successful conversion of a liability into an asset was West Virginia Democrat Gaston Caperton's upset victory over Republican incumbent Arch Moore. Lacking political experience, Caperton used spots to play up his background "as a successful businessman and his independence from West Virginia party politics as well as his championship of education reform, environmental protection, and a development plan for the economically prostrate state" (Guskind & Hagstrom, 1988, p. 2789). The independence theme prevailed in a hard-fought Democratic primary and was used again successfully in the general election. The "I'm no politician" theme was the 1988 version of a preemptive technique pioneered by California gubernatorial candidate Ronald Reagan in the election of 1966.

As in past campaigns a successful attack message must be *believable*, or else the attacker might find that going negative can backfire. This is what happened to one experienced and well-funded candidate, Cleveland's Republican Mayor George V. Voinovich, in his effort to upset Ohio's Democratic Senator Howard Metzenbaum. Voinovich used TV attack ads that accused Metzenbaum of being "soft" on kiddie porn. The attack was viewed as shocking and was widely criticized in the press and in political cartoons. Voinovich's standing in the polls went down. "His ads," said Metzenbaum pollster Mark Mellman (cited in Guskind & Hagstrom, 1988, p. 2788), "boomeranged because 'the kiddie porn charges were simply unbelievable. You can't go out and beat someone over the head caveman style.' "

One of the most disappointing races for Republicans was the 54–46% defeat of Peter Dawkins—Heisman Trophy winner, Rhodes scholar, army general, Wall Street investment banker—to New Jersey Democratic incumbent Frank Lautenberg. The latter had kept such a low profile in office that few voters had a clear image of his record. Dawkins moved to New Jersey to make the race and spent $1 million in introducing television spots in late February of the election year, but they had little impact (Seglem, 1989). Inspired by Cranston's success in 1986, Lautenberg opted for an early incumbent attack strategy before voters could familiarize themselves with Dawkins. Based on their focus group research of the Dawkins introductory ads, Lautenberg's campaign found that people did not believe the Dawkins claim that he came to New Jersey to live because the people made his family feel the most at home. Focus group respondents registered doubts about his sincerity, and this encouraged Lautenberg to exploit the "carpetbagger" theme with tag lines like, "Come on, Pete, be real!" and "Are we just a political pit stop?" (Grove, 1989).

Cranston had run positive ads in his 1986 primary and then launched into an attack strategy in the general election. In New Jersey in 1988, Lautenberg had no primary competition, and this meant his very first campaign message was negative. "It was the first time in memory that an incumbent senator had begun his campaign with a negative ad" (Grove, 1989, p. A14). Moreover, his media drive against Dawkins was unrelentingly negative, with only two of his six commercials having a pro-Lautenberg message (Yang, 1988b, p. A10).

Dawkins tried to fight back. He initially responded with an ad that accused Lautenberg of mudslinging. Then he escalated his counterattack with an ad that accused Lautenberg of taking campaign contributions from New Jersey's worst toxic polluters and claimed that the senator pocketed tens of thousands of dollars trading stocks of companies doing business with the government. Lautenberg countered with a tough ad accusing Dawkins of misleading the people about why he moved to New Jersey, of lying about his Vietnam war record, and of being a hypocrite because he is financed by polluters. A follow-up Lautenberg spot even alleged that when Dawkins was serving with the army in California, he personally polluted an entire beach. The announcer in the spot said, "You know what he did to California's environment. Think of what he could do to New Jersey's" (Guskind & Hagstrom, 1988, p. 2786).

Lautenberg appeared to have the edge in the ad wars, but Dawkins made a serious run at Lautenberg that tightened the race in October with a tough ad on crime in East Camden and a comparative message that he supported the death penalty and Lautenberg did not (Grove, 1989, p. A14). Running out of money, Dawkins called for a truce and pledged to stop all personal attacks and challenged Lautenberg to do the same (Yang, 1988b). Lautenberg refused to do so but also used his money advantage in the final weeks of the campaign to air a positive spot that listed his Senate accomplishments (Grove, 1989, p. A14). The early and continual incumbent attack strategy worked.

Issue and character attacks were rampant in the election of 1988, and a sampling here underscores the point. A clever economic attack was launched by Democratic gubernatorial candidate Bob Jordan against North Carolina's Republican governor, Jim Martin. The ad uses chimpanzees decked out in business suits in a humorous, negative action-type ad with the theme, "Who came up with Jim Martin's budget?" The tag line is: "Had enough monkey business? Bob Jordan for governor" (Aristotle Industries, 1989; Guskind & Hagstrom, 1988). Governor Martin successfully countered with a "good ole boys" humorous attack ad, directed at Bob Jordan (Aristotle Industries, 1989). Both candidates in the North Carolina gubernatorial race preferred the rapier thrust rather than the roundhouse swing, and the use of humor in attack messages indicated a lighter touch.

In most of the country the attack messages were not so humorous. The California Senate race was a virtual bloodbath. Despite Republican Senator Pete Wilson's efforts to preempt domestic issue and environmental attacks, Democratic challenger Leo McCarthy launched a vigorous assault, including ads that attacked Wilson's environmental record and contended that Wilson voted against a bill to help victims of toxic waste because he received extensive political action committee support from corporate polluters. McCarthy also delivered a hard-hitting attack on Wilson's Social Security voting. Wilson hit McCarthy for his support of former California Supreme Court Chief Justice Rose Bird and for his criminal justice votes in the legislature. Another Wilson ad used its own "money theme" and asked how Leo McCarthy could own two luxury condominiums— market value, over a half million dollars. The ad asked, as the camera flashes on a golf course, "Where does all this money come from? Well, we don't know" (Guskind & Hagstrom, 1988, p. 2784). In the end, the incumbent survived a rather bruising attack and counterattack message battle.

In an open seat gubernatorial race in Indiana, thirty-two-year-old Democrat Evan Bayh, son of former liberal Senator Birch Bayh, rode a classic "time for a change" theme to victory (Farney, 1988). Ironically, he used a variety of conservative themes to defeat the Republican lieutenant governor, fifty-two-year-old John Mutz. His strong conservative message was largely negative and effectively communicated through television commercials. The ads hit Mutz hard for tax increases, governmental inefficiency, and even blasted the state's $55 million incentive program to attract a Japanese auto factory to Indiana. Mutz was put on the defensive, as the Democratic challenger rode the conservative themes to victory, the first time a Democrat won the governorship since 1964 (Householder, 1989).

Another attack theme used in 1988 was a Republican spot, "He's Like Mike," that sought to link the Democratic candidate to Michael Dukakis. Nevada Republican incumbent Senator Chic Hecht used this attack to narrow the gap between himself and the Democratic candidate, Governor Richard Bryan (Guskind & Hagstrom, 1988; Reinhold, 1988). Republican Connie Mack also used this attack in his Florida Senate clash with Democrat Buddy McKay. He used an ad that proclaimed, "Hey, Buddy, you and Mike are liberals" (Guskind & Hagstrom, 1988, p. 2785). Mack won despite a poorly run campaign that "lacked such basics as a grassroots organization or a clear message" (Van Gieson, 1989). McKay felt the Dukakis association hurt and said wistfully, "I'd be a hell of a lot better off if Bush was running unopposed" (Baker, 1989, p. 162). Although Hecht's linkage ads helped, he was not able to overcome "a reputation for ineptitude that found him at the bottom of every list of Senators when ranked for effectiveness" (Baker, 1989, p. 168).

Money attacks constituted a popular negative message in 1988. Leo McCarthy's attack on Republican California Senator Pete Wilson, linking a weak vote on toxic waste to political action committee money, and Wilson's counterad on McCarthy's ownership of two luxury condominiums, with the "where does all the money come from" line, are cases in point. The most effective ad of this genre was used by successful Democratic candidate Joseph I. Lieberman in his upset victory of Connecticut incumbent Lowell Weicker. Early in the campaign, Lieberman hit Weicker hard for missing Senate votes while making speeches for fees. It had Weicker standing at a dangerous campaign corner, the intersection of money and politics. "The attacks helped Lieberman, and his eventual victory was but one example of how challengers in 1988 turned the clash between private money and the public interest into a winning issue—even when, as in the case of Weicker's honorarium, it was perfectly legal'' (Alston & Hook, 1988, p. 3366).

In an open House seat in New Jersey, vacated due to the death of Democratic incumbent James Howard, Republicans felt they had an excellent chance due to the changing demographics of the district. Their candidate, former state legislator Joseph Azzolina who owned Foodtown Supermarkets, would be well funded and have Bush at the head of the ticket. A young, poorly funded Democrat, state senator Frank Pallone, however, won with a very strong issue attack on ocean polluting, with a comparative message that he represented the future and would protect the ocean, while Azzolina was an old politician looking for a place to hide in Washington. Due to the cost of television he used direct mail, and his campaign did twelve mailings, all focusing on the ocean coastline issue. Pallone's campaign also did negative mail that "showed how Azzolina's Food-town markets incinerated waste while other grocery chains recycled" (Paolantino, 1989, pp. 23–24).

Character attacks were important factors in the defeat of the few House incumbents who lost. In these races, free media reporting of the charges also plays a decisive role. In Georgia, Republican Pat Swindall lost, and he was indicted shortly before the election on federal perjury charges for allegedly lying to a grand jury in a case involving laundered drug money. Republican Joseph DioGuardi lost in New York, hurt by an "October Surprise" charge in the local press of allegedly receiving an illegal campaign contribution. The House Banking Committee chairman, Democrat Fernand St. Germain of Rhode Island, was accused of underreporting his assets and accused of "serious and sustained misconduct" by the Justice Department. It cost the twenty-eight year incumbent his seat. Democrat Bill Chappell of Florida, chairman of the Defense Appropriations Subcommittee, was not charged formally with wrongdoing but was hurt nevertheless by newspaper reports that "linked Chappell and some staff members to questionable business relationships with some defense contractors" (Baker, 1989, pp. 168–169). With respect to character attacks, it is clear that the money–legislative behavior linkage is a persuasive one.

As in 1986, *response messages* or rebuttals were quite numerous, and in many cases quite creative. It is clear that in most cases, a candidate has to respond or rebut attack charges, lest the unanswered charges are believed. In some races, however, the conventional wisdom about not responding and giving your attacker free publicity is still prudent. Such situations are rare, however, and involve challengers who have low name recognition, lack previous electoral experience, and are inadequately funded. Democratic New York Senator Pat Moynihan, for example, was attacked strongly in a commercial by Republican challenger Bob McMillan for being insensitive to the problem of ocean pollution. The tag line was: "Where was PAT?" (Aristotle Industries, 1989). Moynihan faced a weak, underfunded challenger and chose not to respond. Similarly, Delaware's Republican Senator William Roth chose not to respond to attacks by his Democratic challenger, S.B. Woo, whose attack ads depicted Roth as favoring the rich on taxes and being negligent on the issues of education and child care (Aristotle Industries, 1989; Guskind & Hagstrom, 1988). Like Moynihan, Roth was not seriously threatened and chose not to respond.

The danger of a nonresponse strategy is underscored, however, in Montana Democratic Senator John Melcher's loss to former radio announcer and cattle auctioneer Conrad Burns. Melcher seemed ahead in the polls, and his challenger lacked electoral experience and had difficulty raising funds. Burns used a highly negative television advertising campaign (Melcher's PAC contributors, his votes on anti-drug legislation, his legislative work on a controversial wilderness bill, and his friendliness with former Philippine President Marcos) and visits from President Reagan and Bush to gain a victory. He was helped by Melcher's decision to reject Democratic urgings that he counterattack Burn's harangue of negative ads, until the final days of the race (McAllister, 1988). Melcher's loss confirmed the dictum that in competitive races an attack unanswered eventually becomes an attack agreed to.

The defeat of Republican Lowell Weicker in the Connecticut Senate race is an example of the *failure to use sustained negative counterattacks to offset strong challenger attacks*. Issue postures of the two candidates were somewhat atypical of partisan divisions in the rest of the country, as Weicker, the Republican, opposed the death penalty, called for new taxes, criticized Reagan's use of war planes against Libya, boasted he had never been invited to the Reagan White House, and was endorsed by the state's AFL-CIO. Lieberman, the Democrat, supported Reagan's Libyan strike, backed the death penalty, treaded lightly on the question of new taxes, said he would accept an invitation to the Reagan White House, and was endorsed by an organization called Citizens for Reagan (Perry, 1988).

Weicker was hurt badly by an ad and cartoon that depicted him, "as a grumpy bear who dozed through hundreds of missed votes, waking only to collect speaking fees and to growl about 'negative' campaigning" (Hendrie, 1989, p. 7). He was also hit by other negative ads that attacked him for voting against Social Security increases and for voting for the tobacco industry's interests after taking campaign contributions and honoraria from the Connecticut-leased U.S. Tobacco. Weicker initially refused to respond, and said he did not want to win if he had to use negative ads.

Two weeks before the election, he changed his mind and struck back. He used one ad that showed a dinner two years earlier in which Lieberman praised Weicker and others, that attacked Lieberman as a big taxer while serving as state senate majority leader in the 1970s, and that charged him with a poor attendance record. The counterattack worked, and Lieberman's campaign admitted that Weicker had moved from a dead heat to a ten-point lead in the polls. Then, paradoxically, Weicker ran a sixty-second spot in which he rehashed his attack on Lieberman and called his own ads and Lieberman's "garbage." In it Weicker said, "I don't care if it's mine or his. I have to tell you, I can't exactly stand up and cheer about the direction that campaigns are going. I don't know exactly why it works this way, but it sure as heck works'' (Hendrie, 1989, p. 8). In what proved to be a strategic error, Weicker then pulled his negative ads going into the final weekend, and Lieberman emerged with a razor-thin victory. Weicker's tactic was similar to Pennsylvania Republican gubernatorial candidate William Scranton's in 1986, and both proved unsuccessful. To succeed, negative attacks and counterattacks must continue through the campaign finish.

Several effective 1988 response strategies merit mention. In Nebraska, former governor and Democratic candidate Robert Kerrey ran response ads that blunted the attacks of Republican incumbent David Karnes. He responded to the attacks with a mixture of humor and outrage. On Karnes's effort to attack him on foreign policy and associate him with Jane Fonda, Kerrey, a Medal of Honor winner who lost part of his leg in Vietnam, replied, ''I served in Vietnam, and many friends of mine were hurt as a result of Jane Fonda's visit to [North] Vietnam. So I urge Senator Karnes to associate me with some other liberal that he thinks will hurt me in this campaign or find some other politician to associate with Jane Fonda'' (Kotok, 1989, p. 21). In a Social Security attack response, a Kerrey spot showed an elderly woman sitting at a kitchen table and complaining about Karnes's ''badmouthing.'' Another ad was a takeoff on the now-famous ''Singing Raisins'' of California and used animated models for a humorous ''bad-mouth'' theme (Kotok, 1989).

Some incumbents used respected third-party sources to reply to strong attacks. In California, Republican incumbent Pete Wilson used actor Charlton Heston, who cited newspaper articles criticizing Leo McCarthy's negative ads. Looking peeved, Heston looks at the camera and says, ''The United States Senate is a place for integrity, not Leo McCarthy'' (Guskind & Hagstrom, 1988, p. 2784). After being blasted with Voinovich's kiddie porn attack in Ohio, Senator Metzenbaum used his respected colleague, Democratic Senator John Glenn, to respond. Looking visibly outraged, Glenn faces the camera and says, ''In the past I've known George Voinovich as an honorable man. But this new TV ad is the lowest gutter politics I've seen in a long time. To imply that Howard Metzenbaum, with four daughters and six grandchildren, is somehow soft on child pornography is disgusting'' (Guskind & Hagstrom, 1988, p. 2788).

Some incumbents preferred, however, to respond personally. It was known in the campaign trade as a ''Shame on You'' spot, a counternegative in which the victim turns the charge on the attacker. In Minnesota, Republican Senator Dave Durenberger was attacked by Democratic challenger Skip Humphrey for voting against the elderly and Medicare at least nineteen times. In the response ad, Durenberger looks annoyed, sits on his desk, and says, ''By now, you may have seen Skip Humphrey's new TV ad distorting my record and featuring some nasty personal attacks on me. Skip Humphrey should know better. His late, great father would never have started a campaign this way. Skip's father knew Minnesota'' (Guskind & Hagstrom, 1988 pp. 2786–2787).

Finally, one of the most creative response ads of 1988 was produced for

Mississippi Republican senatorial candidate Trent Lott. His challenger, Wayne Dowdy, used a clever attack ad with an expensive car driving down Mississippi roads, allegedly driven by a chauffeur with Lott in the back reading the *Wall Street Journal*. The driver was a black man named George Awkward, and Dowdy drew on the ad to campaign on the slogan, "Cut George, not Social Security." Lott's response ad used George Awkward, who was a law enforcement officer assigned to Lott as a congressional leader. In Lott's ad, George Awkward stands before the American flag, his shoulder holster in plain view, and personally delivers his angry response, saying, "I've been a detective in a security police force in Washington, D.C. for twenty-seven years. Wayne Dowdy calls me a chauffeur. He offends every law enforcement officer who puts his life on the line every day. Mr. Dowdy, I'm nobody's chauffeur." After a short pause for dramatic effect, Awkward glares at the camera and says, "Got it?" (Guskind & Hagstrom, 1988, p. 2783). Lott's response ad was effective, as Dowdy pulled the original attack ad.

Attack politics had clearly changed dramatically from the outset of the Reagan era. Negative campaigning, compared to positive advertising, was used with greater frequency. It was used by incumbents as well as challengers. The old practice about building up your positives first before attacking was abandoned, and attacks occurred at the start of the campaign as well as the middle and end. Using third-party sources or campaign surrogates to attack or respond was not always viewed as the most effective tactic, and candidates themselves sometimes attacked or responded personally. In some quarters, particularly the media, there were criticisms that attack politics or negative campaigning was getting out of hand. Some individuals even favored some type of government regulation. What could or should be done about the attack politics phenomena, if anything, is the focus of Chapter 4.

Inadequacy of Present Defenses against Attack Messages

Just as the Battle of Agincourt demonstrated the vulnerability of French armor to the British longbow, the 1988 campaign showed the deceptive power of visual association and the weaknesses of the protection [against political attack messages] provided by debates, news broadcasts, counteracting advertising and press coverage.

> —Kathleen Hall Jamieson, Professor of Communication
> (Jamieson, 1988, p. C1)

[On various proposals to regulate political ads:] Even if such proposals were to pass constitutional muster—a doubtful prospect in light of the Supreme Court's interpretation of the First Amendment as applied to speech in political campaigns—it is questionable whether the proposals would either reduce campaign costs or enhance political communication.

> —Dr. Herbert E. Alexander, Director of the Citizen's
> Research Foundation (Alexander & Haggerty, 1988, p. 5)

The 1988 election underscored the inadequacy or limitation of existing defenses against well-conceived and well-focused attack message strategies. One leading authority on political campaign advertising (Jamieson, 1988) said that it was the worst election year ever for lying and distortion. She faults both presidential candidates for advertising distortions and feels the electorate, ''numbed by both the negative campaigns of 1986—and a press corps preoccupied more with ad strategy than content—simply took the visual demagoguery in stride'' (Jamieson, 1988, p. C2).

Author of one of the best scholarly books on the subject, *Packaging the Presidency* (1984), Jamieson recanted her previous position that political attack advertising is little more than a benign irritant, observing: "I concluded a survey of presidential advertising in a recent book on presidential campaigns with the assurance that the public had little to fear from distortions in TV and other ads. I was wrong" (1988, p. C2). Her reassessment is influenced by what took place during the 1986 and 1988 campaigns, in which the use of political attack messages played an increasingly decisive role. Specifically she argues that the 1988 campaign illustrated the power of television attacks, which traditional strategic options are unable to offset.

Jamieson is not alone in such sentiments. Other scholars, media and press people, politicians, and citizen groups have expressed similar concerns and, in some cases, suggested remedies. This chapter examines both existing and proposed defenses against attack messages. It includes analyses of existing legal remedies, calls for voluntary restraints, and the use of participants in the campaign process as a check on abuses by others.

INADEQUACY OF LEGAL REMEDIES

A number of legal options have been put forth as vehicles to limit the use of political attack messages in contemporary campaigns. These include the use of legal suits and/or formal complaints against offenders, the adoption of federal legislation to control campaign practices, and revival of the Fair Campaign Practices Commission to function as an independent referee of political advertising. The efficacy of each of these options, however, is doubtful.

Existing Legal Options

Existing legal remedies involve three possible courses of action: (1) suing for libel, (2) suing for false advertising, and (3) filing a complaint under a state Fair Campaign Act. The problem with the first two options is that the American courts have shown a consistent disposition to safeguard the unfettered expression of what is termed "traditional political speech."

Albert (1986) surveyed existing court cases and legislation concerning false and/or distortive political statements made on radio and television, pointing out their limitations. He (1986, p. 73) observes that a constraining factor in any legal remedy is "the tolerance in this country of wide-open political debate and excesses in campaign rhetoric [which] is borne of constitutional commitment to free speech and the acceptance of the public of such rhetoric as a part of our democratic system of government."

Suits for libel possess very limited possibilities. "The bottom line then is that the opportunity for candidates to recover damages for defamation along the campaign trail is available only in limited circumstances, and the courts have been blunt in acknowledging the fact" (Albert, 1986, p. 44). In addition, the possibility of filing false advertising complaints with the Federal Communication Commission is not encouraging. Albert (1986) maintains that, due to legal barriers against the censorship of political advertising, neither the Federal Communication Commission (FCC) nor the Federal Trade Commission (FTC) is inclined to take action against false or misleading advertising. Injunctive relief from a court is a possibility, but it is a largely unknown and unused remedy, with only one federal district court opinion on the subject.

Albert (1986) concludes his analysis of possible legal remedies by suggesting that an aggrieved candidate's best chance for success is to file a state Fair Campaign complaint. Some twenty-five states have such codes, and he proposes that the other twenty-five states need to adopt one. Albert's analysis and optimism about this remedy is influenced by the courts' receptivity to the enactment of such statutes (Albert, 1986). Most campaign practitioners are not as optimistic, however, particularly as a result of the need for expeditious action backed by sanctions during the heat of a strongly contested campaign. Due to the limitations of existing legal remedies and the increasing use of negative campaign tactics, some have proposed legislative responses as a viable alternative.

Proposed Legislative Responses

Proposed legislative responses to the use of political attack advertising began in earnest in the 98th Congress (1983–84), with succeeding Congresses considering but not adopting restrictions. Most of the proposed reforms center on the use of "talking heads," requiring candidates attacking an opponent in television advertising to make the attack themselves, rather than relying on surrogates or voice-overs coupled with imagery. This requirement involves the use of what Neale (1987, p. 36) terms "scenes, and production materials . . . aimed at increasing a candidate's accountability for his or her messages; presumably, less negative, less strident communication would be the result." The most recent bill, which received considerable attention by a subcommittee of the Senate Commerce Committee in the 101st Congress (1989–1990), also calls for equal television time so that a candidate can respond to an opponent's attack commercial.

Other proposals of critics include a ban on paid television ads, with a requirement that broadcast stations provide free air time for candidates in order to communicate with voters. Still others prefer regulating political advertising. Such proposed regulations include a requirement that commercials be longer than sixty seconds in order to force candidates to reveal more of who they are and what they stand for. Still other proposals "would eliminate voice-overs, anonymous faces, and actors playing the part of politicians, and they would have candidates, party chairpersons, or interest-group leaders speak to the camera full face for the duration of the advertisement" (Alexander & Haggerty, 1988, p. 5).

Curtis Gans, director of the Committee for the Study of the American Electorate, believes that negative campaigns have had an adverse impact on voter turnout and strongly supports the concept of regulation. He contends that three forms of regulation might prove effective. The first is the previously mentioned proposal to abolish all paid political messages and to allocate a limited amount of free television time. This is the policy used in both Great Britain and Canada. Gans concedes, however, that such a reform tends to work better in a system of tight, ideological, and homogeneous parties, where there is a unitary spokesman for the party as a whole. "It becomes more problematical in our system of heterogeneous parties, a candidate-oriented political process and media markets with 40 or more races within them" (Gans, 1989, p. C2).

A second approach, Gans argues, is Charles Guggenheim's suggestion to abolish the fifteen-, thirty-, and sixty-second spots "and allow only larger and presumably more substantive segments, though broadcasters might legitimately object to having to program odd lots of time" (1989, p. C2). A final regulation is an offshoot of what the French require, "a 'uniform format' regulation in which a candidate simply addresses the camera for the duration of the ad. Such a mandated format is embodied in legislation proposed by Senators Daniel Inouye (D–Hawaii) and Warren Rudman (R–N.H.)" (Gans, 1989, p. C2). Gans maintains that this format would fit best within the American system, "permitting free speech so long as an identified individual was doing the speaking, and would return the process to debate, accountability and answerability" (1989, p. C2).

Others feel, however, that such endeavors are excessively restrictive and would run up against the First Amendment's guarantee of free speech. Herbert Alexander, Director of the Citizen's Research Foundation and a leading scholar on electoral reform, examined a variety of the aforementioned proposals. He concluded that "even if such proposals were to pass constitutional muster—a doubtful prospect in light of the Supreme Court's interpretation of the First Amendment as applied to speech in political campaigns—it is questionable whether the proposals would either reduce campaign costs or enhance political communication" (Alexander & Haggerty, 1988, p. 5). On the regulation requiring personal representation in the ad, a 1984 Congressional Research Service constitutional analysis suggests "that it would be difficult for such legislation to satisfy constitutional guarantees of free speech" (cited in Neale, 1987, p. 38). It is instructive that Senator Danforth, who was hit by an exhaustive negative campaign in 1982 and who introduced a 1985 reform bill requiring personal representation, now accepts the view that such restrictions violate candidates' First Amendment rights (Broder, 1989).

The most recent legislation before the Senate has evoked similar reservations. Republican Mitch McConnell, who used the "Hound Dog" commercials to unseat incumbent Walter Dee Huddleston in 1984, expressed strong opposition to this legislation on the grounds that it "would discourage free and robust debate" (cited in Raasch, 1989, p. C1). Others see legislative restrictions on the use of attack messages as providing incumbents with what may prove to be a decisive advantage in all future elections. John McCain (R-Ariz.) testified that legislative restrictions on political attack messages "would discourage a challenger from talking about an incumbent's record,'' thus in effect taking away the only effective tactic against incumbent candidates (cited in Raasch, 1989, p. C1).

Regardless of policy merits, however, most of the proposed legislative remedies, even if they overcome the reservations of interested lawmakers, would still face considerable judicial scrutiny. In order to overcome constitutional barriers, a more recent campaign-reform proposal of Senators Byrd (D-W. Va.) and Boren (D–Okla.) has attempted to deal with it as a small part of a more comprehensive "good-government" and "campaign finance" regulatory proposal. The portion of the bill dealing with negative campaigning attempts "to curtail this tactic and cut costs, by offering low-cost ad rates only to those candidates who substantially identify themselves in their advertisements" (Alston, 1988, p. 3527). It thus attempts to induce compliance by making participation voluntary and providing financial incentives to do so. This bill did not pass in the 100th Congress (1987–88), but is under consideration again in the 101st Congress (1989–90). The Court, of course, would rule on the constitutionality if such a bill ever made it through the legislative process.

Fair Campaign Practices Commission

Jamieson rejects the call for legislative restrictions and contends that any attempt to regulate the format of campaign ads would inevitably give one candidate an edge over another. As an alternative, she suggests the revival of the privately financed Fair Campaign Practices Commission (FCPC), as a referee in the truth and falsity in political ads. She points out that if the advertiser of a commercial product makes undocumented claims suspected of being false, the networks or station could refuse to run the ad or the Federal Trade Commission might even file false advertising charges. Political advertisements, however, enjoy First Amendment free speech protections, and as a result some type of bipartisan commission is needed to assess them (cited in Broder, 1989).

The FCPC operated from 1956 to 1976, but its former director, Bruce Felknor, said it never had substantial resources or a sufficient partisan balance to do the job appropriately. Moreover, the FCPC as a tax-exempt organization was prevented by the IRS from doing anything that could be construed as intervention for a particular candidate. It solicited and publicized complaints about unfair practices but issued no rulings of its own. Felknor observes that what the FCPC tried to do was "to stimulate the press to examine the incident and who smeared whom" (cited in Broder, 1989, p. A22). Given the proper resources and partisan balance, this is a function Jamieson believes a revitalized FCPC could perform in "essentially providing a news peg for the press to do stories about the advertising tactics campaigns are using. But she and others argue that, even in the absence of an FCPC, the press should be doing more 'truth-squadding' than it is" (cited in Broder, 1989, p. A22).

IMPROBABILITY OF VOLUNTARY RESTRAINT

Voluntary action also has been suggested as a way to limit political attack messages. However, very few believe that this approach would work, since it requires consultants and candidates to restrict their strategic options in the face of an increasing perception on the part of both that attack messages are one of the few viable approaches for candidates who trail an opponent (Sabato, 1981).

Professional Code of Ethics

One voluntary approach is adherence to a professional code of ethics. The American Association of Political Consultants (AAPC), for example, has such a code. Among other things, it pledges its members "to appeal to the good and commendable ideals in the American voters and not to indulge in irrational appeals . . . not to disseminate false or misleading information intentionally— [and] not to indulge in any activity which corrupts or degrades the practice of political campaigning . . . '' (Broder, 1989, p. A22). Bradley S. O'Leary, president of the AAPC, said that in thirteen years since the association was founded, none of its approximately 1,000 members have ever been disciplined for violation. One censure was initiated, however, but the threat of a lawsuit caused it to be dropped. Instead O'Leary and other consultants argue that "the marketplace imposes an informal but effective discipline on 'bad actors,' who can lose their bids for future business because other consultants will not work with them or candidates are told that they should be wary of employing them'' (cited in Broder, 1989, p. A22).

Other consultants, though, are critical of the ability of professional codes of ethics and the marketplace to enforce accountability and standards. Republican consultant Douglas Bailey observed: "I don't think there's any sanction at all within the industry, no standards that are generally accepted . . . There's a general body of knowledge of what works and what doesn't, but that's not the same as a code of ethical behavior'' (cited in Broder, 1989, p. A22). Democrat consultants express similar sentiments. Stan Greenberg noted, "I would like to say there is a standard of truthfulness at work. In fact, there is a much more pragmatic standard, which is, 'we'll use whatever the press will let us get away with' '' (cited in Broder, 1989, p. A22). Democratic pollster Geoff Garin said, "In the marketplace the standard is winning, and my sense is that the standards get lower and lower all the time. . . . Consultants get judged in their won–lost records, not on the character of their campaigns'' (cited in Broder, 1989, p. A22). In short, professional codes of ethics, like much in politics, are broad, vague, and lacking in sanctions. They posit ideals that a few individuals of outstanding character might strive for, but for the most part code contents are not widely applied in practice.

Voluntary Agreements by Parties and/or Candidates

Still another possible voluntary approach to attack politics is through self-regulation by the major parties and candidates. Neale observes that "the basis for a joint program exists in the established tradition whereby the Democratic and Republican national chairman have signed, and agreed to abide by the principles of the Code of Fair Campaign Practices (FCPC) during the Presidential election years" (Neale, 1987, p. 44).

In 1987 Paul Kirk, the Democratic party national chairman, issued a program of eight "resolves" for the 1988 Democratic presidential nomination campaign. Released on March 11, 1987, they requested mutual respect among candidates and called for candidates to conduct positive campaigns. A Democratic Unity Task Force of public officials and party activists was established to monitor the "tone and tenor" of the nomination campaign. As Kirk formulated it, the Task Force was to "advise, admonish, and—if necessary—publicly bring political pressure to bear on any candidate, campaign or constituency group indulging in negative campaigning" (Neale, 1987, p. 44).

The 1988 Democratic presidential campaign, by Kirk's standards, did not work well, thus underscoring the limitations of voluntary agreements. In early March of 1988, House Speaker Jim Wright called on all Democratic presidential candidates to stop using negative television advertisements for the rest of the campaign and complained that they distort the political debate and mislead voters. Advertisements attacking party rivals, he argued, tend to "tarnish and muddle the process of democracy. . . . Those overriding principles which bind us as Democrats are far more significant than the things that separate us" (Getlin, 1988, p. 24). Democratic Party Chairman Paul Kirk himself asked Democrats to stop the backbiting and said, "I do think the accumulation of negative ads is not good. We want to be stronger, not weaker" (cited in Rheem, 1988, p. 1). The public rhetoric of both Wright and Kirk suggests that the so-called voluntary intraparty agreement did not work well.

Voluntary interparty agreements fared no better in the general election, as extensive negative campaigning was the order of the day. On September 9, 1987, the U.S. Senate approved unanimously (87–0) a nonbinding resolution (S. Res. 279) on clean campaigns. As Jeremy Gaunt describes it, the resolution urged

its members and party campaign committees—the National Republican Senatorial Committee (NRSC) and the Democratic Senatorial Campaign Committee (DSCC)—to avoid negative and personal attacks during election campaigns. Specifically, candidates and the committees were called upon to engage in positive and constructive campaigns, avoiding negative attacks calculated to impugn the character, integrity or patriotism of a candidate. (Gaunt, 1987, p. 2194)

It is clear that this resolution had little impact on the actual conduct of the 1988 campaign. Recall also that candidate-initiated efforts to stop all future negative advertising have a poor track record as well. Although campaign strategy and resource constraints played a role, 1986 Pennsylvania Republican gubernatorial candidate William Scranton and 1988 New Jersey Republican senatorial candidate Pete Dawkins were both unsuccessful in getting their Democratic counterparts to adhere to such an agreement. It amounted to unilateral campaign disarmament, as Democrats Bob Casey and Frank Lautenberg continued their negative advertising through election day and won the Pennsylvania governorship and New Jersey Senate seat respectively. Voluntary agreements by major parties and candidates are clearly an inadequate defense against attack message politics.

USING PARTICIPANT INTERESTS

The final options involve the participants in the political campaign process, particularly candidates, consultants, and the mass media, who are motivated as a result of the role that each assumes in what is an adversarial process to police the actions of other players.

The Media as Referee

One defense mechanism to assure that attack politics does not get out of control involves the role of the media as a referee. Many consultants take the view that it is the role of the media to police the accuracy and fairness of campaign advertising, although some consultants and many journalists disagree. Democratic media adviser Robert Squire told a 1988 post-election American Press Institute press conference:

The biggest failing of the press was in covering [advertising] spots and media. . . . You should have been much tougher in dealing with us and the stuff we put on. . . . You should treat advertising like a speech and when a candidate says something that is untrue, say so. Don't stand on the sidelines. Be a referee. (cited in Broder, 1989, p. A22)

A Republican consultant, Don Sipple, agreed and stated that it was part of the media's role to inform and to educate voters. Republican pollster Richard Wirthlin, however, disagreed and questioned whether the press ought to be a referee. In Wirthlin's view, the primary, if not sole, responsibility for monitoring should remain with the candidates and campaigns. Many media people tend to side with Wirthlin's position, but some favor a more active role. Richard Threlkeld, for example, did a piece on October 19, 1988, for ABC News that presented a critical analysis of the presidential campaign ads. *Washington Post* journalist Lloyd Grove was impressed with Threlkeld's piece and then wrote some articles of his own that analyzed the ads critically. In retrospect, Grove assessed the media's performance and said, ''I think we probably didn't pay enough attention [to the accuracy of the ads] early on. We treated it too much as a game, and focused too much on tactics rather than content'' (cited in Broder, 1989, p. A22).

Although some media people performed the referee or "truth-squadding" function endorsed by Jamieson, many did not. There appears to be a lack of consensus in the media community about whether and to what extent the media should police the accuracy of political advertising. Until such a consensus develops, the media will not be an adequate counterweight to keep attack politics under control.

It needs to be emphasized, however, that while the media can make a stronger contribution as a defense against excessive attack politics, there is an inherent limitation on its ability to play a primary role. That limitation is the "symbiotic" relationship between journalists on one hand, and governmental officials and politicians on the other. Jay Blumler and Michael Gurevitch (1981) note that there are two paradigms for conceptualizing the relationship between the media and government/politics. One is the "adversary approach" that implies ongoing conflict, and the other is an exchange or "symbiosis" approach that implies ongoing cooperation. Although there is a widespread presumption about the adversarial relationship, partly reinforced by the stellar efforts of *Washington Post* reporters Woodward and Bernstein on the Watergate issue, recent scholarly works have emphasized the development of a largely cooperative or "symbiotic" relationship (Bennett, 1988; Entman, 1989; Hess, 1981; Paletz & Entman, 1981; Press & Verburg, 1988; L. Sigal, 1973).

It is our view that the symbiotic approach is quite applicable to the study of campaign politics. In his classic work, *The Rise of Political Consultants*, Sabato (1981) raised the question why the media has not been more diligent in analyzing the activities of consultants and campaign advertising. His answer lay in the importance of consultants as sources of information for political reporters. The latter depend on consultants for information in much the same way previous generations of reporters depended on key state and county party "bosses."

David Broder, the *Washington Post's* senior political reporter, agrees with Sabato, and notes that Sabato's analysis was borne out in the election of 1988. Broder cites an article by Tim Miller and David Stebenne in the *Gannett Center Journal* to support his point. The Miller–Stebenne study "showed that of the 18 most-often-quoted sources on the 1988 campaign in a dozen leading news outlets, half were professional consultants. Moreover, a much larger stream of unattributed information flows to political journalists from the consultants, who built credibility and credits for themselves and their future clients by their candor in assessing the campaigns in which they are working" (Broder, 1989, p. A22).

In 1988 the role of the media in performing a referee function was mixed at best. Nevada, North Carolina, Texas, and Delaware are states cited by consultants where the media came down hard on campaigns that had distortions in their political ads (Broder, 1989). The Metzenbaum–Voinovich Ohio Senate race, analyzed in an earlier chapter, is yet another example of the media playing a referee role. Some consultants, like Democrat Robert Squire, give the media low marks overall. On the other hand, other analysts shared the view of Sabato, who said of the 1988 election, "I think the press did a better job of policing the

ads than ever before . . . but I still did not see much criticism of consultants''
(cited in Broder, 1989, p. A22). In view of the absence of a consensus of what
the media's role should be and the inherent constraint of the "symbiotic" relationship between media and government/politics, our contention is that media
can never be an exclusive or primary counterweight against the excesses of attack
politics.

Candidate Defenses

As Chapters 1–3 have demonstrated, attack politics is the rule and not the
exception in contemporary campaigns. Given the inadequacies of legal and voluntary restraints, the question remains, How can candidates protect themselves
against political attacks?

There is considerable merit in Jamieson's general position that "the best
available defense seems to be the vigilance of the opposing candidate and party"
(1988, p. C2). There is a question, however, as to what "vigilance" entails.
Jamieson stresses the need for candidates to strategically exploit mass media
news, advertising, and political debates in order to provide direct responses to
an opponent's attack messages.

However, Jamieson's suggestions—using news, advertising, and debates to
provide explicit or implicit rebuttals to an attack—are post hoc. Although they
may be prepared in advance, they are implemented following an opponent's
attack. This inherently limits their effectiveness.

First, it is unclear whether refutation or rebuttal messages can accomplish
much more than to minimize the damage already done by an attack message,
especially in the long term, following the disassociation of the content and its
origins. As a result, the track record of refutation and rebuttal messages is mixed.
Three incumbent senators, Bayh, Church, and McGovern, employed rebuttal
advertising in response to opponents' attacks on their "liberal" voting records
in 1980, but the strategy was only able to reduce their margins of defeat (Hershey,
1984). Rebuttal or refutation messages worked for Melcher in 1982 (Sabato,
1983) and for both Gramm (Aristotle Industries, 1985) and Humphrey (Beiler,
1987) in 1984. However, the very rebuttal message that Humphrey utilized to
deflect his opponent's Social Security attack in 1984 failed when employed by
Abdnor for the same purpose in 1986.

In addition, refutation and rebuttal messages are useless in response to an
opponent's attack that is launched late in a close campaign, thus simply precluding a response. This limitation is particularly important in light of reports
of increasing use of "last-minute" political attacks in a number of 1988 presidential primary contests (Colford, 1988a).

The most effective strategy is for candidates to preempt opponents' attacks
prior to their use, thus militating against their effectiveness. Chapters 2 and 3
delineated numerous examples of the use of preemptive strategies during campaigns from 1982 to 1988. Preemptive messages anticipate specific attacks that

might be initiated by an opponent, answering them through the use of on-point messages delivered in advance of the attacks. However, preemption carries one important weakness: *it requires candidates and their consultants to anticipate all potential attacks, and to prepare and implement specific messages covering all potential vulnerabilities.* This is a difficult and costly undertaking, at best.

A more effective alternative involves the use of a specific form of preemption, the inoculation message strategy. It is a strategy of resistance to the influence of potential political attack messages that holds much promise. Chapter 5 explains the nature of inoculation, and Chapters 6–9 detail the results of an extensive program of research on the efficacy of the inoculation message strategy.

The Nature of Inoculation

The best way to counteract any exaggeration is the well-worn device by which the speaker puts in some criticism of himself.

—Aristotle

(cited in Solmsen, ed., *The Rhetoric and the Poetics of Aristotle,* p. 139)

[A] body of research dealing with the techniques for inducing resistance to change has accumulated. We view this research as a valuable, largely ignored contribution to the literature of persuasion.

—Gerald R. Miller and Michael Burgoon,
Professors of Communication (Miller & Burgoon, 1973, p. 6)

The inoculation message strategy grew out of research on the relative persuasive effectiveness of one-sided versus two-sided messages in the early 1950s. As the titles of these message strategies suggest, the speaker who employs a one-sided message seeks to persuade receivers by presenting arguments supporting only one side of a controversial issue, whereas the speaker who uses a two-sided message attempts to influence by acknowledging both sides of a controversial issue, employing a combination of bolstering and refutation in developing their position.

An unexpected finding of this early research was that the two-sided message made receivers more resistant to subsequent counterpersuasion (Lumsdaine & Janis, 1953). In other words, in addition to the short-term impacts of the messages on receiver attitudes, the two-sided messages offered the additional benefit of fostering attitude persistence, such that receivers were made less vulnerable to subsequent attempts to change their attitudes. This finding, though interesting, required a theoretical position to unlock its full promise. The question was, why do two-sided messages confer resistance to subsequent counterpersuasion?

William J. McGuire, a social psychologist, initially at the University of Illinois and later at Columbia University, tackled this question in a research program that spanned the late 1950s and much of the 1960s. The timing was ripe for the attention to strategies of resistance to persuasion. There was concern for the fact that some American prisoners of war had broken during the Korean War, admittedly under tremendous pressure from North Korean captors, yielding to counterarguments about the validity of the American position on the war and the superiority of the American way of life (United States Senate, 1956). In contrast to the limited effects view of mass media influence that had come to dominate the thinking of academics during the 1950s (Katz & Lazarsfeld, 1955), McGuire was preoccupied with what he termed "the disconcerting vulnerability of people's convictions in forced exposure situations . . . [and particularly] the political indoctrination of captive audiences" (McGuire & Papageorgis, 1961, p. 327).

In addition, resistance to persuasion was an interesting, and at this moment, novel question. Since the 1920s, both academics and practitioners had devoted considerable energy and resources in finding new and better ways to persuade receivers. Gerald Miller and Michael Burgoon (1973, p. 6) acknowledged this preoccupation of the extant literature in social influence: "In examining the writings in the field . . . persuasion is treated almost exclusively as a facilitator of change." Indeed until the late 1950s, there was practically no emphasis on conferring resistance to—protecting people against—persuasion. What was surprising was that this question had been neglected for so long.

DEFINITION AND DESCRIPTION

Inoculation is a message strategy that seeks to promote resistance to attitude change. It attempts to motivate receivers to strengthen attitudes, making them less susceptible to subsequent persuasive attempts.

The initial formulation of inoculation theory utilized a biological analogy to explain how messages confer resistance to persuasion. As McGuire (1970, p. 37) describes, "We can develop belief resistance in people as we develop disease resistance in a biologically overprotected man or animal; by exposing the person to a weak dose of the attacking material strong enough to stimulate his defenses but not strong enough to overwhelm him."

This formulation, employing the biological analogy, assumed "overprotection" and limited the early inoculation research to what McGuire termed "cultural truisms," beliefs uncontaminated by counterarguments and "so generally accepted that most individuals are unaware of attacking arguments" (McGuire, 1970, p. 37). He located four "overprotected " issues in the health care context. Subsequently, McGuire (1970) focused both the attack and the defense messages of his research program on one or more of the following attitudes: the value of an annual medical examination; the benefits of regular toothbrushing; the merits of penicillin; and the advisability of getting a chest X-ray annually to guard against tuberculosis.

McGuire was tempted to frame inoculation in broader terms, maintaining that because people selectively avoid content that runs contrary to existing beliefs, many if not most attitudes are in effect overprotected and thus candidates for inoculation. Indeed, in an initial comparison of supportive and refutational approaches in resistance, McGuire (1961a, p. 184) grounded his predictions on the selective exposure thesis, "that people tend to defend their beliefs by avoiding exposure to counterarguments rather than by developing positive supports for the beliefs." Subsequently, however, he found it safer to restrict inoculation to "cultural truisms" because of conflicting research findings on selective exposure, a particularly popular topic for research in social influence during the 1950s (Anderson & McGuire, 1965).

Inoculation theory posits that refutational pretreatments, which raise the specter of potentially damaging content to the receiver's attitude while simultaneously providing direct refutation of that content in the presence of a supporting environment, threaten the individual, triggering the motivation to bolster arguments supporting the receiver's attitudes, thereby conferring resistance (Papageorgis & McGuire, 1961). Figure 5.1 illustrates this process.

It is important that inoculation is more than preemptive refutation, the process of responding to counterarguments in advance. Indeed, if the construct were limited to preemptive refutation, it would afford limited utility since communicators would need to prepare specific preemptive messages corresponding to each and every anticipated attack. Instead, a refutational pretreatment includes the use of threat, usually operationalized as a warning of an impending and potentially persuasive attack. It is threat that triggers the motivation to bolster attitudes, thus fostering resistance to counterpersuasion.

Thus, preemptive refutation of specific counterarguments is a necessary, but not sufficient, ingredient in inoculation. The process works by motivating receivers to bolster attitudes, an internal process, and not by simply providing answers to specific counterarguments. As McGuire (1962, p. 248) maintains, "The resistance conferred by the refutational defense . . . derives not only from the assimilation and retention of the bolstering material . . . but also from the motivational effect of the preexposure to threatening material."

The threat component of the pretreatment message is the integral element in inoculation, motivating receivers to defend against any potential attack, rather than rehearsing for specific arguments and rendering themselves defenseless against different arguments that might be encountered (Miller & Burgoon, 1973, p. 40). This suggests that inoculation carries tremendous potential since, through threat and preemptive refutation, it is able to spread a blanket of protection over the receiver against a wide array of potential counterarguments.

Figure 5.1
The Inoculation Process

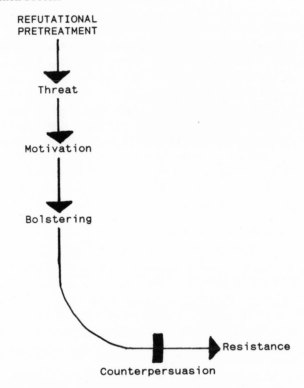

EARLY RESEARCH FINDINGS

The early research on inoculation supported the viability of the theoretical construct, confirming the superiority of the refutational as opposed to the supportive approach in conferring resistance; confirming the theory that refutational pretreatments provide resistance to both same and different counterarguments, a very important implication of the original theory; and providing a good deal of specific information involving the implementation of inoculation, including placement, decay, and reinforcement.

The design of this early research followed a common model, although the specific variables examined depended on the focus of each of the investigations. Attack messages were written on one or more "cultural truisms," and appropriate treatment messages (e.g., supportive, inoculation same, inoculation different, etc.) were prepared for each of the attack messages. The treatment messages were administered in advance of the attack messages.

The supportive messages sought to bolster existing receiver attitudes, whereas the refutational or inoculation messages were designed first to threaten receivers, warning of the prospect of a potentially persuasive attack, and then to provide

Figure 5.2
Typical Inoculation Design

SESSION	ATTACK ONLY (CONTROL)	INOCULATION FOLLOWED BY ATTACK		INOCULATION; NO ATTACK	CONTROL; NO INOCULATION; NO ATTACK
		SAME	DIFFERENT		
First	_____	_____	_____	X	X
Second	X	X	X	X	X

Note: X identifies the assessment of subjects' beliefs. To
determine an inoculation effect, Second Session subjects' beliefs
in both the Inoculation Same and Inoculation Different conditions
were compared to subjects' beliefs in the Attack Only (Control)
condition. No Attack, No Inoculation and No Attack conditions
were utilized as manipulation checks.

Source: "The generality of immunity to persuasion produced by
preexposure to weakened counterarguments" by D. Papageorgis and
W. J. McGuire, 1961, Journal of Abnormal and Social Psychology,
62.

refutation, which was specific to the content of the impending attack in the
inoculation same condition and generic (on the same subject as, but not addressing
the specific content of, the impending attack) in the inoculation different condition. For example, one of the issues used in McGuire's research concerned
the desirability of annual medical examinations. As McGuire (1970) explains
the process, receivers overwhelmingly accepted the wisdom of such examinations. Consequently, subsequent attack messages would stress that annual examinations were costly and turned people into hypochondriacs (McGuire, 1970).
However, prior to the attack, receivers were administered one of three pretreatments. The supportive pretreatments simply reinforced this attitude, indicating
that checkups insure early detection of potential health problems (McGuire,
1970). By contrast, the inoculation same pretreatments warned of an impending
attack against the receiver's attitude, and provided specific refutation of the
arguments that were to appear in the attack; whereas the inoculation different
pretreatments warned of impending attack, and provided refutation of arguments
against examinations other than those that were to appear in the attack message
(McGuire, 1970).

The effectiveness of the various treatments was assessed by comparing the
strength of receiver beliefs following exposure to the attack messages in the
treated and untreated (control) conditions. A design used in one of the studies
is illustrated in Figure 5.2.

Superiority of the Refutational Approach

The focus of the first laboratory research on inoculation concerned the relative superiority of refutational as opposed to supportive pretreatments in conferring resistance to subsequent attacks. This research was sparked by the unexpected finding, noted previously, that two-sided messages provide an additional benefit over one-sided messages in making receivers resistant to counterpersuasion (Lumsdaine & Janis, 1953).

The superiority of refutational pretreatments was essential to the logical underpinning of inoculation theory, and thus the early research concentrated on this issue. Since motivation is essential to the theory, refutational pretreatments should prove more effective. Aside from preparing receivers for the content of subsequent attacks, the refutational pretreatment threatens receivers, thus triggering the motivation to bolster attitudes, thereby promoting resistance (Papageorgis & McGuire, 1961). Supportive pretreatments solely consist of arguments that support receiver beliefs, completely ignoring potential counterarguments contrary to those beliefs (McGuire, 1962). Thus, supportive pretreatments don't threaten receivers and therefore lack the basic capacity to motivate receivers to bolster their attitudes. In fact, the supportive pretreatment may serve to falsely reassure receivers of their beliefs, thus making them more vulnerable to subsequent attacks.

In a series of direct comparisons of the two approaches, most investigators reported that refutational pretreatments were superior to supportive (Anderson & McGuire, 1965; McGuire, 1961a, 1962; McGuire & Papageorgis, 1961, 1962; Papageorgis & McGuire, 1961; Tannenbaum, Macaulay & Norris, 1966; Tannenbaum & Norris, 1965), although a few of the studies concluded that the use of both was superior to using either separately (Anatol & Mandel, 1972; Burgoon & Chase, 1973; McGuire, 1961a, 1962; Tannenbaum & Norris, 1965).

Controversy arose over why the combined approach conferred more resistance. McGuire (1961a) attributed the added effectiveness of the combined pretreatments to the threatening component of the refutational pretreatment. On the other hand, Percy Tannenbaum and Eleanor Norris (1965) used congruity theory to explain the effectiveness of the combined pretreatments, maintaining that each pretreatment simply boosts the other, thus increasing the inconsistency of the subsequent counterarguments.

These findings provided a solid foundation of support for the underlying premise of inoculation theory. Most subsequent research would explore more intricate issues in inoculation.

Refutational Same and Different Pretreatments

Because inoculation confers resistance through motivation, and not simply by providing refutational preemption on specific content, a question arises as to whether an inoculation effect extends beyond the specific content of the pretreatment. If it does, inoculation becomes a powerful construct in persuasion, because inoculation would enable the communicator to utilize a single refutational pretreatment to spread a large umbrella of protection over a broad content area. Thus, the early research addressed the relative effectiveness of inoculation in fostering resistance to both refutational same and refutational different counterarguments.

In the first study of inoculation and same and different counterarguments, Papageorgis and McGuire (1961) found that the refutational pretreatments conferred resistance to both same and different counterarguments. Although the pattern of the means indicated a slight superiority of refutational same defenses, the differences were not statistically significant. Following up on this finding, McGuire's (1961b, 1962, 1970) research program provided further support for the prediction that inoculation confers resistance to both same and different counterarguments.

These findings confirm that refutational pretreatments serve to motivate receivers, as opposed to providing specific answers to counterarguments. The threatening pretreatment triggers an internal process in receivers, motivating them to bolster their attitudes, thus making them resistant to counterarguments that contain both same and different content than the pretreatment. In subsequent studies, investigators manipulated threat levels, finding that greater threat affords more resistance (McGuire, 1962, 1964; McGuire & Papageorgis, 1961, 1962).

Other Findings

One of the important outcomes of the early research, beyond the theoretical concerns, was providing information about the specific implementation of inoculation pretreatments. Thus, the early research findings informed future research and practice in indicating the optimal placement of pretreatments, the rate of decay of pretreatments, the role of reinforcement in militating decay, and other information.

Prerefutation versus Postrefutation. Because inoculation theory posits that threat triggers the motivation to resist attacks, the theoretical construct implies that refutation is more effective if it precedes rather than follows exposure to an attack message. Ironically, this basic assumption received very little attention in the early research. Tannenbaum and Norris (1965) tested the relative effectiveness of refutation administered before and after an attack. While the differences weren't statistically significant, the authors (1965, p. 157) concluded that "immunization allows for the introduction of more defense arousal. . . ." A year later, Tannenbaum, Macaulay, and Norris (1966) conducted a similar experiment, concluding that while both approaches conferred resistance, the refutation–attack sequence was somewhat more effective.

Pretreatment Decay and Reinforcement. It makes intuitive sense that inoculation pretreatments decay with the passage of time. The threat generated and the specific content provided should dissipate over time, much as any message stimulus would. Many of the early studies on inoculation employed relatively short intervals between the administration of the inoculation treatment and the persuasive attack. The delay between inoculation and attack ranged from a few minutes (McGuire, 1970; Pryor & Steinfatt, 1978; Tannenbaum & Norris, 1965) to a maximum of two weeks (McGuire, 1970; Ullman & Bodaken, 1975). Most of the early studies did not examine the effectiveness of inoculation at multiple time periods. But the few that did indicated that inoculation diminishes over time (McGuire, 1962, 1970; Pryor & Steinfatt, 1978).

Also, the early research indicated that the effectiveness of inoculation over time depends to some degree on the type of inoculation message employed. McGuire (1962) and Burt Pryor and Thomas Steinfatt (1978) found that the decay of inoculation was less with refutational different in contrast to refutational same pretreatments. This is consistent with the central role of threat, and consequently motivation, in inoculation. Although receivers may forget the specific content of a message, the motivational effect lingers because the inoculation process has triggered an internal process in which receivers are motivated to seek additional arguments and information in support of their attitudes.

Very little early research concentrated on the role of reinforcement in inoculation. McGuire (1961b), in testing the superiority of "active" and "passive" inoculation pretreatments (in the active condition subjects were asked to write an essay that showed how the counterarguments could be refuted), reported that while "single defenses" were effective with both same and different counterarguments, "double defenses" provided a significant boost with same counterarguments. In another study, Tannenbaum, Macaulay, and Norris (1966) found that "concept-boost" messages provided a slight increase in resistance compared to a single message, but the difference fell short of statistical significance.

EXTENDING THE DOMAIN OF INOCULATION

The early research on inoculation focused on what McGuire termed "cultural truisms," germ-free beliefs uncontaminated by counterarguments. As indicated previously, McGuire was tempted to frame inoculation in broader terms, maintaining that because people selectively avoid content that runs contrary to existing beliefs, many if not most attitudes are in effect overprotected, and thus candidates for inoculation. However, he was concerned about the conflicting research findings on selective exposure (Anderson & McGuire, 1965). In addition, McGuire (1962) posited that it would be more difficult to threaten receivers on more controversial topics, and since threat served as the theoretical lynchpin in inoculation theory, that it would not be possible to replicate the early findings on more controversial issues.

This question involving the domain of inoculation theory was the focus of scholars during the 1960s and 1970s. Insko (1967) argued that inoculation theory was limited to germ-free beliefs, and as a result, that its applicability was restricted. Pryor and Steinfatt (1978) responded that McGuire's rationale was faulty, that the biological analogy applies to specific arguments and not to topics. "In the biological case, there are no cultural truisms, no totally unattacked organs. What is required is that the beliefs in question must not have been attacked by a *particular* virus (argument or position), not that they must have never been attacked at all" (p. 219). In other words, as long as the receiver has not been previously exposed to the specific content contained in the pretreatment and subsequent attack, it would be possible to inoculate, even on more controversial issues.

However, Pryor and Steinfatt (1978) failed in an effort to extend inoculation theory to middle-level or high-level beliefs. They reasoned that refutational pretreatments would prove more effective than supportive in fostering resistance with higher level beliefs. Instead, they found supportive pretreatments to be very successful at all belief levels. In explaining their results, they noted the possibility that language intensity had contributed to the effectiveness of the supportive pretreatments, a variable that has been shown to affect resistance outcomes in a series of studies (Burgoon & Chase, 1973; Burgoon, Cohen, Miller & Montgomery, 1978; Burgoon & King, 1974; Burgoon & Miller, 1971; Miller & Burgoon, 1979).

Clearly, there is nothing in the original message sidedness research that warrants a limitation of inoculation to germ-free beliefs. Indeed, the Lumsdaine and Janis (1953) study described earlier employed a highly controversial propaganda message and found that the two-sided message fostered resistance to attacks. In explaining the resistance finding, they (Lumsdaine & Janis, 1953, p. 318) reasoned

if the initial communication is . . . a two-sided one it will already have taken into account both the positive and negative arguments and still have reached the positive conclusion. When the listener is then subsequently exposed to the persuasion of opposing arguments . . . he is less likely to be influenced by them . . . [since] he has been given an advanced basis for ignoring or discounting the opposing communication and, thus "inoculated," he will tend to retain the positive conclusion.

It is reasonable to conclude that the two-sided message is the prototypical refutational pretreatment, complete with threat, and that it contains the potential to motivate receivers to bolster attitudes on both noncontroversial and controversial topics.

A number of studies during the 1970s (Burgoon et. al., 1976; Burgoon & Chase, 1973; Burgoon, Cohen, Miller & Montgomery, 1978; Burgoon & King, 1974; Freedman & Steinbruner, 1964; Infante, 1975; McCroskey, 1970; McCroskey, Young & Scott, 1972; Miller & Burgoon, 1979; Tate & Miller, 1973; Ullman & Bodaken, 1975) applied a number of the basic tenets of inoculation theory to more controversial topics. Burgoon, Cohen, Miller, and Montgomery (1978, p. 38) and Miller and Burgoon (1979, p. 312), in the process of positing and testing alternative resistance models, offered a rationale to support broader application. "While earlier research spent effort attempting to specify optimal pretreatment strategies, [these investigations provide] evidence to suggest that ... any message may affect the persuasive efficacy of a subsequent persuasive attack."

This rationale suggests that the boundaries of inoculation theory are broader than McGuire initially posited, encompassing both noncontroversial and controversial topics. This affords greater utility to inoculation theory, since most of the issues that are important enough to warrant an inoculation effort are also more controversial in nature.

One domain that contains issues that are important enough to warrant an inoculation effort involves political attack messages. As the results of our research program confirm, the inoculation message approach is a viable strategy to deflect the persuasive impact of political attack messages (Pfau & Burgoon, 1988; Pfau, Kenski, Nitz & Sorenson, 1989a). The nature, results, and implications of this program of research on inoculation in political campaign communication is the focus of Chapters 6–9.

Chapter 6

Application of Inoculation to Political Campaigns

[The Abdnor–Daschle race] has become more immersed in punch–counterpunch television exchanges—and has strayed closer to character assassination—than any other in the nation.

Jerry Hagstrom and Robert Guskind, Political Analysts
(Hagstrom & Guskind, 1986, p. 2623)

Dukakis marched to his own drummer. He did not believe in attack politics.

—Marjorie Randon Hershey, Professor of Political Science
(Hershey, 1989, p. 78)

Inoculation and preemption are what win campaigns.

—Jim Innocenzi, Consultant
(cited in Ehrenhalt, 1985, p. 2653)

While the extant literature in political communication has viewed persuasion as central to political campaigns (McBath & Fisher, 1969), it also has treated conversion as synonymous with persuasion (Miller & Burgoon, 1973). Thus, practice and research involving political campaigns have focused largely on attempts to change receiver attitude and voting behavior (Kraus & Davis, 1976).

This research program adopts the view of Miller and Burgoon (1973) regarding the objectives of persuasion. They distinguish the attempt to change attitudes and behaviors from the effort to foster resistance to change in existing attitudes and behaviors. "The former objective has been extensively studied by students of persuasion; the latter has been relatively unexplored" (Miller & Burgoon, 1973, p. 16).

Thus, this research program assumes that, just as political messages can be designed to convert receivers, they also can be structured so as to foster resistance in receivers to potential conversion. This research program operationalized resistance in terms of McGuire's inoculation theory, applying the construct to the political campaign communication context.

The application of inoculation theory to political campaign communication is both useful and important to scholars as well as practitioners. As a result of the rising tide of attack messages in contemporary campaigns, increasing attention has focused on a practical question, What can be done to combat attack messages?

Few answers have appeared to date. The more popular and obvious options contain serious shortcomings. As discussed in Chapter 4, legislative efforts to restrict attack messages are unlikely to survive judicial scrutiny, given the Court's firm support for the unfettered expression of "traditional political speech" (Alexander & Haggerty, 1988; Broder, 1989; Neale, 1987). The voluntary surrender of the attack option is unlikely since attack messages are perceived to be an effective strategic tool, particularly for candidates who trail opponents (Sabato, 1981).

Another possibility is to attack first. Such a strategy can be effective, as the 1986 Cranston and 1988 Lautenberg senatorial campaigns demonstrate. It is less likely to be used, however, because it is a high-risk strategy and because most American politicians are, by nature, risk averse. Still another option is to counterattack, but this allows the opponent to establish the initial definition of candidate images, and thus is at best a damage containment strategy.

Finally, the post-hoc refutation of the content of political attacks, the most common strategic response to date, provides limited potential. First, it is unclear whether refutation messages can do much more than to minimize the damage already done by an attack message, especially in the long term, following the disassociation of the content and the source of the attack (Hagstrom & Guskind, 1986; Pfau, Kenski, Nitz & Sorenson, 1989b). Second, post-hoc refutation messages are of no value against an opponent's attack that is launched late in a close campaign, thus simply precluding any response.

As a result, political consultants have begun to explore refutational preemption as a strategic option in response to the attack message. Republican consultant Jim Innocenzi (cited in Ehrenhalt, 1985, p. 2563) claims that "inoculation and preemption are what win campaigns." Consultant Charlie Black agrees, stating that "if you know what your negatives are, you can preempt" (cited in Ehrenhalt, 1985, p. 2563). Salmore and Salmore (1985, p. 80) advise incumbents to "anticipate negatives and preempt them." Stephen Frantzich's (1989, pp. 220–221) interviews with active political consultants revealed that "potential subjects of attack often use 'inoculation letters'. A preemptive letter outlining your position on a sensitive issue protects you from future negative information the voter might receive."

However, refutational preemption is a necessary but not a sufficient ingredient in inoculation. As discussed in Chapter 5, inoculation promotes resistance through the use of a warning of an impending attack, *employed in conjunction with* refutational preemption. The warning of an impending attack is designed to threaten the individual, triggering the motivation to bolster arguments supporting attitudes, thereby conferring resistance to subsequent counterpersuasion (Anderson & McGuire, 1965; McGuire, 1964, 1970; Papageorgis & McGuire, 1961). It is the two elements in tandem, threat plus refutational preemption, that distinguish inoculation from other message strategies.

The present research program constitutes the first attempt to apply inoculation theory to the political campaign context, examining its potential in promoting resistance to the influence of attack messages among potential voters.

DESCRIPTION OF THE 1986 AND 1988 STUDIES

The effectiveness of inoculation was assessed in two large, experimental field investigations, the first using a data set from the 1986 campaign between Republican incumbent James Abdnor and Democratic challenger Tom Daschle for the U.S. Senate from South Dakota, and the second employing a data set involving the 1988 general election presidential campaign between Republican George Bush and Democrat Michael Dukakis.

The Research Setting

The 1986 investigation featured two highly respected and well-known opposing candidates (Fialka, 1986). Abdnor had won the Senate seat in 1980 over incumbent George McGovern. Prior to declaring his candidacy for the U.S. Senate, Daschle had served four terms in the House of Representatives.

Both candidates made extensive use of political advertising during the campaign. Altogether, Abdnor and Daschle spent $6.6 million, most of which was targeted for media advertising. The $6.6 million amounted to $9.40 for each South Dakota resident or more than $22 for each vote cast in the election (Brokaw, 1986). One journalist estimated in late October that the average South Dakota resident had been exposed to more than 300 political advertisements on behalf of the two candidates (Fialka, 1986). To put this in some kind of perspective, Hagstrom and Guskind (1986, p. 2619) commented during the days before the election that "by election day, South Dakotans will have seen more television commercials this year for Republican Sen. James Abdnor and his opponent, Rep. Thomas A. Daschle, than for Coca Cola, Budweiser or Chrysler cars." The study was conducted during October 1986.

In addition, some of the commercial messages, particularly the Abdnor attack on Daschle for his association with actress Jane Fonda (an implicit charge that Daschle was too "liberal" for South Dakota), which Abdnor used to close the gap on Daschle, but which Daschle finally answered with an advertisement that showed stereotypic political "pols" gathered in a "smoke-filled room" discussing ways to smear Daschle, were singled out for national network coverage as among the most aggressive messages in the 1986 campaigns (Stengel, 1986). Hagstrom and Guskind (1986, p. 2623) termed the Abdnor and Daschle race as "more immersed in punch–counterpunch television exchanges—and . . . closer to character assassination—than any other in the nation."

The 1988 investigation involved the first presidential campaign absent an incumbent candidate in twenty years. Republican George Bush, a two-term vice-president, and Democrat Michael Dukakis, the governor of Massachusetts, captured their party's respective nominations following stiff intraparty challenges.

The election featured a radical reversal in support for the candidates. Bush, who trailed Dukakis by as much as 17% in July, mounted an aggressive campaign to win the election by a comfortable margin of 8% (Farah & Klein, 1989). The Bush campaign employed attack advertisements that were successful in defining Dukakis as left of center (Farah & Klein, 1989). As a result, one analyst (Hershey, 1989, p. 96) commented, "It would be hard to find more convincing proof of the efficacy of attack politics. The campaign did make a difference." The study was conducted from middle September through early November of 1988.

The 1988 investigation used the direct mail communication channel to administer inoculation pretreatments. The direct mail communication channel has become an increasingly important vehicle for candidates in contemporary political persuasion, in part because of the ability to tailor messages to specific voter subgroups (Heller, 1987), and in part because of the low profile of direct mail communication compared to television and radio communication (Armstrong, 1988).

Subjects

Potential voters in the Sioux Falls metropolitan area served as subjects for both studies. The Sioux Falls metropolitan area is divided into forty-three voting precincts. In both investigations, two adjacent, approximately two-square block, predominantly residential areas were selected at random from each precinct. A total of 733 potential voters served as subjects for the 1986 study; 314 in the 1988 study. In both investigations, subjects were randomly assigned to the various treatment conditions and the control condition.

Design and Data Analysis

Both studies employed a factorial analysis of variance (ANOVA) design, initially involving three independent variables: attack message approach; treatment condition; and political party orientation. The factorial provided a direct comparison of the relative persuasiveness of the attack messages in the various treatment conditions and the control condition, taking into account the political party affiliation of subjects.

When further analysis was warranted, one of two procedures was employed. If theory predicted a particular relationship among three or more means of a significant main effect or an interaction effect, thus providing an explanatory calculus for a specific prediction, planned comparisons were computed using Dunn's multiple comparison procedure (Kirk, 1982). The planned comparison procedure is confirmatory, and both Roger Kirk (1982) and Geoffrey Keppel (1982) recommend as many as a–1, planned comparisons at the set alpha level. By contrast, if the omnibus ANOVA revealed an unpredicted interaction or main effect, then a more conservative procedure was employed. First, appropriate tests of simple effects were conducted, and then, only if the results warranted, post-hoc tests were employed to examine the differences in means. The Bon-ferroni post-hoc procedure was used in the 1986 study, whereas the Scheffe post-hoc test was employed in the 1988 study.

Independent Variables

In all analyses in the 1986 study and in one analysis in the 1988 study, the independent variable, treatment condition, was operationalized as no inoculation (control), inoculation same, and inoculation different. Subjects in the no inoc-ulation (control) category were exposed to an attack message without having first received a pretreatment. By contrast, subjects in the inoculation groups received a pretreatment message prior to exposure to an attack message. These subjects received either an inoculation same pretreatment, featuring an explicit rebuttal of the content of the subsequent attack message, or an inoculation different pretreatment, consisting of a generic defense of the candidate.

The 1988 study attempted a more ambitious assessment of various treatment options. Hence, with the single exception noted above, treatment condition was operationalized as no treatment (control), inoculation, inoculation plus reinforce-ment, and post-hoc refutation. Once again, those subjects in the no inoculation (control) category simply received an attack message, while subjects in the inoculation group received either a same or different inoculation pretreatment prior to exposure to an attack message. Subjects in the inoculation plus rein-forcement group received an inoculation pretreatment plus a reinforcement message prior to exposure to an attack message, whereas those subjects in the post-hoc refutation category were first exposed to an attack message, and then received an explicit rebuttal message to the content of the attack.

In the 1986 study, the independent variable, political party orientation, was operationalized as strong identifiers (Democrats and Republicans), weak iden-tifiers (Democrats and Republicans), no identification (apathetic and Indepen-dents), and crossover (Democrats who supported the Republican candidate and Republicans who supported the Democratic candidate). In the 1988 study, the political party orientation variable was trichotomized as strong identifiers, weak identifiers, and nonidentifiers, but absent the crossover category. The crossover cell was not used in the 1988 study because, unlike 1986, the initial surveys identified very few party identifiers who supported the nominee of the opposite political party. For subsequent analyses in both studies, a narrower variable, political party identification, was inserted in place of political party orientation in the design. Political party identification was operationalized as either Democratic or Republican identifiers who supported the candidate endorsed by their respective party.

In both investigations, the effectiveness of the treatment conditions in deflecting the persuasive attacks was assessed by comparing the attitudes of receivers who received one of the treatments versus those who received no treatment, following exposure to the attack messages. Hence, the attack message variable served an integral function in the studies. The two attack message approaches consisted of issue attacks, which involved specific positions taken by the candidate, as well as character attacks, which focused on personal qualities of the candidate. Both issue and character attack messages were included in the design because of the possibility that the effectiveness of the treatments may vary depending upon whether the attack messages contain issue or character content.

In subsequent analyses, other variables were incorporated into the design in place of the political party orientation and political party identification variables. In both studies, threat was included in the design as a manipulation check. It was trichotomized based on subjects' average scores across the threat dimension. Average scores on a seven-point metric of 2.5 or less were classified as low; more than 2.5 but less than 4.5 as moderate; and 4.5 or more as high.

In both the 1986 and 1988 investigations, the time interval separating inoculation and attack was examined. Time interval was operationalized as short, moderate, or long, based on intervals of one, two, and three weeks, respectively. Other individual difference factors were incorporated into the design in the place of the political party variables. In both studies, receiver gender was analyzed. And in the 1988 study, which employed a more detailed initial questionnaire so as to allow additional individual difference variables to be included in the design, both receiver age and education levels were examined.

Dependent Variables

Both investigations employed the same primary dependent variable: receiver attitude following exposure to the attack messages, as operationalized in terms of attitude toward the candidate supported in the attack message, attitude toward the position advocated in the attack message, and the likelihood of voting for the candidate supported in the attack message. In addition, both studies used a secondary dependent variable: the receiver's perception of the source credibility of the candidate supported in the attack message.

Three measures were employed to assess receiver attitude. Attitude toward the candidate supported in the attack message and attitude toward the position advocated in the attack message were evaluated using six semantic differential items adapted for the political communication context from a four-item measure employed previously by Burgoon, Cohen, Miller, and Montgomery (1978) and Miller and Burgoon (1979). Both scales featured six semantic differential items, including wise/foolish, positive/negative, acceptable/unacceptable, favorable/unfavorable, right/wrong, and good/bad. The reliabilities of the two attitude scales were high: in the 1986 study, attitude toward the candidate supported in the attack message (.87), and attitude toward the position advocated in the attack message (.91); and in the 1988 study, attitude toward the candidate supported in the attack message (.94), and attitude toward the position advocated in the attack message (.96). Likelihood of voting for the candidate supported in the attack message was assessed in both investigations using a 0–100 probability scale.

Threat, a manipulation check in both studies, was assessed in the 1986 study with a three-item scale, modified from one developed by Burgoon, Cohen, Miller, and Montgomery (1978) and used subsequently by Miller and Burgoon (1979) and Burgoon, Pfau, Birk, and Clark (1985). The scale, which included the semantic differential items of dangerous/safe, threatening/nonthreatening, and anxious/calm, did not attain satisfactory reliability (.50). Thus, the scale was modified in the 1988 study to include five semantic differential items: safe/dangerous, not risky/risky, unintimidating/intimidating, nonthreatening/threatening, and not harmful/harmful. The reliability of the 1988 threat scale was satisfactory (.83).

Finally, both investigations also assessed the source credibility of the candidate supported in the attack message. The factors and scales employed to measure credibility were based on previous factor analytic research by McCroskey, Holdridge, and Toomb (1974). The studies employed fifteen seven-interval semantic differential items designed to evaluate five dimensions of source credibility. The dimensions and their respective indicators included *character*, comprising selfish/unselfish, good/bad, and honest/dishonest; *competence*, including qualified/unqualified, competent/incompetent, and intelligent/unintelligent; *composure*, consisting of poised/nervous, tense/relaxed, and anxious/calm; *extroversion*, involving energetic/tired, outgoing/withdrawn, and aggressive/meek; and *sociability*, comprising cheerful/gloomy, pleasant/unpleasant, and good-natured/irritable.

The obtained alpha reliabilities for the five dimensions of source credibility were satisfactory in both investigations: in the 1986 study, character (.77), competence (.83), composure (.77), extroversion (.79), and sociability (.79); and in the 1988 study, character (.85), competence (.89), composure (.85), extroversion (.74), and sociability (.85).

Message Construction

Since both investigations sought to assess the comparative efficacy of distinct strategies in conferring resistance to political attack messages, it was necessary to prepare a number of messages for administration. In both studies, experimenters prepared a total of four attack messages, after identifying the most salient issue and character concerns in the campaigns on the basis of available

Figure 6.1
Inoculation and Attack Message Configuration

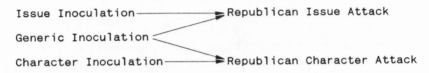

DEMOCRATIC CANDIDATE

Issue Inoculation ────────────► Republican Issue Attack

Generic Inoculation ◄

Character Inoculation ──────────► Republican Character Attack

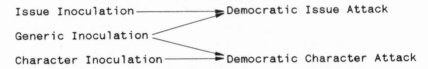

REPUBLICAN CANDIDATE

Issue Inoculation ────────────► Democratic Issue Attack

Generic Inoculation ◄

Character Inoculation ──────────► Democratic Character Attack

polling data. Experimenters used the existing pool of candidate campaign communication (position papers, print and electronic commercial messages, and the complete and partial accounts of candidate speeches) to construct the attack messages. Sponsorship of the attack messages in both studies was attributed to the interest group, Citizens for an Informed Electorate.

In the 1986 study, the polling data pinpointed four chief concerns, which were subsequently used as the basis for the focus of the respective attack messages. The Abdnor messages attacked Daschle for his "liberal" voting record and for opposition to President Reagan and his agenda, whereas the Daschle messages attacked Abdnor for his endorsement of Republican farm policies and for failing to speak effectively for rural America in the Senate.

In the 1988 study, the Bush messages attacked Dukakis for being weak on crime and for deception involving his record as governor of Massachusetts. The Dukakis messages attacked Bush for his support of agricultural and development policies that have hurt rural America and for insensitivity to the plight of the average working person.

Inoculation pretreatment messages were prepared in response to each of the attack messages. An inoculation same message was written for each candidate as an implicit rebuttal to each issue and character attack message, whereas an inoculation different message was constructed for each candidate as a generic defense of the respective candidate, absent any rebuttal of the content of the corresponding attack message. Figure 6.1 illustrates the specific inoculation and attack message configuration utilized in both investigations.

Inoculation theory operates on the central premise that threat triggers the motivation to bolster existing attitudes, thereby making them resistant to subsequent attacks (Anderson & McGuire, 1965; McGuire, 1964; Papageorgis & McGuire, 1961). Anderson and McGuire (1965, p. 44) describe the role that threat plays in the inoculation process, as follows: "To stimulate the person to develop his defenses and acquire resistance to persuasion, it is necessary to threaten him rather than reassure him about the validity of his belief.'' Thus, the first paragraph of each inoculation message was designed to threaten receivers.

Threat was operationalized as a warning of impending and potentially persuasive attacks against the candidate supported by the receiver. The warning was specific to the content of the subsequent attacks in the inoculation same condition and general in the inoculation different condition. In addition, in the 1988 study, reinforcement messages were written to bolster the content of each of the six initial inoculation messages.

Each inoculation message, as well as each reinforcement message in the 1988 study, attempted to replicate the written style and design of their corresponding attack message. Burgoon, Cohen, Miller, and Montgomery (1978, p. 33) have previously stressed the need for influence studies to employ messages that are relatively similar.

Thus, each pair of inoculation messages, as well as the corresponding reinforcement messages in the 1988 study, were constructed in such a way as to match as closely as possible the writing style and overall comprehensibility of the respective attack message. Particular attention was paid to the total length, average sentence length, verb tenses, and modifiers used in the inoculation, reinforcement, and attack messages (Burgoon, Cohen, Miller & Montgomery, 1978). Total word counts and the Index of Contingency, developed by Selwyn Becker, Alex Bavelas, and Marcia Braden (1961) to assess the comprehensibility of messages, were used to evaluate message equivalence.

As Table 6.1 indicates, the total word counts and the Index of Contingency ratings of the inoculation messages and their respective attack messages employed in the 1986 investigation were similar. And, as Table 6.2 illustrates, the word counts and Contingency ratings of the inoculation messages, reinforcement messages, and their corresponding attack messages used in the 1988 study were similar.

Procedure

Undergraduate senior students attached to the Center for the Study of Communication served as interviewers for both of the investigations. Prior to the study, interviewers received six to eight hours of training, consisting of formal instruction followed by supervised practice interviews to insure uniformity in the administration of the instruments employed in the studies. Interviewers were assigned randomly to all conditions.

The 1986 Study. The first phase of the 1986 study was designed to inoculate receivers and was conducted from October 1 to October 8. During this phase, interviewers informed subjects that they were conducting research for the Center for the Study of Communication. Interviewers asked subjects to read a political message and then to respond to a few questions about the message. Subjects

Table 6.1
Comparison of 1986 Inoculation and Attack Messages

Possible Message Combinations	Total Words	Contingency Index
Abdnor Issue Inoculation	242	8.8
Daschle Issue Attack	240	10.8
Abdnor Character Inoculation	248	7.6
Daschle Character Attack	254	10.2
Abdnor Generic Inoculation	249	13.5
Daschle Issue Attack	240	10.8
Daschle Character Attack	254	10.2
Daschle Issue Inoculation	228	7.9
Abdnor Issue Attack	238	10.1
Daschle Character Inoculation	256	9.1
Abdnor Character Attack	231	8.4
Daschle Generic Inoculation	236	7.5
Abdnor Issue Attack	238	10.1
Abdnor Character Attack	231	8.4

Note: The Index of Contingency evaluates the readability of sentences. A low Index of Contingency indicates significant diversity in word use. A high Index of Contingency signifies significant repetition in word use.

received a message consistent with their previously expressed candidate preference. Interviewers administered the pretreatment instruments—a brief demographic questionnaire and a manipulation check—and inoculation messages to 530 Sioux Falls area potential voters (59% response).

The second phase of the study was implemented from October 11 through October 28. Interviewers asked subjects to read a political message on behalf of one of the candidates. Subjects were told that the messages were prepared by the interest group, Citizens for an Informed Electorate. This deception was needed to maximize realism in the message administration and minimize demand characteristics posed by the presence of the interviewer. All treatment and control subjects received a message at odds with their candidate preference. After subjects read the message, interviewers administered the posttreatment instruments.

This phase consisted of two simultaneous components. The interviewers ad-

Table 6.2

Comparison of 1988 Inoculation, Reinforcement, and Attack Messages

Possible Message Combinations	Total Words	Contingency Index
Bush Issue Inoculation	246	7.13
Bush Issue Reinforcement	244	7.77
Dukakis Issue Attack	244	7.31
Bush Character Inoculation	249	6.58
Bush Character Reinforcement	245	8.74
Dukakis Character Attack	247	7.01
Bush Generic Inoculation	246	7.06
Bush Generic Reinforcement	244	9.05
Dukakis Issue Attack	244	7.31
Dukakis Character Attack	247	7.01
Dukakis Issue Inoculation	246	9.04
Dukakis Issue Reinforcement	246	8.98
Bush Issue Attack	244	8.10
Dukakis Character Inoculation	245	6.50
Dukakis Character Reinforcement	244	8.85
Bush Character Attack	245	8.12
Dukakis Generic Inoculation	245	7.47
Dukakis Generic Reinforcement	246	8.11
Bush Issue Attack	244	8.10
Bush Character Attack	245	8.12

Note: The Index of Contingency evaluates the readability of sentences. A low Index of Contingency indicates significant diversity in word use. A high Index of Contingency signifies significant repetition in word use.

ministered the posttreatment instruments and attack messages to those adults who had received an inoculation pretreatment. Altogether, 341 subjects completed this phase (64%), 85 refused (16%), and 104 could not be reached (20%). At the same time, the interviewers administered posttreatment instruments and attack messages to a separate group of 392 Sioux Falls area adults (57% response rate) who functioned as a control group in the study.

The 1988 Study. The 1988 study was more intricate in its administration. The first phase of the study was conducted from September 12 to September 24. Using the *City Directory*, which organizes resident telephone numbers according to street address, callers completed interviews with 529 households in designated areas in each voting precinct (46% completion rate). The interviewers asked one potential voter in each of the households their preference among the candidates in the presidential race, their political party affiliation, general demographic information, and whether they would be willing to participate in an on-going investigation of candidate political messages during the presidential campaign.

The second phase of the study involved the direct mailing of inoculation and reinforcement messages to a randomly assigned portion of the sample population. On September 28, researchers mailed inoculation pretreatment messages to 95 Bush supporters and 114 Dukakis supporters. On the same day, they mailed attack messages to a separate group of 34 Bush supporters and 33 Dukakis supporters who would constitute the refutation condition in the study. The third phase was completed on October 5. Researchers mailed reinforcement messages to 47 of the 95 inoculated Bush supporters and to 56 of the 114 inoculated Dukakis supporters. On the same day, they mailed refutation messages to the 34 Bush supporters and the 33 Dukakis supporters who had previously received attack messages.

The fourth phase of the study was conducted from October 10 to October 22. This phase consisted of three simultaneous steps, all requiring researchers to interview subjects in their homes. First, researchers administered attack messages and posttreatment instruments to those adults who had received previously either an inoculation or inoculation-plus-reinforcement pretreatment via direct mail. Altogether, 163 of these participants completed this phase of the study (78%), 11 refused further participation (5%), and 35 could not be reached (17%) despite repeated efforts. Second, the researchers administered attack messages and post-treatment instruments to a separate group of 52 Bush supporters and 55 Dukakis supporters who constituted the control condition in the study. A total of 91 control subjects completed this phase of the study (85%), 4 refused (4%), and 12 could not be reached (11%). Third, researchers administered posttreatment instruments to the 34 Bush supporters and the 33 Dukakis supporters who had previously received both an attack and refutation message via direct mail. Altogether, 60 of these participants completed this phase of the study (90%), 2 refused (3%), and 5 could not be reached (8%) despite repeated efforts.

The remaining 146 phase one participants all expressed no preference between the candidates and were a part of a separate analysis involving the immediate and delayed impact of political attack messages. The flow sheet in Figure 6.2 sequentially depicts the steps involved in the 1988 study.

VERIFICATION OF THE THREAT MANIPULATION

A manipulation check was conducted to confirm the presence of sufficient threat levels among inoculated subjects in both studies. Since threat serves as the motivational catalyst which triggers the internal process of resistance in receivers, both the 1986 and 1988 investigation attempted to assess threat levels among inoculated subjects.

Figure 6.2
Flow Chart of the Administration of the 1988 Study

PHASE 1
Sept. 12-24

Initial Phone Interviews (n=529)

INOCULATION CONDITION   POST-HOC REFUTATION   CONTROL CONDITION

PHASE 2
Sept. 28

Mail Inoculation   Mail Attack Messages
Messages to Bush &   to Bush & Dukakis
Dukakis Supporters   Supporters (n=67)
   (n=209)

PHASE 3
Oct. 5

Mail Reinforcement   Mail Post-Hoc
Messages to Half of   Refutation Messages
  Bush & Dukakis   to Bush & Dukakis
Supporters (n=103)   Supporters (n=67)

PHASE 4
Oct. 10-22

Administer Attack   Administer Measures   Administer Attack
Messages & Measures   to Bush & Dukakis   Messages & Measures
to Bush & Dukakis   Supporters (n=60)   to Bush & Dukakis
Supporters (n=163)   Supporters (n=91)

The 1986 Investigation

In the 1986 study, a 3 (threat levels) $\times$ 2 (inoculation pretreatment) $\times$ 2 (attack message approach) factorial analysis of variance was computed for each of the dependent variables. The results revealed a main effect for threat on the dependent measures of likelihood of voting for, $F(2, 329) = 3.49$, $p < .05$; $\hat{\omega}^2 = .01$, and composure, $F(2, 329) = 3.33$, $p < .05$; $\hat{\omega}^2 = .01$. In addition, threat approached significance on the credibility dimension of character, $F(2, 329) = 2.66$; $p < .10$; $\hat{\omega}^2 = .01$. The results of a planned comparison of the attack message means at low, moderate, and high threat on the credibility dimension of composure indicated that the high threat condition promoted more resistance than the low or moderate threat conditions, $F(1, 330) = 8.08$, $p < .05$; $\hat{\omega}^2 = .02$.

However, results of the analysis of variance identified an interaction involving threat and attack message approach which achieved statistical significance on the dependent measure of attitude toward candidate, F (2, 329) = 3.82, $p <$ .05; $\hat{\omega}^2$ = .02, and approached statistical significance on the measures of attitude toward position, F (2, 329) = 3.01, $p <$ .10; $\hat{\omega}^2$ = .01; likelihood of voting for, F (2, 329) = 2.37, $p <$ .10; $\hat{\omega}^2$ = .01; and character, F (2, 329) = 2.42, $p <$ .10; $\hat{\omega}^2$ = .01.

The possible interaction of threat and attack message approach warranted further post-hoc explorations. Tests of simple effects were computed on issue and character attack message approaches across the three levels of threat. They revealed that issue attacks did not, but character attacks did, produce a statistically significant difference across threat levels on the dependent measure of attitude toward candidate, F (2, 174) = 3.23, $p <$ .05; $\hat{\omega}^2$ = .03; attitude toward position, F (2, 174) = 4.14, $p <$ .05; $\hat{\omega}^2$ = .04; and character, F (2, 174) = 6.28, $p <$ .05; $\hat{\omega}^2$ = .06; and nearly significant differences across threat levels on the dependent measure of likelihood of voting for, F (2, 174) = 2.72, $p <$ .10; $\hat{\omega}^2$ = .02.

Examination of the character attack means suggested a common pattern: attitude change increased from low to moderate threat levels, and then dropped from moderate to high threat levels. However, further tests of the character attack means offered little support for this claim. They did indicate that the effectiveness of the attack messages fell as threat increased from moderate to high on the credibility dimension of character, t (1, 329) = -2.83, $k = 3$, $p <$ .05, two-tailed, but they fell short of statistical significance on the measures of attitude toward candidate, attitude toward position, and likelihood of voting for.

Thus, while the inoculation pretreatments in the 1986 study did generate threat, the overall level was insufficient. The most plausible explanation was that measurement of the threat dimension in this study was deficient. The relatively low alpha reliability (.50) called into question the overall internal consistency of the three-item measure. This problem was dealt with in the 1988 study by changing to a five-item threat measure, employed previously by Burgoon, Cohen, Miller, and Montgomery (1978) and Miller and Burgoon (1979) with quite satisfactory alpha reliability outcomes.

Another explanation for the low threat level involves the operationalization of threat in the 1986 study. The initial studies on inoculation operationalized threat in terms of the placement of two counterarguments in the first paragraph of an inoculation message (McGuire, 1961a, 1961b). Later, McGuire (1964) operationalized "high threat" as the use of as many as four counterarguments in an inoculation message. Of course, McGuire's inoculation messages, administered in laboratory settings, were lengthy, running 500–600 words.

The 1986 investigation, conducted in field conditions, employed much shorter inoculation messages (228–256 words). As a result, a single counterargument was raised in the opening paragraph of each inoculation message. While the use of a single counterargument may not be adequate to generate the requisite threat levels, the alternative, the use of more than one counterargument, would require more lengthy inoculation messages, which in turn may impair subject participation in a field setting.

One final explanation is that the low threat levels were an idiosyncrasy of the Abdnor and Daschle pairing. Polls indicated that both candidates were extremely popular at the outset of the campaign (Fialka, 1986), and consequently, voters who expressed a preference for a particular candidate may have been less worried than usual about the prospect that the opponent's attacks might persuade them to alter their preference.

In any event, the primary purpose of a manipulation check is to protect against Type II error, the possibility of rejecting research hypotheses when they are true. The results of the 1986 study supported inoculation theory, thus reducing concerns about sufficient threat levels.

The 1988 Investigation

In the 1988 investigation, a 3 (threat level) $\times$ 4 (treatment condition) $\times$ 2 (attack message approach) factorial analysis of variance was computed on the primary dependent variable. The $4 \times 3 \times 2$ factorial ANOVA indicated a nearly significant main effect for the treatment condition on the dependent variable of threat level, $F(3, 279) = 2.13, p < .10; \hat{\omega}^2 = .01$. A planned comparison was computed to assess the combined inoculation means against the no inoculation mean. It revealed that the combined inoculation conditions produced significantly greater threat levels than the control condition, $F(1, 279) = 8.56, p < .05; \hat{\omega}^2 = .03$. Thus, the manipulation check confirmed the presence of significant threat levels among subjects who received inoculation pretreatment, but not among subjects in the control condition.

These results indicate that the five-item measure is the most appropriate instrument to assess threat, thus offering support for the rationale provided previously to explain the relatively low threat levels generated in the 1986 study. But the 1988 results, while statistically significant, nonetheless failed to account for sizable variance in dependent variables.

This may be an intrinsic feature of inoculation when applied in a political campaign context. Threat levels in a political campaign, where it is customary for receivers to be exposed to messages which run opposite their own attitudes, inherently may be lower than in other circumstances. Most past resistance research was confined to laboratory conditions, using messages which focussed on salient issues designed to threaten attitudinal freedom. The results in the 1986 and 1988 investigations suggest that it may be necessary to rethink the notion of threat in a political campaign context.

Chapter 7

The Viability of the Inoculation Strategy

Silence is perceived as guilt, but undoing a negative is difficult.
—Consultant Robert Goodman, Media Consultant
(cited in Hagstrom & Guskind, 1986, p. 2621)

The value of persuasion as an inhibitor of [attitude and/or behavioral] change is undeniable.
—Gerald R. Miller and Michael Burgoon,
Professors of Communication (Miller & Burgoon, 1973, pp. 5–6)

The 1986 study, which examined inoculation in a campaign for the U.S. Senate, was the first scientific effort to apply inoculation in a political context. Hence, the primary focus of the investigation was the potential of the inoculation approach to deflect the influence of political attack messages. The 1988 investigation went further, examining the effectiveness of inoculation against post-hoc refutation in fostering resistance to political attacks, assessing the potential of inoculation-plus-reinforcement in providing a boost to the initial inoculation pretreatments, and employing direct mail as the communication channel for all the pretreatment messages. The two investigations, taken together, offer a solid foundation of findings concerning the effectiveness of inoculation in political campaign communication.

The results of both studies indicate that inoculation is a viable and promising strategy of resistance to the influence of political attack messages. The results suggest that inoculation deflects the impact of political attack messages in a number of ways: it undermines the potential influence of the source of such attacks, in a general sense and with regard to specific dimensions of source credibility; it deflects the specific content of the attacks; and it reduces the likelihood that the political attacks will influence receiver voting intention. In addition, because inoculation precedes attack, it even provides defenses against attacks that are launched late in a campaign in order to preempt a post-hoc refutation response. These initial results concerning the viability of the inoculation strategy will be reported and explained in this chapter.

THE 1986 INVESTIGATION

The 1986 investigation, which tested the effectiveness of inoculation in the Abdnor and Daschle race for the U.S. Senate in South Dakota, provided the first evidence that inoculation could confer resistance to the influence of political attack messages.

General Effectiveness of Inoculation

A 2 (attack message approach) $\times$ 3 (inoculation condition) $\times$ 4 (political party orientation) factorial analysis of variance was initially computed to test the effectiveness of inoculation pretreatments. The results revealed a significant main effect for inoculation condition on the primary dependent measures of attitude toward the candidate supported in the attack message, F (2, 709) = 14.09, p < .05; $\hat{\omega}^2$ = .03; attitude toward position advocated in the attack message, F (2, 709) = 11.02, p < .05; ω^2 = .02; and the likelihood of voting for the candidate supported in the attack message, F (2, 709) = 6.44, p < .05; $\hat{\omega}^2$ = .01. The main effects indicated differences in the inoculation condition means. A question remained, however, as to the precise nature of those differences.

Two additional approaches were employed to provide direct tests of the effectiveness of the inoculation pretreatments. Both provided further support for the prediction that inoculation pretreatments, whether same—featuring an explicit rebuttal of the content of a subsequent attack message, or different—consisting of a generic defense of a candidate, confer resistance to attitude change following exposure to a persuasive attack.

First, modified Bonferroni comparisons were computed to compare the combined same and different inoculation pretreatment means against the no inoculation means. They revealed statistically significant differences between the combined treatment and control means on the main dependent measures of attitude toward candidate, F (1, 709) = 21.32, p < .05; $\hat{\omega}^2$ = .03; attitude toward position, F (1, 709) = 16.90, p < .05; $\hat{\omega}^2$ = .02; and likelihood of voting for, F (1, 709) = 10.73, p < .05; $\hat{\omega}^2$ = .01.

While the combined inoculation pretreatment means were significantly lower than the no inoculation condition means on all three dependent measures, thus affirming the broad, overall effectiveness of the inoculation approach, the comparisons also indicated that the inoculation same and different means did not differ significantly from one another, thus revealing viability for each of the two

Table 7.1

Summary of the Inoculation Condition Means on Receiver Attitude

Dependent Measure	Inoculation Condition		
	None	Same	Different
Attitude toward Candidate			
Mean *	3.91 (n=392)	3.41 (n=232)	3.33 (n=109)
SD	1.26	1.23	1.32
Attitude toward Position			
Mean *	3.78 (n=392)	3.38 (n=232)	3.14 (n=109)
SD	1.44	1.41	1.51
Likelihood of Voting for			
Mean *	18.96 (n=392)	13.91 (n=232)	10.89 (n=109)
SD	19.89	20.35	18.81

Note: Ratings of receivers' attitude toward the candidate supported in the attack message and receivers' attitude toward the position taken by the candidate supported in the attack message are based on seven-point scales. Assessment of the likelihood of voting for the candidate supported in the attack message is based on a 100-point probability scale. The higher the rating or assessment, the more persuasive the attack message.

* $p < .05$.

inoculation approaches. The inoculation condition means are displayed in Table 7.1.

The inoculation same and different pretreatment means were treated separately to provide a direct test of effectiveness. A simple analysis of variance was computed on the difference between the treatment and control conditions on all dependent variables. The results verified that *each* of the inoculation pretreatment approaches fosters resistance to subsequent attack messages. The inoculation same pretreatment conferred resistance on the dependent measures of attitude toward candidate, $F (1, 622) = 20.50$, $p < .05$; $\hat{\omega}^2 = .03$; attitude toward position, $F (1, 622) = 10.98$, $p < .05$; $\hat{\omega}^2 = .02$; and likelihood of voting for, $F (1, 622) = 6.72$, $p < .05$; $\hat{\omega}^2 = .01$. The inoculation different pretreatment conferred resistance on the dependent measures of attitude toward candidate, F

$(1, 499) = 14.81, p < .05; \hat{\omega}^2 = .03$; attitude toward position, $F (1, 499) = 15.38, p < .05; \hat{\omega}^2 = .03$; and likelihood of voting for, $F (1, 499) = 9.70, p < .05; \hat{\omega}^2 = .02$.

The results on source credibility were mixed. There was a significant main effect for inoculation condition on the source credibility dimension of extroversion, $F (2, 709) = 9.98, p < .05; \hat{\omega}^2 = .02$. A planned comparison of the combined same and different pretreatment means and the no inoculation means confirmed that inoculation pretreatments confer resistance to subsequent attack messages, $F (1, 709) = 228.91, p < .05; \hat{\omega}^2 = .14$. Also, the results indicated that inoculation condition approached statistical significance on the credibility dimension of composure, $F (2, 709) = 2.39, p < .10; \hat{\omega}^2 = .00$. However, comparisons involving the combined same and different pretreatment means and the no inoculation means indicated that these differences were not significant.

When inoculation same and different pretreatments were examined separately, the inoculation same pretreatments produced a statistically significant effect on the source credibility dimensions of competence, $F (1, 622) = 3.23, p < .05$, one-tailed; $\hat{\omega}^2 = .00$, and extroversion, $F (1, 622) = 8.84, p < .05; \hat{\omega}^2 = .01$. The inoculation different pretreatments resulted in statistically significant impacts on the source credibility dimensions of competence, $F (1, 499) = 2.88, p < .05$, one-tailed; $\hat{\omega}^2 = .00$; composure, $F (1, 499) = 4.27, p < .05; \hat{\omega}^2 = .00$; and extroversion, $F (1, 499) = 15.63; p < .05; \hat{\omega}^2 = .03$.

Effectiveness of Inoculation over Time

It makes intuitive sense that the effect of inoculation pretreatments decays over time. As noted in Chapter 4, two of the early inoculation studies indicated that the impact of inoculation diminishes with the passage of time, and that the decay is less with inoculation different than same pretreatments (McGuire, 1962; Pryor & Steinfatt, 1978).

A 3 (small, moderate, and large interval) $\times$ 2 (same and different inoculation pretreatment) $\times$ 2 (issue and character attack message approach) factorial analysis of variance was computed to assess the viability of inoculation over time.

The factorial analysis of variance indicated a significant main effect for time interval on the major dependent measures of attitude toward candidate, $F (2, 329) = 3.75, p < .05; \hat{\omega}^2 = .01$; and attitude toward position, $F (2, 329) = 6.13, p < .05; \hat{\omega}^2 = .03$.

Subsequent planned comparisons verified that inoculation decays over time. The results indicated that inoculation pretreatments are more effective in deflecting attack messages at small intervals as opposed to moderate or large intervals on the measures of attitude toward candidate, $F (1, 329) = 6.86, p < .05; \hat{\omega}^2 = .02$, and attitude toward position, $F (1, 329) = 6.93, p < .05; \hat{\omega}^2 = .02$, and that inoculation is more effective at moderate than long intervals on attitude toward position, $F (1, 329) = 6.91, p < .05; \hat{\omega}^2 = .02$.

These significant main effects, in conjunction with the planned comparison results involving the attitude toward candidate and attitude toward position measures, suggest that inoculation effectiveness wears off over time. However, the absence of any interactions involving inoculation pretreatment and time interval suggests no support for the position that the decrease in effectiveness is less with the inoculation different than the inoculation same approach.

The results of the factorial on the secondary measures of source credibility failed to support either of these positions. Although the factorial analysis of variance identified main effects for time interval on the credibility dimensions of character, $F(2, 329) = 5.02$, $p < .05$; $\hat{\omega}^2 = .02$; competence, $F(2, 329) = 5.78$, $p < .05$; $\hat{\omega}^2 = .03$; and sociability, $F(2, 329) = 7.92$, $p < .05$; $\hat{\omega}^2 = .04$; a triple interaction involving time interval, inoculation condition, and attack message approach was significant on the dimension of extroversion, $F(2, 329) = 3.26$, $p < .05$; $\hat{\omega}^2 = .01$, and overrode the main effects on the dimensions of character, $F(2, 329) = 3.08$, $p < .05$; $\hat{\omega}^2 = .01$, and competence, $F(2, 329) = 3.67$, $p < .05$; $\hat{\omega}^2 = .01$.

In all three instances, there were consistent patterns of differences involving the means which suggested that inoculation same pretreatments varied in their effectiveness in deflecting character attacks as opposed to issue attacks at large intervals, whereas inoculation different pretreatments varied in their effectiveness in deflecting character as opposed to issue attacks at moderate intervals. A 2 × 2 factorial analysis of variance involving attack message approach (issue, character) and inoculation pretreatment (same, different) was computed at each time interval (small, moderate, large) as a prerequisite to further post-hoc explorations.

Although all attack message approach and inoculation pretreatment at moderate and large time intervals on the dimensions of character, competence, and extroversion approached statistical significance, the two-way analysis of variance identified only one significant interaction, at large intervals on the credibility dimension of competence, $F(1, 108) = 4.49$, $p < .05$; $\hat{\omega}^2 = .03$. Further analysis of the means indicated that at large intervals same inoculation pretreatments were significantly more effective in deflecting character attacks as opposed to issue attacks, $t(1, 329) = -3.04$, $k = 6$, $p < .05$, two-tailed.

A planned comparison was computed to follow up on the finding of a main effect for time interval on the credibility dimension of sociability. The results indicated that inoculation pretreatments were more effective in promoting resistance to attack messages at small intervals as opposed to moderate or large intervals, $F(1, 329) = 15.52$, $p < .05$; $\hat{\omega}^2 = .04$.

Finally, the factorial revealed a significant two-way interaction involving time interval and attack message condition on the credibility dimension of composure, $F(2, 329) = 3.37$, $p < .05$; $\hat{\omega}^2 = .01$. A test of simple effects on both issue and character attacks across the three time intervals indicated that the means of issue attack messages, but not character attack messages, varied significantly over time, $F(2, 161) = 6.25$, $p < .05$; $\hat{\omega}^2 = .06$. Further examination of the means revealed that issue attacks were much more effective at small time intervals in contrast to moderate, $t(1, 329) = -2.52$, $k = 3$, $p < .05$, two-tailed, and

Table 7.2
Summary of the Time Interval Means on all Dependent Measures

Dependent Measure	Time Interval Means		
	Short (n=99)	Moderate (n=130)	Long (n=112)
Attitude toward Candidate			
Mean *	3.12	3.39	3.60
SD	1.13	1.35	1.22
Attitude toward Position			
Mean *	3.01	3.19	3.68
SD	1.23	1.46	1.52
Likelihood of Voting for			
Mean	9.95	13.62	14.81
SD	15.53	21.51	21.20
Character			
Mean *	3.30	3.60	3.86
SD	0.96	1.25	1.40
Competence			
Mean *	3.64	4.06	4.31
SD	1.36	1.40	1.42
Composure			
Mean	3.17	3.46	3.65
SD	1.32	1.46	1.61
Extroversion			
Mean	4.36	4.72	4.74
SD	1.37	1.36	1.38
Sociability			
Mean *	3.35	3.88	4.14
SD	1.28	1.42	1.54

Note: Ratings of receivers' attitude toward the candidate supported in the attack message, attitude toward the position taken by the candidate supported in the attack message, and source credibility of the candidate supported in the attack message are based on seven-point scales. Assessment of the likelihood of voting for the candidate supported in the attack message is based on a 100-point probability scale. The higher the rating or assessment, the more persuasive the attack message.

* $p < .05$.

large, t (1, 329) $=$ -3.46, $k = 3$, $p < .05$, two-tailed, intervals. These results suggest a more intricate pattern than has been previously thought between decay and inoculation pretreatment.

Discussion of the 1986 Findings

The most important finding of the 1986 study was that the inoculation pretreatments, whether same or different, confer resistance to attitude change following exposure to political attack. This effect was found with all primary dependent variables, accounting for 3% of variance in attitude toward the candidate supported in the attack message, 2% of variance in attitude toward the position taken by the candidate supported in the attack message, and 1% of variance in the likelihood of voting for the candidate supported in the attack message. The effect of inoculation also was found with the secondary source credibility dimension of extroversion, and to a lesser degree, with the dimensions of competence and composure.

The 1986 results offer support for McGuire's theoretical model (McGuire 1961a, 1961b, 1962, 1970; McGuire & Papageorgis, 1961, 1962; Papageorgis & McGuire, 1961) and for the extension of the model to more controversial topics (Burgoon et al., 1976; Burgoon & Chase, 1973; Burgoon, Cohen, Miller & Montgomery, 1978; Burgoon & King, 1974; Freedman & Steinbruner, 1964; McCroskey, 1970; McCroskey, Young & Scott, 1972; Miller & Burgoon, 1979; Pryor & Steinfatt, 1978; Tate & Miller, 1973; Ullman & Bodaken, 1975), such as those found in the political campaign context. Results of this initial application of inoculation theory in political campaign communication are promising, especially given the rise of the attack strategy in contemporary campaigns, coupled with the lack of viable defenses against this strategy.

Nonetheless, despite the broad presence of statistically significant main effects for inoculation, the results failed to account for much of the overall variance in dependent variables. However, the level of variance accounted for in no way diminishes the importance of the findings of the 1986 study.

The significance of variance cannot be assessed solely by mathematical means. Other considerations also must be examined. For example, the 1986 investigation utilized an axiomatic theory to explain the efficacy of a fourth political message strategy in campaigns. Consequently, the findings are undergirded by the explanatory calculus of inoculation theory, thus requiring less variance accounted for. Furthermore, in tight political races, the variance accounted for in the 1986 investigation could prove sufficient to put one candidate over the top. Or, as Jeffries (1986, p. 259) writes, "even slight changes may be significant in close elections."

In addition, inoculation should prove most effective when employed prior to the formation of, or the solidification of, voter perceptions about candidates and issues. Research suggests more volatility in voter perceptions, and thus more potential for influence, during the initial phase of political campaigns (Becker

Table 7.3

Summary of Inoculation Pretreatment Means Based on Issue and Character Attack Message Approach for Short, Moderate, and Long Time Intervals on the Dimensions of Source Credibility

Inoculation Pretreatment

ISSUE ATTACK MESSAGES

Dependent Measure	Small Intervals		Moderate Intervals		Large Intervals	
	Same (n=31)	Different (n=17)	Same (n=41)	Different (n=15)	Same (n=42)	Different (n=18)
Character						
Mean	3.60	2.98	3.89	4.09	4.28	3.80
SD	0.87	1.33	1.12	1.20	1.46	1.54
Competence						
Mean	3.82	3.16	4.16	4.37	4.72	4.54
SD	1.53	1.19	1.46	1.35	1.34	1.60
Composure						
Mean	3.09	2.73	3.64	3.80	4.15	3.54
SD	1.57	1.29	1.30	1.33	1.58	1.70
Extroversion						
Mean	4.82	3.88	4.91	5.13	5.13	4.59
SD	1.38	1.63	1.19	1.11	1.35	1.32
Sociability						
Mean	3.42	3.24	4.11	4.80	4.62	4.28
SD	1.56	0.92	1.46	1.23	1.68	1.56

CHARACTER ATTACK MESSAGES

	Small Intervals		Moderate Intervals		Large Intervals	
	Same ($\underline{n}$=35)	Different ($\underline{n}$=16)	Same ($\underline{n}$=51)	Different ($\underline{n}$=23)	Same ($\underline{n}$=32)	Different ($\underline{n}$=20)
Character						
Mean	3.26	3.15	3.51	2.99	3.38	3.83
SD	0.87	1.33	1.12	1.20	1.46	1.54
Competence						
Mean	3.86	3.35	3.97	3.62	3.50	4.52
SD	1.26	1.37	1.29	1.54	1.33	1.54
Composure						
Mean	3.48	3.13	3.28	3.30	3.19	3.50
SD	0.97	1.64	1.48	1.75	1.68	1.48
Extroversion						
Mean	4.20	4.31	4.69	4.15	5.13	4.70
SD	1.16	1.52	1.34	1.73	1.66	1.08
Sociability						
Mean	3.43	3.19	3.59	3.51	3.54	3.98
SD	1.15	1.40	1.40	1.49	1.39	1.46

Note: Ratings of receivers' perceptions of the source credibility of the candidate supported in the attack message are based on seven-point scales. The higher the rating, the more persuasive the attack message.

& McCombs, 1978; Gopoian, 1982; Kennamer & Chaffee, 1982; Trent & Friedenberg, 1983; Williams, Weber, Haaland, Mueller & Craig, 1976). Thus, the
inoculation strategy should prove to be most effective early in a political campaign, prior to the total saturation of the political environment with campaign
messages, and against a lesser-known opponent.

By contrast, the 1986 investigation tested the viability of inoculation under
the most unfavorable circumstances. The study targeted for influence only the
least susceptible receivers, those already committed to a candidate. In addition
the 1986 study was conducted during the last month of an intense campaign, in
which the average voter had been exposed to more than 300 political advertisements on behalf of the two candidates, and which featured known and respected
opponents (Fialka, 1986).

Finally, the 1986 investigation employed a single message stimulus (the treatment condition consisted of an inoculation message, subsequently followed by
an attack message; the control condition consisted of a single attack message)
administered during the last month of an intense campaign. In actual use in a
political campaign, practitioners would inoculate via multiple messages administered over a period of time using a variety of communication channels, but
particularly television. Thus, the results of the 1986 study are conservative. The
potential of the inoculation message strategy may be greater than the 1986 results
indicate.

The results offer some support for the position that inoculation decays over
time. The 1986 study affirmed decay on both attitude toward candidate and
attitude toward position measures. However, contrary to the previous findings
of both McGuire (1962) and Pryor and Steinfatt (1978), the results failed to
support a difference in the rate of decay between inoculation same and different
pretreatments.

The triple interaction, involving time interval, inoculation condition, and attack
message approach on the source credibility dimensions of character and competence are interesting because the interactions seem to suggest a consistent
pattern of differences in which inoculation same pretreatments varied in their
effectiveness in deflecting character attacks as opposed to issue attacks at large
intervals, whereas inoculation different pretreatments varied in their effectiveness
in deflecting character as opposed to issue attacks at moderate intervals.

While there is no theoretical rationale to account for this finding, this pattern
of results suggests that the relationship between inoculation, time interval, and
attack message may be more intricate than previously thought and carries important nuances for practitioners who employ inoculation pretreatments aimed
at specific attack messages and who are interested in their durability over time.

THE 1988 INVESTIGATION

The 1988 investigation examined inoculation as a direct mail strategy during
the Bush and Dukakis presidential campaign. This investigation attempted to

build on the results of the 1986 study. Thus, it assessed the effectiveness of inoculation in both absolute and relative terms.

A 4 (treatment condition) $\times$ 2 (attack message approach) $\times$ 3 (political party orientation) factorial analysis of variance was initially computed to examine the relative effectiveness of the inoculation approach. The four treatment conditions included inoculation, inoculation-plus-reinforcement, post-hoc refutation, and control.

Relative Effectiveness of Inoculation

The factorial indicated a significant main effect in the treatment condition means on the primary dependent variables of attitude toward the candidate supported in the attack message, $F (3, 289) = 14.32, p < .05; \hat{\omega}^2 = .11$; attitude toward position advocated in the attack message, $F (3, 290) = 11.00, p < .05$; $\hat{\omega}^2 = .09$; and likelihood of voting for the candidate supported in the attack message, $F (3, 287) = 15.15, p < .05$ $\hat{\omega}^2 = .11$, with a triple interaction involving treatment condition, political party orientation, and attack message approach, $F (6, 287) = 2.34, p < .05; \hat{\omega}^2 = .02$, overriding the main effect of treatment condition on likelihood of voting for.

In addition, the factorial revealed significant main effects in the treatment condition means on the following dimensions of source credibility: character, $F (3, 286) = 41.22, p < .05; \hat{\omega}^2 = .05$; competence, $F (3, 289) = 57.08, p < .05; \hat{\omega}^2 = .06$; extroversion, $F (3, 290) = 15.98, p < .05; \hat{\omega}^2 = .02$; and sociability, $F (3, 289) = 46.76, p < .05; \hat{\omega}^2 = .06$.

Modified Bonferroni comparisons were conducted to further explore these differences in the treatment means for all main effects revealed by the factorials, with the exception of the main effect which was overridden by the triple interaction. The triple interaction on the dependent measure of likelihood of voting for the candidate supported in the attack message will be examined later in this chapter.

Initial Analyses. Planned comparisons were computed to compare inoculation and inoculation-plus-reinforcement means against the no inoculation means on the two primary dependent variables for which simple main effects were reported. Results revealed that the combined inoculation means were significantly lower than the control means on attitude toward candidate, $F (1, 289) = 41.54, p < .05; \hat{\omega}^2 = .11$, as well as attitude toward position, $F (1, 290) = 28.50, p < .05; \hat{\omega}^2 = .08$. Thus, the results indicated that the political attack messages exerted significantly less influence on the inoculated receivers. The various treatment condition means are displayed in Table 7.4.

Planned comparisons were also computed on the treatment means for the four dimensions of source credibility that revealed main effects. Once again, the results indicated that the combined inoculation means were significantly lower than the control means on the dimensions of character, $F (1, 286) = 15.75, p < .05; \hat{\omega}^2 = .04$; competence, $F (1, 289) = 4.47, p < .06; \hat{\omega}^2 = .01$;

Table 7.4
Summary of the Treatment Condition Means on Receiver Attitude

Dependent Measure	Treatment Condition Means			
	Control	Refutation	Inoculation	Inoculation Plus Reinforcement
Attitude toward Candidate				
Mean *	4.26 (n=90)	3.30 (n=60)	2.98 (n=89)	2.97 (n=74)
SD	1.60	1.57	1.43	1.22
Attitude toward Position				
Mean *	3.96 (n=91)	2.71 (n=60)	2.75 (n=89)	2.84 (n=74)
SD	1.81	1.54	1.48	1.41
Likelihood of Voting for				
Mean *	39.62 (n=89)	22.55 (n=60)	17.50 (n=88)	11.68 (n=74)
SD	33.38	32.12	24.89	18.01

Note: Ratings of receivers' attitude toward the candidate supported in the attack message and the receivers' attitude toward the position taken by the candidate supported in the attack message are based on seven-point scales. Assessment of the likelihood of voting for the candidate supported in the attack message is based on a 100-point probability scale. The higher the rating or assessment, the more persuasive the attack message.

* $p < .05$.

extroversion, $F (1, 290) = 5.66, p < .05; \hat{\omega}^2 = .02$; and sociability, $F (1, 289) = 13.43, p < .05; \hat{\omega}^2 = .04$.

Another planned comparison was computed, following up the main effect revealed in the omnibus ANOVA, to determine whether inoculation (the inoculation and inoculation-plus-reinforcement means were combined for this test) is more effective than simple post-hoc refutation in conferring resistance to attitude change following exposure to a political attack message.

Since inoculation theory posits that threat triggers the motivation to resist attacks, the theoretical construct implies that refutation is more effective if it precedes, rather than follows, exposure to an attack message. Ironically, this basic assumption has received scant attention in the extant literature, aside from two early tests on attack-refutation sequence which were described under "Other Findings" in Chapter 5 (Tannenbaum, Macaulay & Norris, 1966; Tannenbaum & Norris, 1965).

The results of the planned comparison provided partial support for the prediction that inoculation is superior to post-hoc refutation in conferring resistance to attitude change following exposure to a political attack message. The combined inoculation means were lower than the post-hoc refutation means on attitude toward candidate, $F(1, 289) = 2.66, p < .10; \hat{\omega}^2 = .01$, and the source credibility dimensions of competence, $F(1, 289) = 16.84, p < .05; \hat{\omega}^2 = .05$, and sociability, $F(1, 289) = 6.40, p < .05; \hat{\omega}^2 = .02$, with the result approaching statistical significance on character, $F(1, 286) = 2.18, p < .10; \hat{\omega}^2 = .00$.

However, subsequent post-hoc analysis of the triple interaction involving the treatment condition, attack message approach, and political party orientation means on the dependent measure of likelihood of voting for the candidate supported in the attack message provided further support for the superiority of inoculation over post-hoc refutation. This interaction will be discussed below.

Finally, planned comparisons were computed to determine whether inoculation plus follow-up reinforcement is superior to inoculation alone in conferring resistance to attitude change following exposure to a political attack message. The planned comparisons indicated no support for this prediction on the dependent measures of attitude toward candidate or attitude toward position or on four of the credibility dimensions. The only support for this prediction was on the source credibility dimension of extroversion, $F(1,290) = 3.97, p < .05; \hat{\omega}^2 = .01$.

Interaction Effect. As indicated previously, the omnibus ANOVA indicated a triple interaction involving the independent variables of treatment condition, attack message approach, and political party orientation on the primary dependent measure of likelihood of voting for the candidate supported in the attack message. To further probe this interaction, two-way factorial analyses of variance were computed involving treatment condition and attack message approach for strong party identifiers, weak identifiers, and nonidentifiers on the dependent measure of likelihood of voting for.

Two-way factorial involving weak political party identifiers indicated a two-way interaction involving treatment condition and attack message approach, $F(3, 101) = 3.40, p < .05; \hat{\omega}^2 = .06$. Further analysis of these differences involving weak party identifiers revealed an interesting pattern. In comparison with the control condition, both post-hoc refutation, $t(1, 287) = 3.50, p < .05$, and inoculation-plus-reinforcement, $t(1, 287) = 2.82, p < .05$, deflected the influence of issue attacks, but inoculation did not. However, refutation was completely ineffective in dealing with character attacks. Compared to the control condition, both inoculation, $t(1, 287) = 2.80, p < .05$, and inoculation-plus-reinforcement, $t(1, 287) = 3.02, p < .05$, reduced the impact of character attacks, whereas refutation did not. In fact, the refutation approach was so

Table 7.5
Summary of the Treatment Condition Means on Issue and Character Attack
Messages for Weak Political Party Identifiers on the Dependent Variable of
Likelihood of Voting for the Candidate Supported in the Attack Message

| | Treatment Condition Means | | | |
	Control	Refutation	Inoculation	Inoculation Plus Reinforcement
Attack Message				
Issue Attacks				
Mean *	36.37 (n=19)	9.44 (n=9)	21.45 (n=20)	14.64 (n=11)
SD	27.05	11.30	27.29	19.22
Character Attacks				
Mean *	22.82 (n=17)	42.70 (n=10)	21.14 (n=14)	19.44 (n=9)
SD	24.07	41.47	24.44	20.98

Note: Assessment of the likelihood of voting for the candidate supported in the attack message is based on a 100-point probability scale. The higher the rating or assessment, the more persuasive the attack message.

* p < .05.

ineffective that it produced a boomerang impact, such that the character attacks were even more persuasive in the refutation than the control condition, t (1, 287) = 2.58, p < .05.

The remaining two-way factorials revealed main effects for treatment condition, but no interactions. This was true for both strong party identifiers, F (3, 143) = 11.98, p < .05; $\hat{\omega}^2$ = .18, and for nonidentifiers, F (3, 143) = 4.49, p < .05; $\hat{\omega}^2$ = .16. Further analysis of these differences revealed a consistent pattern of results, with inoculation and inoculation-plus-reinforcement proving superior to the refutation approach in deflecting the influence of political attack messages.

Among strong party identifiers, in contrast to the control condition, inoculation, t (1, 287) = 6.41, p < .05; inoculation-plus-reinforcement, t (1, 287) = 8.40, p < .05; and post-hoc refutation were more effective in suppressing the influence of attack messages, but inoculation-plus-reinforcement also proved superior to post-hoc refutation, t (1, 287) = 2.82, p < .05. Among noniden-

Table 7.6
Summary of the Treatment Condition Means for Strong Political Party Identifiers and for Nonidentifiers on the Dependent Variable of Likelihood of Voting for the Candidate Supported in the Attack Message

	Treatment Condition Means			
	Control	Refutation	Inoculation	Inoculation Plus Reinforcement
Party Orientation				
Strong Party Identifiers				
Mean *	43.33 (n=33)	18.54 (n=37)	14.75 (n=40)	6.02 (n=41)
SD	38.82	29.57	23.97	12.20
Nonidentifiers				
Mean *	50.85 (n=20)	38.75 (n=4)	16.07 (n=14)	21.62 (n=13)
SD	36.29	31.82	23.00	25.39

Note: Assessment of the likelihood of voting for the candidate supported in the attack message is based on a 100-point probability scale. The higher the rating or assessment, the more persuasive the attack message.

* $p < .05$.

tifiers, the inoculation, t (1, 287) $=$ 3.80, $p < .05$, and inoculation-plus-reinforcement, t (1, 287) $=$ 3.27, $p < .05$, conditions, but not the post-hoc refutation approach, were more effective in deflecting the persuasiveness of attack messages.

Further Analyses. As in the 1986 study, this investigation sought to determine whether both same and different inoculation approaches confer resistance to attitude change following exposure to a political attack message. The treatment condition was reconfigured as inoculation same, inoculation different, and control to test this prediction, and a 3 (treatment condition) $\times$ 3 (political party orientation) $\times$ 2 (attack message approach) factorial analysis of variance was computed.

The factorial revealed a significant main effect for treatment condition on the major dependent variables of attitude toward candidate, F (1,235) $=$ 22.13, $p < .05$; $\hat{\omega}^2 = .14$; attitude toward position, F (1, 236) $=$ 14.99, $p < .05$; $\hat{\omega}^2$

= .10; and likelihood of voting for the candidate supported in the attack message, F (1, 233) = 23.55, p < .05; $\hat{\omega}^2$ = .15.

Planned comparisons were computed to assess the same and different inoculation means versus the control mean. The results verified that *each* inoculation approach fosters resistance to subsequent attack messages. The comparisons revealed significant differences in the inoculation same and control means on attitude toward candidate, F (1, 235) = 31.40, p < .05; $\hat{\omega}^2$ = .10; attitude toward position, F (1, 236) = 18.70, p < .05; $\hat{\omega}^2$ = .06; and the likelihood of voting for, F (1, 233) = 33.98, p < .05; $\hat{\omega}^2$ = .11; and in the inoculation different and control means on attitude toward candidate, F (1, 235) = 29.65, p < .05; $\hat{\omega}^2$ = .10; attitude toward position, F (1, 236) = 23.67, p < .05; $\hat{\omega}^2$ = .08; and likelihood of voting for, F (1, 233) = 32.58, p < .05; $\hat{\omega}^2$ = .10. These means are displayed in Table 7.7.

The factorial also indicated significant main effects for treatment condition on the source credibility dimensions of character, F (2, 233) = 9.83, p < .05; $\hat{\omega}^2$ = .07; competence, F (2, 236) = 11.49, p < .05; $\hat{\omega}^2$ = .08; extroversion, F (2, 236) = 4.74, p < .05; $\hat{\omega}^2$ = .03; and sociability, F (2, 235) = 10.09, p < .05; $\hat{\omega}^2$ = .07; with the results approaching statistical significance on the dimension of composure, F (2, 236) = 2.60, p < .10; $\hat{\omega}^2$ = .01.

The subsequent planned comparisons revealed that each inoculation approach conferred resistance, following the same pattern of results as with the primary dependent measures. The comparisons indicated significant differences on the inoculation same and control means on character, F (1, 233) = 29.27, p < .05; $\hat{\omega}^2$ = .05; competence, F (1, 236) = 13.49, p < .05; $\hat{\omega}^2$ = .05; composure, F (1, 236) = 3.17, p < .05; $\hat{\omega}^2$ = .01; extroversion, F (1, 236) = 7.16, p < .05; $\hat{\omega}^2$ = .02; and sociability, F (1, 235) = 14.27, p < .05; $\hat{\omega}^2$ = .05. In addition, the comparisons found significant differences in the inoculation different and control means on character, F (1, 233) = 16.73, p < .05, $\hat{\omega}^2$ = .06; competence, F (1, 236) = 21.08, p < .05; $\hat{\omega}^2$ = .07; composure, F (1, 236) = 3.33, p < .05; $\hat{\omega}^2$ = .01; and sociability, F (1, 235) = 13.64, p < .05; $\hat{\omega}^2$ = .05; but not on the credibility dimension of extroversion.

The 1988 investigation also sought to replicate the 1986 findings on inoculation pretreatments and time interval. The 1986 results indicated that inoculation decays over time and that inoculation same and different approaches vary in their capacity to deflect issue or character attacks depending on the time interval which separates the pretreatment and the attack. Once again, a 3 (small, moderate, and large interval) × 2 (same and different inoculation pretreatment) × 2 (issue and character attack message approach) factorial analysis of variance was computed to assess the viability of inoculation over time.

Contrary to the 1986 findings, the factorial analysis of variance failed to reveal any main effect for time interval on primary or secondary dependent measures. However, the factorial did indicate five triple interactions involving time interval, inoculation pretreatment, and attack message approach on the primary dependent measure of attitude toward candidate, F (2, 141) = 5.14, p < .05; $\hat{\omega}^2$ = .05,

Table 7.7
Summary of the Same and Different Inoculation Means and the Control Means on the Primary Dependent Measures

Dependent Measure	Treatment Condition Means		
	None	Same	Different
Attitude toward Candidate			
Mean *	4.26 (n=90)	2.96 (n=109)	3.00 (n=54)
SD	1.60	1.30	1.40
Attitude toward Position			
Mean *	3.96 (n=91)	2.84 (n=109)	2.70 (n=54)
SD	1.81	1.47	1.42
Likelihood of Voting for			
Mean *	39.62 (n=89)	14.67 (n=108)	15.19 (n=54)
SD	33.38	21.42	23.48

Note: Ratings of receivers' attitude toward the candidate supported in the attack message and the receivers' attitude toward the position taken by the candidate supported in the attack message are based on seven-point scales. Assessment of the likelihood of voting for the candidate supported in the attack message is based on a 100-point probability scale. The higher the rating or assessment, the more persuasive the attack message.

* $p < .05$.

and on secondary source credibility dimensions of character, F $(2, 139) = 5.09$, $p < .05$; $\hat{\omega}^2 = .07$; competence, F $(2, 141) = 6.10$, $p < .05$; $\hat{\omega}^2 = .07$; composure, F $(2, 141) = 5.03$, $p < .05$; $\hat{\omega}^2 = .06$; and sociability, F $(2, 140) = 3.69$, $p < .05$; $\hat{\omega}^2 = .04$.

In all five instances, there were consistent patterns of differences involving the means which suggested that inoculation same and different pretreatments varied in their effectiveness in conferring resistance to attack messages across time intervals. Thus, a 2×2 factorial analysis of variance involving attack message approach (issue and character) and inoculation approach (same and different) was computed at each time interval (small, moderate, large) as a prerequisite to further post-hoc analyses.

The two-way analyses of variance identified significant interactions at small intervals on the primary dependent measure of attitude toward candidate, F (1, 73) = 3.67, $p < .05$; $\hat{\omega}^2 = .03$, and on the credibility dimension of competence, F (1, 73) = 4.69, $p < .05$; $\hat{\omega}^2 = .05$. Further analyses of the means indicated that at small time intervals same inoculation pretreatments were more effective in deflecting character attacks than issue attacks on the measures of attitude toward candidate, t (1,141) = 2.89, $p < .05$, two-tailed, and competence, t (1, 141) = 2.68, $p < .05$, two-tailed, and that inoculation same messages were more effective than inoculation different messages in conferring resistance to character attacks on the measures of attitude toward candidate, t (1, 141) = 3.31, $p < .05$, two-tailed, and competence, t (1, 141) = 2.44, $p < .10$, two-tailed. These means are shown in Table 7.8.

At moderate time intervals, the two-way factorial only identified one main effect, indicating that inoculation different pretreatments were superior to inoculation same in providing resistance to attack messages on the secondary dependent measure of competence, F (1, 50) = 5.90, $p < .05$; $\hat{\omega}^2 = .09$.

However, the two-way analyses of variance indicated a number of significant interactions at large intervals on the dependent measures of attitude toward candidate, F (1, 18) = 4.81, $p < .05$; $\hat{\omega}^2 = .15$; character, F (1, 18) = 7.76, $p < .05$; $\hat{\omega}^2 = .24$; competence, F (1, 18) = 5.54, $p < .05$; $\hat{\omega}^2 = .17$; composure, F (1, 18) = 12.45, $p < .05$; $\hat{\omega}^2 = .34$; and sociability, F (1, 18) = 6.63, $p < .05$; $\hat{\omega}^2 = .21$.

Further analyses of these means identified a consistent pattern for all dependent measures. Post-hoc tests indicated that at large time intervals inoculation same were more effective than inoculation different pretreatments in deflecting issue attacks on: attitude toward candidate, t (1, 141) = 4.13, $p < .05$, two-tailed; character, t (1, 139) = 4.31, $p < .05$, two-tailed; competence, t (1, 141) = 3.91, $p < .05$, two-tailed; composure, t (1, 141) = 4.90, $p < .05$, two-tailed; and sociability, t (1, 140) = 3.70, $p < .05$, two-tailed; and that inoculation different messages were more effective in conferring resistance to character as opposed to issue attacks on attitude toward candidate, t (1, 141) = 3.31, $p < .05$, two-tailed; character, t (1, 139) = 4.39, $p < .05$, two-tailed; competence, t (1, 141) = 4.17, $p < .05$, two-tailed; composure, t (1, 141) = 4.75, $p < .05$, two-tailed; and sociability, t (1, 140) = 3.64, $p < .05$, two-tailed.

The pattern of results provides a more complete picture of the relative effectiveness of inoculation pretreatments in conferring resistance to persuasion across small, moderate, and large time intervals. The 1986 results hinted at some subtle variations in inoculation effectiveness with issue as opposed to character attacks over time, whereas the 1988 results indicate clear patterns. At small time intervals between the inoculation pretreatment and the subsequent attack message, inoculation same pretreatments were more effective in deflecting character than issue attacks, and also were superior to inoculation different pretreatments in providing resistance to character attacks. At moderate time intervals, the differences in the effectiveness of inoculation same and different pretreatments were negligible.

However, at large intervals, the relative superiority of the inoculation pretreatments varied according to attack message approach: inoculation same pretreatments were most effective in conferring resistance to issue as opposed to character attacks, whereas inoculation different pretreatments were most effective in providing resistance against character attacks as opposed to issue attacks.

Discussion of 1988 Findings

The results of the 1988 investigation offer further support for the effectiveness of the inoculation message strategy as a vehicle to confer resistance to the influence of attack messages, thus enabling a candidate to provide an umbrella of protection against the full force of an opponent's attack messages. The results bolster the 1986 findings, indicating that inoculation pretreatments, whether same or different, deflect the overall persuasiveness of subsequent political attacks.

In addition, the results extend the scope of inoculation to a new domain, suggesting viability for this resistance strategy via the direct mail communication channel, clearly an important application given the rapid growth of direct mail communication in political campaigns (Armstrong, 1988; Godwin, 1988; Sabato, 1981) and the most recent use of direct mail as a conduit for strong, targeted political attacks (Armstrong, 1988; Heller, 1987). The combined inoculation and reinforcement conditions produced a significant impact, accounting for sizable variance in receivers' responses to the source and content of subsequent attack messages.

These results suggest that Armstrong (1988) is on target with his claim that most people open and at least glance at virtually every piece of mail, particularly personalized political correspondence. Since inoculated and control subjects in this study were alike *in virtually every respect*, including exposure to campaign events (e.g., mass media news, political advertisements, and debates), differing only in that the inoculated subjects had received a direct mail inoculation message and the control subjects had not, the greater resistance shown by inoculated subjects to the persuasive attack messages suggests that many of them read and internalized the inoculative material.

However, as a caveat, it must be stressed that South Dakota demographics are particularly favorable to the use of the direct mail communication channel, since the typical resident is more likely to read direct mail than people in many other states. ABC News/*Washington Post* exit poll data comparing South Dakota and the nation in 1988 indicated that a typical state resident is more likely to be Caucasian (+9.0%)—particularly of German and Scandinavian backgrounds— and a high school graduate (+9.7%), and less likely to be eighteen to twenty-four years old (-2.5%) and to earn higher incomes, such as from $40,000 to $49,999 a year (-6.2%) or more than $50,000 a year (-12.6%).[1] Thus, the results of the 1988 investigation may overestimate the viability of the direct mail communication channel when generalized nationally.

The initial results failed to support the prediction that reinforcement messages

Table 7.8

Summary of Inoculation Pretreatment Means Based on Issue and Character Attack Message Approach for Short and Long Time Intervals on Attitude toward Source Measures

SMALL TIME INTERVALS

Dependent Measure	Attack Message Approach			
	Inoculation Same Pretreatments		Inoculation Different Pretreatments	
	Issue (n=29)	Character (n=24)	Issue (n=17)	Character (n=7)
Attitude toward Candidate				
Mean	3.22	2.47	2.93	3.33
SD	1.05	1.09	1.39	1.12
Source Credibility: Character				
Mean	3.19	2.79	3.65	3.43
SD	1.34	1.28	1.57	0.88
Source Credibility: Competence				
Mean	3.95	2.92	3.22	3.86
SD	1.55	1.36	1.62	1.02
Source Credibility: Composure				
Mean	3.57	3.56	3.73	3.38
SD	1.34	1.81	1.47	1.01
Source Credibility: Sociability				
Mean	3.52	2.85	3.53	3.05
SD	1.34	1.72	1.42	0.91

LARGE TIME INTERVALS

	Inoculation Same Pretreatments		Inoculation Different Pretreatments	
	Issue ($\underline{n}$=8)	Character ($\underline{n}$=6)	Issue ($\underline{n}$=4)	Character ($\underline{n}$=4)
Attitude toward Candidate				
Mean	2.44	3.44	4.71	2.79
SD	1.43	1.47	1.62	1.58
Source Credibility: Character				
Mean	2.63	3.67	5.17	2.58
SD	1.45	1.46	0.84	1.91
Source Credibility: Competence				
Mean	3.17	4.06	5.75	3.00
SD	1.83	1.60	1.20	2.23
Source Credibility: Composure				
Mean	2.58	4.11	5.67	2.67
SD	1.29	1.59	1.41	1.56
Source Credibility: Sociability				
Mean	2.79	3.89	5.17	2.83
SD	1.36	1.49	1.14	2.05

Note: Ratings of receivers' attitude toward the candidate supported in the attack message and perceptions of the source credibility of the candidate supported in the attack message are based on seven-point scales. The higher the rating, the more persuasive the attack message.

increase the effectiveness of inoculation pretreatments. This would seem to indicate that the initial inoculative stimulus, which triggers an internal motivational process to bolster arguments supporting attitudes, carries considerable persistence. This outcome is consistent with the findings of Chaiken (1987), Petty (1977), and Petty and Cacioppo (1979, 1984) that message strategies producing higher receiver involvement tend to enhance attitude persistence. Previous laboratory research involving college undergraduates (McGuire, 1961b; Tannenbaum, Macaulay & Norris, 1966) reported small reinforcement effects, while results of the 1986 study, as reported above, concluded that inoculation pretreatments experience limited decay over a period of three weeks, at least in terms of receiver voting intention.

However, the 1988 investigation failed to rule out one other explanation for the initial failure of reinforcement messages to enhance the effectiveness of the inoculation pretreatments. It may be that the amount of reinforcement is crucial and that it requires more than a single reinforcement to significantly boost the effectiveness of inoculation pretreatments.

The pattern of results of the 1988 study provides modest support for the position that the inoculation message strategy, which was represented in the treatment condition of the study by both inoculation and inoculation-plus-reinforcement, is more effective than post-hoc refutation in deflecting attitude change following exposure to a political attack message. The omnibus ANOVA and subsequent planned comparisons indicated some advantage for inoculation over post-hoc refutation on the primary measure of attitude toward candidate and the secondary measures of competence and sociability.

However, the triple interaction, involving the independent variables of treatment condition, political party orientation, and attack message approach, on the dependent measure of likelihood of voting for the candidate supported in the attack message is particularly revealing with regard to the relative effectiveness of the inoculation approach versus post-hoc refutation. The subsequent two-way factorial and post-hoc analyses point to a consistent pattern of results, indicating the superiority of the inoculation approach over post-hoc refutation among strong political party identifiers as well as nonidentifiers.

Among weak party identifiers, however, the effectiveness of inoculation and post-hoc refutation varied somewhat depending on attack message approach. The results indicated that, while post-hoc refutation and inoculation-plus-reinforcement are more effective than inoculation alone in deflecting issue attack messages, inoculation and inoculation-plus-reinforcement are vastly superior to post-hoc refutation in combating character attacks, with post-hoc refutation actually resulting in a boomerang effect. There is no theoretical explanation that can account for this finding, and these results could be explained as an idiosyncrasy of the 1988 Bush and Dukakis pairing or even an artifact of measurement. Nonetheless, the impact of inoculation, inoculation-plus-reinforcement, and post-hoc refutation on issue and character attack messages among weak party identifiers should be examined further, since additional support for the pattern of results revealed in this study suggests important nuances for political professionals in their efforts to design and target defenses to political attack messages.

The pattern of results pointing to the conclusion that the inoculation strategy is superior to post-hoc refutation in deflecting political attacks is both useful and important. On a theoretical level, it adds to the initial work of Tannenbaum and Norris (1965) and Tannenbaum, Macaulay, and Norris (1966), providing confirmation in a field research setting that the sequence of refutation-attack confers more resistance to persuasion than attack-refutation. In addition, the finding confirms the central role of threat in any strategy designed to mitigate political attack messages. Threat is the motivational trigger for resistance, as inoculation theory posits (Anderson & McGuire, 1965; McGuire, 1962, 1964, 1970; Papageorgis & McGuire, 1961), and the inoculation approach intrinsically is capable of generating higher threat levels than refutation through the use of a warning of impending attack prior to the actual attack.

On a practical level, this finding informs the practice of political campaign communication. In the first direct comparison of the two alternative strategic responses to political attacks, the inoculation strategy generally proved more effective than post-hoc refutation in combating the influence of political attacks, with the one exception involving issue attacks among weak political party identifiers.

The design of both investigations rules out campaign events as contaminants for all the results with the possible exception of the inoculation and post-hoc refutation finding of the 1988 study. Both investigations measured the effectiveness of the inoculation treatments by comparing the persuasiveness of the political attack messages administered among subjects who had received a pretreatment and those who had not. Since both the treatment and control groups in both studies were the product of random assignment, it is reasonable to assume that the two groups were the same in every respect, including exposure to the full range of campaign events, except for the pretreatment messages that were administered exclusively to the treatment groups. Since the treatment groups were less influenced by the political attack messages that were subsequently administered to both the treatment and control groups, the only plausible explanation is that it was the pretreatments that were responsible for this difference.

However, the finding that the inoculation strategy is more effective than post-hoc refutation in deflecting the impact of political attack messages in the 1988 investigation may have been tainted by campaign events. To make this assessment, the order of treatment and attack was altered. Those subjects in the inoculation condition received an inoculation pretreatment during phase two and received an attack message and measurement in phase four. Subjects in the post-hoc refutation condition received an attack during phase two, a post-hoc refutation message in phase three, with measurement following in phase four. This change in the order of treatment and attack, while necessary in order to test the effectiveness of inoculation versus post-hoc refutation, renders the results vulnerable to the contamination of campaign events, such as candidate advertising and the first Bush and Dukakis debate on September 25, one day following the completion of the first phase of the investigation and three days after the start of the second phase of the study.

However, three of the four content areas selected for use in the 1988 investigation—the Dukakis attacks against Bush that Republican farm policy had crippled rural America and that he was insensitive to the plight of the average working person, and the Bush attack against Dukakis that he had deceived the public concerning his record as governor of Massachusetts—were not employed as the basis of major attacks by the candidates prior to October 10 (phases one, two, and three of the study were completed from middle September to early October, whereas phase four commenced October 10).

One of the content areas, the Bush attack against Dukakis that he was soft on crime, was used as the basis of an attack, receiving considerable emphasis in Bush's advertising and some attention in the September 25 televised debate (Hershey, 1989). Thus, the use of the crime attack by the Bush campaign serves as a potential confound to the finding that the inoculation approach is superior to post-hoc refutation.

However, there is reason to believe that the impact of this contaminant was small. First, Bush's attack that Dukakis was soft on crime was not a major feature of the first debate. In a content analysis of that debate, Hershey (1989, p. 90) revealed that twelve other issue and image concerns received more attention by Bush and Dukakis than crime. Second, a check of area television station logs affirmed that the first regional appearance of Bush's "furlough" advertisement occurred in this area of dominant influence (ADI) on October 10 (also, Americans for Bush, the independent organization that sponsored a similar attack on Dukakis, made no television buys in this ADI prior to October 10).[2] Third, the results of this study indicated that all four attack messages administered in the investigation, including the Bush attack that Dukakis was soft on crime, generated significant persuasive impact on receivers.

The results of the 1988 investigation provide further confirmation that the relationship involving inoculation, time interval, and attack message approach is an intricate one. The five triple interactions on the primary dependent measure of attitude toward candidate and the secondary source credibility dimensions of character, competence, composure, and sociability, involving time interval, inoculation condition, and attack message approach are particularly interesting.

The five triple interactions point to a consistent pattern of differences in the means and thus provide useful information to practitioners who seek to design inoculation messages for candidates. The results generally indicate that inoculation same pretreatments are the most effective at short time intervals and with issue attacks at long intervals, but that inoculation different pretreatments are the most effective at moderate intervals and with character attacks at long intervals.

As in the 1986 study, the interactions only surfaced on the source measures, but this time they appeared on all but one of the measures. Thus, the relationship involving inoculation strategy, attack message approach, and time interval appears confined to receiver attitudes about the source of attack messages. There is no theoretical rationale to account for this finding.

NOTES

1. The data were originally collected by ABC News/*Washington Post*, and then made available by the Inter-University Consortium for Political and Social Research.

2. Telephone conversations with Roger Ailes, media consultant to the Bush–Quayle campaign, and Sky Baab, Midwest Region Political Director, confirmed that extensive use of the "furlough" message in the campaign's paid advertising did not begin in this region until around October 10.

Chapter 8

Inoculation and Political
Party Disposition

Partisanship is the single most important single influence on political
opinions and voting behavior.
> —William H. Flanigan and Nancy H. Zingale, Professors
> of Political Science (Flanigan & Zingale, 1987, pp. 28–29)

Political parties [act]...as intermediaries between voters and the
decision the voters must reach....They limit alternatives to ones
the voter can easily understand.
> —Louis Maisel and Paul M. Sacks, Professors of Political Science
> (Maisel & Sacks, 1975, p. 9)

The findings of the 1986 and 1988 investigations indicate that candidates can
inoculate supporters against the influence of potential attack messages that might
be launched by an opponent in a political campaign. While these findings clearly
document the viability of the inoculation message strategy in political campaign
communication, questions remain concerning inoculation and the political party
disposition of receivers. This chapter will address those questions.

IMPACT OF POLITICAL PARTY DISPOSITION IN
INFLUENCE

It stands to reason that factors that influence the overall effectiveness of
political attack messages should also affect the ability of inoculation messages
to confer resistance to attitude change. The voting behavior literature indicates
that attitude toward party (the general tendency to identify or not, which we

refer to as party orientation, as well as a specific disposition, which we term party identification) exerts substantial pressure on political cognition (Campbell, Munro, Alford & Campbell, 1986). As Miller, Miller, and Schneider (1980, p. 79) stress, "it is the relative stability of the impact that party identification has on subsequent evaluations of candidates and policies which makes it an important attitude to monitor over time."

Indeed, ever since Campbell, Gurin, and Miller (1954) and Campbell, Converse, Miller, and Stokes (1960) posited the psychological theory of voting in two election studies during the 1950s, political scientists have emphasized the substantial influence of political party disposition on political cognition. This theory posits that, absent psychological cross pressures in the form of short-term forces, like candidate image or issues, which are unique to the circumstances of any particular election, party identification is the most significant influence on voter attitudes about candidates.

However, it is true that recent studies document a weakening of party identification during the last two decades and its relationship to the vote (Abramson, 1983; Axelrod, 1972, 1974, 1978, 1982, 1986; Beck, 1988; Norpoth, 1987; Petrocik, 1980, 1981, 1987; Stanley, Bianco & Niemi, 1986; Wattenberg, 1986). An excellent review of this literature, which treats party identification both as a dependent and an independent variable, appears in Campbell, Munro, Alford, and Campbell (1986).

The general weakening of party identification has swelled the nonaffiliated ranks (a combination of politically apathetic and independent) to over one-third of the electorate (*Public Opinion*, 1984, p. 21) and increased the amount of crossover voting (Republican party identifiers who vote for Democratic candidates and vice versa) to more than one-seventh of the electorate (Mann & Wolfinger, 1984, p. 273).

In addition to the general erosion of party identification, revisionists have underscored the fact that partisanship is more unstable over time than was previously assumed. They contend, therefore, that party identification is a much less predictable variable in voting decisions than James E. Campbell and others maintained.

More recently, there additionally has been a revision of the revisionists. These scholars emphasize the continual force of political party identification in structuring the immediate context of electoral decisions (Markus & Converse, 1979; Stanga & Sheffield, 1987; Whiteley, 1988). Whiteley (1988), for example, employed Granger-causality analysis to demonstrate convincingly that the stability of partisanship is a separate issue from its exogeneity in affecting voting decisions. He (1988, p. 961) contends that "partisanship is a tally of affective evaluations, which are quite distinct from issue-based evaluations. Partisanship, candidate evaluations, and issues all independently Granger-cause voting behavior, and the former is more important than the latter in determining the vote choice."

In short, party identification remains the most reliable predictor of the vote.

Democratic pollster Peter Hart conceded after the 1984 election that party attachment today is less strong and susceptible to change, but he went on to emphasize that "party identification continues to be the single best predictor of what an individual will do" (Moving Right Along? . . . , 1985, p. 63). Shively (1980, p. 236) characterizes the role of party identification on political attitudes and behaviors in contemporary campaigns as "still dominant in many people's decisions on how to vote, and . . . still one of the few factors transcending immediate elections." Abramson (1983) maintains that despite a weakening of the relationship between party identification and electoral choice since 1964, it remains an important variable that contributes to opinion formation and influences voting behavior. More recently, Abramson, Aldrich, and Rohde (1983), Stanga and Sheffield (1987), Kenski and Lockwood (1988), and Whiteley (1988) have underscored the continual force of party identification in voter decisions.

INOCULATION AND POLITICAL PARTY ORIENTATION

Party identification affects persuasibility in a number of ways. Chaffee and Choe (1980), for example, report that higher political involvement of identifiers reduces persuasibility. King (1977) observes that affiliated receivers are more inclined to selective perception of their candidate's message, a claim that has received considerable support to date (Atkin, 1971; Blumler & McQuail, 1969; Sherrod, 1971; Weisberg & Rusk, 1970). Nonetheless, in an increasingly volatile electoral environment, more and more partisans, even strong political party identifiers, occasionally defect, casting their vote for candidates of the opposite political party (Niemi & Weisberg, 1984). Consequently, inoculation, which attempts to minimize defections, is a relevant strategy for political party identifiers.

Although strong partisans are less numerous today (29% in 1984) than they were in 1952 (35%), a leading text on parties and elections by Frank Sorauf and Paul Beck (1988) emphasizes the importance of strong partisans for politics generally and for political parties and candidates in particular. Strong partisans are more likely to follow campaigns in the media; communicate with and attempt to persuade others; perceive sharper differences in political parties; and manifest overt signs of active involvement (e.g., voting, volunteering, contributing, etc.).

In addition, strong partisans may prove more receptive to inoculation than either weak partisans or nonpartisans. The very presence of higher levels of political involvement should render strong party identifiers particularly susceptible to inoculation because it facilitates threat. As explained in Chapters 5 and 7, the inoculation process uses threat, consisting of a warning of impending attack, as the catalyst to receiver motivation.

Both the 1986 and 1988 investigations examined the overall effectiveness of inoculation in fostering resistance to attack messages, in general terms and in terms of the political party orientation of potential voters. The findings of both studies indicate that, while inoculation is a viable strategy among all groups—

nonpartisans, weak partisans, and strong partisans—it confers more resistance to the subsequent exposure to political attack messages among receivers who are strong party identifiers.

The 1986 Investigation

Initially, as reported in Chapter 7, the 2 (attack message approach) $\times$ 3 (inoculation condition) $\times$ 4 (political party orientation) factorial analysis of variance identified main effects for political party orientation on the primary attitude measures of attitude toward the candidate supported in the attack message, attitude toward position taken in the attack message, and the likelihood of voting for the candidate supported in the attack message, and on four of the secondary source credibility dimensions.

However, to accurately assess the relative effectiveness of inoculation among the political party orientation conditions it was necessary to confine the analysis to inoculated subjects. Thus, a 2 (attack message approach) $\times$ 2 (inoculation approach) $\times$ 4 (political party orientation) factorial analysis of variance was computed.

The factorial analysis of variance indicated significant main effects for political party orientation (none, weak, strong, crossover) on the primary dependent measures of attitude toward candidate, F (3, 325) = 5.37, $p < .05$; $\hat{\omega}^2 = .04$; attitude toward position, F (3, 325) = 12.20, $p < .05$; $\hat{\omega}^2 = .08$; and likelihood of voting for, F (3, 325) = 4.66, $p < .05$; $\hat{\omega}^2 = .03$. These results are shown in Table 8.1.

However, an interaction involving inoculation pretreatment and political party orientation overrode the main effect finding on attitude toward position. Two tests of simple effects were computed, on inoculation same and different pretreatments, across political party orientation. These tests of simple effects revealed that inoculation same pretreatments, F (3, 228) = 7.47, $p < .05$; $\hat{\omega}^2 = .08$, and inoculation different pretreatments, F (3, 105) = 6.80, $p < .05$; $\hat{\omega}^2 = .14$, varied significantly across political party orientation on attitude toward position.

Further examination of the means indicated that inoculation same pretreatments were more effective in deflecting attack messages among strong identifiers than among nonidentifiers, t (1, 325) = -3.15, $k = 6$; $p < .05$, two-tailed; weak identifiers, t (1, 325) = -3.54, $k = 6$; $p < .05$, two-tailed; or crossovers, t (1, 325) = -3.42, $k = 6$; $p < .05$, two-tailed. By contrast, the inoculation different pretreatments were more effective with weak party identifiers, t (1, 325) = -2.93, $k = 6$; $p < .05$, two-tailed; strong identifiers, t (1, 325) = -3.46, $k = 6$; $p < .05$, two-tailed; and crossovers, t (1, 325) = -3.41, $k = 6$; $p < .05$, two-tailed, than with nonidentifiers. These means are displayed in Table 8.2.

Political party orientation exerted minimal impact on the dimensions of source credibility. The only significant effect involving political party orientation was

Table 8.1
Summary of Political Party Orientation Means on Receiver Attitude

Dependent Measure	Political Party Orientation			
	None (n=82)	Weak (n=94)	Strong (n=121)	Crossover (n=44)
Attitude toward Candidate				
Mean *	3.65	3.51	3.05	3.53
SD	1.28	1.39	1.38	1.24
Attitude toward Position				
Mean *	3.80	3.49	2.76	3.45
SD	1.48	1.42	1.48	1.46
Likelihood of Voting for				
Mean *	15.21	15.03	7.84	18.32
SD	26.00	15.03	18.01	23.51

Note: Ratings of receivers' attitude toward the candidate supported in the attack message and receivers' attitude toward the position taken by the candidate supported in the attack message are based on seven-point scales. Assessment of the likelihood of voting for the candidate supported in the attack message is based on a 100-point probability scale. The higher the rating or assessment, the more persuasive the attack message.

* $p < .05$.

a main effect on the dimension of sociability, $F (3, 325) = 3.05$, $p < .05$; $\hat{\omega}^2 = .02$.

Planned comparisons were then computed for the political party orientation means on the three remaining dependent variables for which significant main effects were reported: attitude toward candidate, likelihood of voting for, and sociability.

The results of the first comparison revealed that persuasive attacks following inoculation exert less influence on strong party identifiers than on nonidentifiers, weak identifiers, and crossovers. This was true on the dependent measures of attitude toward candidate, $F (1, 325) = 9.76$, $p < .05$; $\hat{\omega}^2 = .03$; likelihood of voting for, $F (1, 325) = 10.26$, $p < .05$; $\hat{\omega}^2 = .03$; and the source credibility dimension of sociability, $F (1, 325) = 3.61$, $p < .05$; $\hat{\omega}^2 = .01$.

The second comparison examined weak party identifiers against nonidentifiers and crossovers. The modified Bonferroni comparisons indicated no significant differences involving the dependent variables of attitude toward candidate, likelihood of voting for, or sociability.

The results of the 1986 study reveal that the inoculation strategy provides more resistance to political attack messages among strong political party iden-

Table 8.2
Summary of the Inoculation Approach Means for None, Weak, Strong, and Crossover Political Orientation Conditions on the Dependent Variable of Attitude toward Position

Inoculation Approach	Political Party Orientation			
	None	Weak	Strong	Crossover
Inoculation Same				
Mean	3.62	3.72	2.80*	3.69
	(n=52)	(n=68)	(n=79)	(n=33)
SD	1.30	1.27	1.29	1.60
Inoculation Different				
Mean	4.11*	2.91	2.69	2.71
	(n=30)	(n=26)	(n=42)	(n=11)
SD	1.45	1.27	1.51	1.05

Note: Ratings of receivers' attitude toward the position taken by the candidate supported in the attack message are based on seven-point scales. The higher the rating, the more persuasive the attack message.

* $p < .05$.

tifiers. The main effect on attitude toward candidate, likelihood of voting for, and the source credibility dimension of sociability, coupled with the post-hoc finding for inoculation same pretreatments on the measure of attitude toward position, all support the position that inoculation is more effective in deflecting attack messages among strong party identifiers as opposed to nonidentifiers, crossovers, or weak identifiers. This provides further support for the position that strong partisans are less susceptible to political influence in all circumstances (Atkin, 1971; Blumler & McQuail, 1969; Chaffee & Choe, 1980; King, 1977; Sherrod, 1971; Shively, 1980; Weisberg & Rusk, 1970).

However, the post-hoc finding that inoculation different pretreatments were more effective among all party identifiers, weak, strong, and crossovers, in contrast to nonidentifiers, cannot be explained by extant theory. These findings do suggest that inoculation same and different pretreatment approaches should be adapted to political party orientation for maximum results.

The 1988 Investigation

The 1986 study examined inoculation and political party orientation in a Senate campaign. Just as party identification remains an important variable influencing voting decisions in presidential campaigns (Abramson, 1983; Abramson, Aldrich & Rohde, 1983; Shively, 1980; Stanga & Sheffield, 1987; Whiteley, 1988), it also plays an instrumental role as a decision criterion for voting in Senate, gubernatorial, and House campaigns (Kenski & Lockwood, 1988). Indeed, party identification once was thought to exert even more influence in nonpresidential elections (Campbell, Munro, Alford & Campbell, 1986). However, Kostroski's (1973) study reported that the impact of party identification on voting has declined in Senate elections, following the same pattern previously observed in presidential elections. Thus, the 1988 investigation anticipated that the 1986 finding, that inoculation fosters more resistance among strong party identifiers, would generalize to a presidential election campaign, and the results indicated that it did.

A 4 (treatment condition) $\times$ 2 (attack message approach) $\times$ 3 (political party orientation) factorial analysis of variance was initially computed and indicated modest support for the position that inoculation pretreatments confer more resistance to the subsequent exposure to an attack message among strong political party identifiers than among weak political party identifiers or nonidentifiers with differences in political party orientation means approaching statistical significance on primary dependent measures of attitude toward candidate, F (2, 289) = 2.46, $p < .10$; $\hat{\omega}^2 = .01$, and the likelihood of voting for F (2, 287) = 2.79, $p < .10$; $\hat{\omega}^2 = .01$, but the triple interaction, reported in Chapter 7, overrode the latter effect. The omnibus factorial revealed no main or interaction effects involving the political party orientation means on the secondary source credibility dimensions.

Two planned comparisons were computed to further explore the differences in political party orientation means on the measure of attitude toward candidate. The means of strong political party identifiers was compared with the means of weak identifiers and nonidentifiers. The results indicated that strong identifiers were significantly less influenced by attack messages across all treatment conditions, F (1, 289) = 5.90, $p < .05$; $\hat{\omega}^2 = .01$. There were no significant differences involving weak identifiers and nonidentifiers. However, when the same planned comparisons were computed among inoculation and inoculation-plus-reinforcement subjects on the measure of attitude toward candidate, the direction of means was the same, but the differences were not statistically significant.

Thus, the 1988 investigation provided further support for the position that inoculation pretreatments are most effective with strong party identifiers. However, the triple interaction, discussed in Chapter 7, provides useful information which could assist practitioners in targeting potential voters of various political party orientations with inoculation pretreatments. Although further confirmation of this pattern of means should be sought in subsequent studies, the initial findings suggest that inoculation generally is superior to post-hoc refutation among both strong party identifiers and nonidentifiers. However, among weak party identifiers, an important target group for inoculation in most political campaigns, reinforcement is needed to optimize inoculation against issue attacks, whereas a single inoculation pretreatment is sufficient in deflecting character attacks.

INOCULATION AND POLITICAL PARTY IDENTIFICATION

The general weakening of party identification documented earlier in this chapter has proven to be the most pronounced among Democrats. Although Axelrod (1972, 1982, 1986) and Norpoth and Rusk (1982) pinpoint a loosening of Democratic party ties among all demographic segments since 1964, sizable shifts among white Southerners, blue-collar workers, and Catholics are particularly noteworthy because they demonstrate the erosion of the New Deal coalition. As a result, McWilliams (1985, p. 168) concludes that "The New Deal strategy has played out . . . It [the New Deal coalition] is exhausted." In fact, the weakening of voter loyalty to the Democratic party is the primary support for the claims of Caddell (1985), Ginsberg and Shefter (1985), Hargrove and Nelson (1985), Lowi (1985), and others that a political dealignment is in progress.

One manifestation of this development is that Democrats are more likely than Republicans to abandon their party's candidates during a political campaign. This is apparent in the higher proportion of Republican party identifiers who vote consistently with party identification. Shively (1980, p. 233) reports that 86% of strong Democrats and 96% of strong Republicans, and 66% of weak Democrats and 84% of weak Republicans, vote consistently for their party's candidate in presidential elections. This pattern has held in more recent elections. For example, in 1984 93% of Republicans voted for Reagan, while 75% of Democrats supported Mondale (Pomper, 1989, p. 133), and in 1988 *New York Times*/CBS News exit polling data indicated that 91% of Republicans voted for Bush and 82% of Democrats cast ballots for Dukakis.[1] This rationale suggests that after inoculation, political attack messages should exert less impact on Republican than on Democrat identifiers.

The 1986 and 1988 investigations also attempted to determine the effectiveness of inoculation among potential voters who are loyal Democratic and Republican identifiers. As argued above, it was expected that following inoculation, attack messages would produce less impact on Republican party identifiers as opposed to Democratic identifiers. However, results of both studies failed to support this position and, in the 1986 study, suggested the opposite pattern.

The 1986 Investigation

A 2 (inoculation message strategy) × 2 (attack message approach) × 2 (political party affiliation) factorial analysis of variance was computed to examine the relative effectiveness of the inoculation pretreatments among party identifiers. The factorial did identify differences in the means of Democratic and Republican party identifiers. These differences attained statistical significance on the source credibility dimensions of competence, $F (1, 207) = 8.20$; $df = 1/207$, $p < .05$;

$\hat{\omega}^2 = .03$; composure, $F(1, 207) = 15.18, p < .05$; $\hat{\omega}^2 = .06$; and extroversion, $F(1, 207) = 34.99, p < .05$; $\hat{\omega}^2 = .13$; and approached statistical significance on the primary attitude measures of attitude toward candidate supported in the attack message, $F(1, 207) = 3.10, p < .10$; $\hat{\omega}^2 = .01$, and likelihood of voting for the candidate supported in the attack message, $F(1, 207) = 3.39, p < .10$; $\hat{\omega}^2 = .01$.

However, further analysis of the direction of these differences revealed that, contrary to what was anticipated, inoculation pretreatment messages conferred more resistance to political attacks among Democratic party identifiers than among Republican identifiers. These means are displayed in Table 8.3.

The 1986 study revealed that inoculation pretreatments seem to confer more resistance to subsequent attack messages among Democratic identifiers than Republican identifiers. This finding was contrary to the prediction that, since Republican party identifiers are less susceptible to political persuasion, attack messages following inoculation should exert less impact on them.

The results of the 1986 study rule out the most parsimonious explanation for this finding: that the attack messages directed toward Republican identifiers were somehow more effective than the attack messages directed toward Democratic identifiers. However, the results indicated no significant inoculation or attack message and party affiliation interaction. This suggests that the explanation for the finding that inoculation confers more resistance among Democratic identifiers must lie elsewhere.

One explanation that cannot be completely ruled out is that the greater impact of inoculation among Democratic as opposed to Republican identifiers is an idiosyncrasy of South Dakota politics. Since South Dakota is a rural plains state, the composition of the Democratic and Republican parties is unique.

ABC News/*Washington Post* exit polling during the 1986 election revealed that compared to national norms, among South Dakota residents there are fewer union members (− 5.8%) and hourly wage earners (− 9.2%),[1] two of the groups frequently identified with the overall weakening of the New Deal coalition in recent years (Axelrod, 1972, 1982, 1986; Norpoth & Rusk, 1982).

In addition, according to ABC News/*Washington Post* data, South Dakota residents in 1986 were more concerned about the federal budget deficit (+ 8.9%) and the state of their local economy (+ 7.1%), felt they were worse off financially than in 1981 (+ 13.2%), and consequently, were more likely to disapprove of Reagan's job performance (+ 9.4%) than people throughout the nation. This may have bolstered the effectiveness of Daschle's attack message against Abdnor on Republican farm policy, and at the same time, undermined Abdnor's attack on Daschle for not being more supportive of President Reagan's legislative agenda. In any event, the effectiveness of inoculation among party identifiers should be explored further in order to eliminate idiosyncrasy as a possible explanation.

The persuasion literature suggests one plausible additional explanation which is also consistent with the position, so firmly established in theory and research, that Democratic identifiers are more persuasible than Republican identifiers (Cad-

Table 8.3
Summary of the Party Affiliation Means on Receiver Attitude

Dependent Measure	Party Affiliation	
	Democrat (n=109)	Republican (n=106)
Attitude toward Candidate		
Mean **	3.10	3.41
SD	1.28	1.18
Attitude toward Position		
Mean	2.93	3.24
SD	1.41	1.26
Likelihood of Voting for		
Mean **	8.57	13.47
SD	17.86	18.41
Source Credibility: Character		
Mean	3.54	3.59
SD	1.46	1.15
Source Credibility: Competence		
Mean *	3.69	4.27
SD	1.60	1.35
Source Credibility: Composure		
Mean *	3.08	3.86
SD	1.55	1.40
Source Credibility: Extroversion		
Mean *	4.09	5.11
SD	1.33	1.13
Source Credibility: Sociability		
Mean	3.75	3.79
SD	1.53	1.51

Note: Ratings of receivers' attitude toward the candidate supported in the attack message, attitude toward the position taken by the candidate supported in the attack message, and perception of the source credibility of the candidate supported in the attack message are based on seven-point scales. Assessment of the likelihood of voting for the candidate supported in the attack message is based on a 100-point probability scale. The higher the rating or assessment, the more persuasive the attack message.

* $p < .05$.
** $p < .10$.

Table 8.4

Comparative Political Profile of South Dakota with the Nation

Variable	Nation		South Dakota		
	n	Percent	n	Percent	Percentage Difference
PARTY IDENTIFICATION					
Democrat	7,529	44.0	448	42.0	- 2.0
Republican	5,825	34.1	483	45.3	+11.2
Independent	3,420	20.0	124	11.6	- 8.4
Other	329	1.9	12	1.1	- 0.8
FINANCIAL WELL-BEING (COMPARED TO 1981)					
Better Off	6,847	38.9	291	26.7	-12.2
Worse Off	3,960	22.5	389	35.7	+13.2
About the Same	6,091	34.6	378	34.6	0.0
No Response	723	4.1	33	3.0	+ 1.1
STATE OF ECONOMY					
Excellent	755	4.3	19	1.7	- 2.6
Good	8,163	46.3	345	31.6	-14.7
Not So Good	6,312	35.8	493	45.2	+ 9.4
Poor	1,675	9.5	202	18.5	+ 9.0
No Response	716	4.1	32	2.9	- 1.2
WHICH PARTY TRUSTED TO DO A BETTER JOB					
Republicans	7,949	45.1	455	41.7	- 3.4
Democrats	7,596	43.1	501	45.9	+ 2.8
No Response	2,076	11.8	135	12.4	+ 0.6
REAGAN APPROVAL					
Approve	10,361	58.8	553	50.7	- 8.1
Disapprove	6,183	35.1	485	44.5	+ 9.4
No Response	1,077	6.1	53	4.9	- 1.2

Source: ABC News/Washington Post Exit Poll, 1986.

dell, 1985; Ginsberg & Shefter, 1985; Hargrove & Nelson, 1985; Lowi, 1985; McWilliams, 1985; Norpoth & Rusk, 1982; Shively, 1980). Greater persuasibility renders Democratic identifiers more vulnerable to political attacks.

Of course, greater persuasibility should also render such receivers more susceptible to inoculation. In addition, *because inoculation precedes attack, it may produce more influence* than subsequent attack messages, particularly among receivers higher in persuasibility. One possible reason involves the presence of an assimilation effect (Sherif & Sherif, 1967). Subjects higher in persuasibility possess a wide range of acceptance/noncommitment, facilitating the influence of the first message in a conflicting message sequence. However, the impact of the initial message alters the receiver's anchor, thus narrowing the latitude of acceptance/noncommitment for the second, and opposing, message. Another possible reason is that the inoculation message gets a unique boost due to a primacy effect based on superior recall and influence of the first message in a conflicting message sequence (Burgoon, 1975). A primacy effect is even more pronounced when the content area is both interesting and familiar to receivers (Rosnow & Robinson, 1967), as should have been true for the inoculation messages geared toward party identifiers. The possibility of enhanced inoculation impact among more persuasible receivers, either due to an assimilation or primacy effect, needs to be examined further.

The 1988 Investigation

The 1988 study attempted to provide more support for the unexpected 1986 finding that inoculation messages confer more resistance to attack messages among Democratic than Republican identifiers. The 1988 investigation configured inoculation somewhat differently, retaining control subjects in the inoculation condition. Hence, a 2 (attack message approach) $\times$ 3 (inoculation condition) $\times$ 2 (political party affiliation) factorial was employed to assess the relative effectiveness of inoculation pretreatments with Democratic and Republican identifiers.

The results indicated modest differences in inoculation based on party affiliation. Just two results, a main effect on the source credibility dimension of competence, $F(1, 193) = 3.35, p < .10; \hat{\omega}^2 = .01$, and a triple interaction on attitude toward the candidate supported in the attack message, $F(1, 193) = 2.73, p < .10; \hat{\omega}^2 = .01$, approached statistical significance. A two-way analysis of variance was computed in attack message approach and inoculation condition for both Republican and Democratic party identifiers. It revealed a main effect for inoculation, $F(2, 97) = 7.88, p < .05; \hat{\omega}^2 = .12$, for Democratic identifiers.

Subsequent post-hoc tests indicated that among Democratic identifiers, while both inoculation pretreatment approaches were effective in conferring resistance, inoculation same messages were more effective than inoculation different messages, $t(1, 193) = 2.35, p < .10$, two-tailed. This finding on the relative superiority of inoculation same pretreatments among Democratic identifiers cannot be explained via extant theory.

Thus, the pattern of results of the two investigations, taken together, provides no clear pattern regarding the relative effectiveness of inoculation among Democratic and Republican party identifiers. Indeed, the failure of the 1988 study to support the unexpected 1986 finding that inoculation is more effective with Democratic identifiers increases the likelihood that the former was an idiosyncrasy of the 1986 political race between Abdnor and Daschle, as argued previously.

NOTE

1. The data were originally collected by ABC News/*Washington Post*, and then made available by the Inter-University Consortium for Political and Social Research.

Chapter 9

Inoculation and Individual Differences

The results regarding the relationships between any given individual-difference variable and susceptibility to social influence tend to be extremely complex and seemingly contradictory.
—William J. McGuire, Professor of Psychology
(McGuire, 1969, p. 243)

Sex role turns out to be one of the most important determinants of human behavior.
—David McClelland, Professor of Psychology
(cited in Gilligan, 1982, p. 14)

The results presented thus far clearly indicate that the inoculation message strategy is a viable option for candidates who seek to provide a blanket of resistance to the influence of political attack messages. Chapter 7 documented the general efficacy of inoculation, whereas Chapter 8 demonstrated that, while inoculation works with all potential voters, its impact is greatest among strong party identifiers.

The remaining question concerns the relative effectiveness of the inoculation strategy among potential voters who differ in terms of gender, age, and education. This will be the focus of Chapter 9.

Much previous research has examined the relationship between general persuasibility and a myriad of individual difference variables. These variables are important because, as McGuire (1969, p. 247) observes, "[Individual difference variables] . . . interact with other aspects of the communication situation (source, message, etc.) in affecting attitude change." As a result, there is a possibility that inoculation same and different pretreatments may vary in their capacity to provide resistance to issue and/or character attacks with different receiver groups.

Both the 1986 and 1988 investigations explored the relative effectiveness of inoculation pretreatments among receivers who vary in terms of gender. The 1988 investigation also probed the impact of inoculation messages among receivers who vary in terms of age as well as educational background. The results suggest useful insights concerning the design and implementation of the inoculation message strategy on each of the three individual difference variables.

INOCULATION AND RECEIVER GENDER

Gender was singled out in this investigation for three reasons. First, gender (along with age and self-esteem) is viewed as "strategic" by McGuire (1969, p. 247) due to "the relatively high quantity and quality of research devoted to [it]." Second, gender is one of the few individual difference variables which has been examined in past inoculation research. And third, given the recent emphasis on "gender gap" in the political communication literature, there is reason to believe that political messages may exert unique influence upon female and male receivers (Frankovic, 1982).

Gender has been examined extensively in persuasion, but the extant research has failed to provide a clear sense of the general relationship between receiver gender and persuasibility. As Littlejohn and Jabusch (1987, p. 84) recently put it, "Sex is one of the most studied and most confusing variables related to persuasibility."

There was a time when influence scholars accepted without reservation or qualification the premise that women are more persuasible than men. McGuire's (1969, p. 251) examination of the status of the extant literature maintained that "There seems to be a clear main-order effect of sex on influenceability such that females are more susceptible than males. Examples can be found over the whole range of social influence situations. . . . " Cronkhite's (1969, p. 136) synthesis of extant research findings similarly concluded, "The evidence seems to indicate overwhelmingly that women are generally more persuasible than men."

The primary reason provided for the early research findings that women are more persuasible than men is socialization. This rationale posits that from early childhood on, females are initially taught and subsequently rewarded for more cooperative behaviors, whereas men are trained to be more aggressive (Petty & Cacioppo, 1981), and that this fundamental difference makes women less resistant to persuasive appeals than men (Burgoon, Jones & Stewart, 1975; Janis & Rife, 1959; Scheidel, 1963).

However, this rationale also implies that as socialization norms change the effect will be to mitigate past differences in persuasibility. This was the premise behind another extensive look at past sex and persuasibility studies. Rosenfeld and Christie (1974) did find that the results varied: at times women were more persuasible; at times no difference in persuasibility was reported; and at times some third factor (e.g., arguments, content, etc.) was more powerful than sex in determining overall yielding. Nonetheless, to the extent that sex differences were manifest, it was women that were reported to be more persuasible.

During the 1970s two extensive secondary reviews of gender and persuasibility continued to question the claim that women were more persuasible than men. Maccoby and Jacklin (1974, p. 268) found "no overall difference in susceptibility to social influence." Eagly's classification (1978, p. 91) of such studies using the criterion of statistical significance concluded that "the most common finding by far is no sex difference."

More recent examinations of the gender and persuasibility literature have employed meta-analysis techniques to provide an integrated and more powerful assessment of extant research. Meta-analysis statistically combines independent experiments in order to integrate their findings, and thus is viewed as more systematic, precise, and powerful than the more traditional secondary literature review (Rosenthal, 1984).

Cooper's meta-analysis (1979) is instructive. Although Cooper focused exclusively on gender differences and degree of conformity, the meta-analysis examined the same studies that had been previously reviewed by Maccoby and Jacklin (1974) and Eagly (1978) in this area and reached the opposite conclusion. Cooper (1979, p. 142) explained that the power of the minority findings for gender differences "is so substantial as to be almost impossible to create by chance." A second meta-analysis focused specifically on the gender and influence literature. Eagly and Carli (1981, p. 10) reported, "When probabilities were combined across studies, significant differences were obtained: Males were less influenced than females . . . even when studies not reporting a probability and assumed to show no effect . . . were included."

The claim that women are more persuasible than men is less equivocal in political influence because of the nature of the content area. Research suggests that the receiver's interest in the influence topic is an important factor that accounts for part of the difference in the response of women and men to influence attempts. Sloan, Love and Ostrom (1974) and Eagly (1978) report that men are more interested than women in political topics. This difference is important because, as Sistrunk and McDavid (1965 & 1971) and Maslach, Santee, and Wade (1987) report, the finding that women are more persuasible than men is true only for more "masculine" topics, such as politics.

This explanation, that the content area is responsible for most gender differences in persuasibility, is the most accepted rationale among contemporary scholars. As Petty and Cacioppo (1981, pp. 261–262) conclude: "There is now widespread agreement that the sex differences observed in most investigations have been due to the fact that women were less familiar with the issue under consideration than men were." What is important, however, is that for political topics, contemporary theory and past and present research point to the greater persuasibility of women as opposed to men.

The few inoculation studies which incorporated gender into their designs suggest modest differences between women and men. For example, although

Stone (1969) reports no gender differences overall, he did find that females showed more change than males when the communication placed more emphasis on source as opposed to message. In addition, Dean, Austin, and Watts (1971) report an interaction between forewarning and sex. For male receivers, forewarning inhibited attitude change; however, for females it facilitated change. The limited inoculation findings add further support for the claim that women are more vulnerable than men to political attack messages.

The issue of gender and persuasibility is particularly relevant in political campaign communication as a result of the identification of "a gender gap" (Mandel, 1982). The growing gap is based on women's negative response to Ronald Reagan's and George Bush's personalities and positions (Benenson, 1982; Carlson, 1988; Carroll, 1989; Dowd, 1984; Farah & Klein, 1988; Goodman, 1986; Kenski, 1988).

Although the gender gap is relatively new in terms of its electoral salience, there is a long history of differences in political attitudes between women and men. During the 1940s, 1950s, and 1960s, one of the largest differences was in the expressed levels of political information and interest, with a much higher proportion of women responding that they had either no opinion or no interest in political issues (Opinion Roundup, 1982). Although a gap still exists, these differences have declined noticeably in the last two decades (Shapiro, Mahajan & Veith, 1984).

The largest issue difference historically has been on the use of force in international affairs, with women more opposed than men (Carroll, 1989). More recently, attitude differences between women and men have surfaced in a number of opinion surveys that show that women are "less supportive than men of high defense spending, more worried about war, less willing to support intervention in foreign affairs, more opposed to the death penalty, more in favor of gun control, and more resistant to certain kinds of intrusions like wiretapping" (Opinion Roundup, 1982, p. 27).

A new issue difference that emerged during the 1970s has been termed the "compassion dimension," with women placing more emphasis than men on the role of government in providing jobs for people and assisting people in need (Opinion Roundup, 1982). In his analysis of the 1984 election, Miller (1988) reported support for Carol Gilligan's (1982) position that women's political attitudes are more inclined toward a "morality of responsibility." Miller (1988, p. 280) states: "It is evident that even economic worries for women are more suggestive of a compassionate concern for the welfare of people in general, rather than reflecting narrow self-interest considerations." A final issue difference is the emergence during the 1970s and 1980s of what has been termed a "risk dimension," with women more likely than men to favor government action to protect the environment (Opinion Roundup, 1982; Poole & Ziegler, 1985).

Thus, the recent phenomenon of the gender gap (Frankovic, 1982), coupled with issue differences on force, compassion, and risk, provides further support for the view that women and men may respond differently to political attacks and/or may respond differently to efforts designed to inoculate against attacks. The results of the 1986 investigation indicated that the effectiveness of inoculation against subsequent exposure to an attack message is different for women than for men (that inoculation interacts with receiver gender in determining resistance to a political attack message).

The 1986 Investigation

Based on the literature involving gender and persuasibility, particularly in a political context, the 1986 study predicted that the effectiveness of inoculation following subsequent exposure to an attack message is different for women than for men (that inoculation interacts with receiver gender in determining resistance to a political attack message). The $2 \times 2 \times 2$ factorial analysis of variance revealed no effects involving gender on two of the attitude measures: attitude toward candidate supported in the attack message or attitude toward position advocated in the attack message. However, the factorial analysis of variance revealed that gender exerts both direct and indirect influence on receiver ratings of source credibility of the candidate supported in the attack message.

Results. The factorial analysis of variance indicated main effects for gender on the credibility dimensions of composure, $F (1, 333) = 5.92, p < .05; \hat{\omega}^2 = .01$, and extroversion, $F (1, 333) = 4.80, p < .05; \hat{\omega}^2 = .01$. This pattern of results suggests that the inoculation pretreatments rendered male receivers more resistant following exposure to attack messages.

In addition, gender interacted with inoculation pretreatment and attack message approach on the credibility dimensions of character, $F (1, 333) = 9.20, p < .05; \hat{\omega}^2 = .02$; competence, $F (1, 333) = 5.30, p < .05; \hat{\omega}^2 = .01$; and sociability, $F (1, 333) = 4.20, p < .05; \hat{\omega}^2 = .01$. To further explicate these interactions, two-way factorial analysis of variance was computed involving inoculation pretreatment and attack message approach for both female and male receivers on each of the three source credibility dimensions.

The two-way analysis of variance indicated significant interactions involving inoculation pretreatment and attack message approach for female receivers on the credibility dimension of character, $F (1, 222) = 5.91, p < .05; \hat{\omega}^2 = .02$, and for male receivers on the dimension of character, $F (1, 111) = 4.29, p < .05; \hat{\omega}^2 = .03$. In addition, interactions approached significance for female receivers on the credibility dimension of competence, $F (1, 222) = 3.05, p < .10; \hat{\omega}^2 = .01$ and for male receivers on the dimension of sociability, $F (1, 111) = 2.74, p < .10; \hat{\omega}^2 = .01$.

Further analysis of these differences revealed a consistent pattern involving gender, inoculation pretreatment, and attack message approach. For female receivers, there was a difference involving the effectiveness of inoculation same pretreatments, consisting of specific responses to the content of a subsequent attack message, in deflecting issue versus character attacks, but no difference regarding the effectiveness of the inoculation different pretreatments, consisting

Table 9.1

Summary of the Inoculation Pretreatment Means on Issue and Character Attack Messages for Females and Males on the Character, Competence, and Sociability Dimensions of Source Credibility

Dependent Measure	Attack Message Approach	
	Issue	Character

FEMALES

Inoculation Same	($\underline{n}$=80)	($\underline{n}$=72)
Source Credibility: Character		
Mean	4.03	3.37
SD	1.33	1.14
Source Credibility: Competence		
Mean	4.37	3.71
SD	1.48	1.33
Source Credibility: Sociability		
Mean	4.27	3.48
SD	1.75	1.31
Inoculation Different	($\underline{n}$=37)	($\underline{n}$=37)
Source Credibility: Character		
Mean	3.42	3.65
SD	1.24	1.42
Source Credibility: Competence		
Mean	3.95	4.01
SD	1.41	1.62
Source Credibility: Sociability		
Mean	4.03	3.82
SD	1.42	1.44

Table 9.1 (continued)

Dependent Measure	Attack Message Approach	
	Issue	Character

MALES

	Inoculation Same	(n=34)	(n=46)
Source Credibility: Character			
Mean		3.78	3.44
SD		1.09	1.19
Source Credibility: Competence			
Mean		4.06	3.96
SD		1.44	1.24
Source Credibility: Sociability			
Mean		3.74	3.61
SD		1.24	1.34
	Inoculation Different	(n=13)	(n=22)
Source Credibility: Character			
Mean		4.13	2.76
SD		1.51	1.14
Source Credibility: Competence			
Mean		4.64	3.59
SD		1.82	1.43
Source Credibility: Sociability			
Mean		4.23	3.18
SD		1.40	1.45

Note: Ratings of the receivers' perceptions of the source credibility of the candidate supported in the attack message are based on seven-point scales. The higher the rating, the more persuasive the attack message.

of a generic defense of a candidate, on the measure of character, t (1, 333) = 2.64; k = 6; $p < .10$, two-tailed.

By contrast, for male receivers, there was a difference involving the effectiveness of inoculation different messages in deflecting issue versus character attacks, but there was no difference regarding the effectiveness of inoculation same pretreatments. This pattern appeared on the dependent measures of character, t (1, 333) = 3.73; k = 6; $p < .05$, two-tailed, and sociability, t (1, 333) = 2.22; k = 6; $p < .10$, two-tailed.

Discussion. The pattern of results of the 1986 study provides somewhat equivocal but nonetheless revealing support for the prediction that the effectiveness of inoculation against subsequent exposure to a political attack message is different for women than for men. The results fail to support a gender effect based on two of the attitude measures: attitude toward the candidate supported in the attack message and attitude toward the position advocated in the attack message.

However, the results provide strong support for a gender effect based on receiver ratings of the source credibility of the candidate supported in the attack message. Indeed, the differences between female and male receivers impact all five dimensions of source credibility. This finding is important given the research that points to the significance of source credibility factors, particularly character, in voter decision criteria (Allen, Long, O'Mara & Judd, 1987; Anderson & Kibler, 1978; Asher, 1980; DeVries & Tarrance, 1972; Graber, 1989; Hellweg, 1979; Hellweg, King & Williams, 1988; O'Keefe, 1975; Pomper, 1975; Post, 1983; Shapiro, 1969).

The results indicate a main effect for gender on two of the dimensions of source credibility: composure and extroversion. The results suggest that inoculation pretreatments render male receivers more resistant than female receivers following the subsequent exposure to an attack message. This finding provides further support for the position that men are less vulnerable than women to persuasive attacks (Cronkhite, 1969; Eagly & Carli, 1981; McGuire, 1969), particularly involving political content (Maslach, Santee & Wade, 1987; Sistrunk & McDavid, 1965, 1971). The finding also supports the view, which past inoculation research intimates (Dean, Austin & Watts, 1971; Stone, 1969), that following an inoculation pretreatment, men are less susceptible than women to persuasive attacks. Or, put another way, inoculation strengthens resistance among both male and female receivers, but leaves male receivers more resistant overall.

However, the triple interactions, involving inoculation pretreatment, attack message approach, and gender on the three source credibility dimensions of character, competence, and sociability, are both interesting and revealing. The results suggest a consistent pattern, involving the relative effectiveness of the two variants of inoculation pretreatment messages. Remember that inoculation same messages constitute an explicit rebuttal to a subsequent attack message, whereas inoculation different messages involve the same topic but provide neither an explicit or implicit rebuttal to a subsequent attack message.

The results suggest that the relative effectiveness of inoculation pretreatment varies for character and issue attack messages depending upon receiver gender. For female receivers, inoculation same pretreatments are more effective in deflecting character as opposed to issue attacks, while inoculation different pretreatments are equally effective against both types of attack. By contrast, for male receivers, inoculation different pretreatments were more effective in deflecting character as opposed to issue attacks, while inoculation same pretreatments were equally effective against both types of attack.

One possible theoretical explanation that may account for these findings involves the greater sensitivity of women to relational concerns. Gilligan (1982) argues that women are more concerned with the relational dimension of communication. She maintains that women are oriented more to interdependence and cooperation, and that this disposition informs both the way that women communicate and the way they respond to the communication of others. Gilligan (1982, p. 29) says that men are more likely to respond to communication in terms of "logic and law," women in terms of "relationship." Eagly (1978) sees this as a plausible explanation for gender differences in persuasibility.

If women are more sensitive to "person concerns," then it *may require more specific information* to alter women's than men's judgments about candidate credibility. This would explain the unanticipated finding that inoculation same pretreatments are more effective in deflecting character attacks among female receivers, but that the opposite is true for male receivers. This rationale is also consistent with Stone's (1969) finding that women are more sensitive to communication that places more emphasis on source factors.

The impact of inoculation pretreatment, attack message approach, and gender on source credibility should be examined further, since additional support for the pattern of results revealed in this study suggests important nuances for political professionals in their efforts to design and target inoculation pretreatment messages.

The 1988 Investigation

The 1988 investigation, examining inoculation in the Bush and Dukakis presidential campaign, provided another opportunity to examine the relative effectiveness of inoculation same and different pretreatments in conferring resistance to issue and character attack messages based on receiver gender. The 1986 results suggested an intricate pattern, with the effectiveness of inoculation pretreatments on the different dimensions of source credibility varying among female and male receivers according to attack message type.

However, the 1986 investigation involved a Senate campaign, whereas the 1988 study concerned a presidential campaign. Based on recent research, this makes a difference in the impact that the various source credibility dimensions exert on candidate evaluation decisions, quite apart from gender considerations. In a 1984 study of comparative candidate evaluation criteria in presidential, vice-presidential, mayoral, and judicial races, Hellweg, King, and Williams (1988) reported that competence was the dominant factor in assessing presidential candidates, whereas character was the primary factor in evaluating vice-presidential and mayoral candidates. Thus, it is possible that in the 1988 study, the competence dimension of source credibility will exert even more influence on voter decisions, and the character and sociability dimensions less.

Results. A 2 (attack message approach) $\times$ 3 (inoculation condition) $\times$ 2 (gender) factorial analysis of variance was computed to examine the relative effectiveness of inoculation pretreatments and attack message approach among female and male receivers. The factorial indicated that inoculation is an effective strategy for both women and men, but did not reveal a main effect for gender on primary attitude or secondary source credibility measures. But, as in the 1986 study, the pattern of results suggests that inoculation pretreatment approach interacts with receiver gender on dimensions of the source credibility of the candidate supported in the attack message.

The factorial analysis of variance revealed a statistically significant two-way interaction involving the independent variables of inoculation pretreatment approach and gender on the source credibility dimension of competence, F (2, 240) = 3.47, $p < .05$; $\hat{\omega}^2 = .02$, and a nearly significant two-way interaction involving the same variables on the credibility dimension of character, F (2, 237) = 2.28, $p < .10$; $\hat{\omega}^2 = .01$. When the source credibility dimensions were collapsed, once again the factorial indicated a nearly significant two-way interaction involving inoculation pretreatment and gender, F (2, 236) = 2.27, $p < .10$; $\hat{\omega}^2 = .01$.

To further explicate these findings, one-way ANOVAs were computed for female and male receivers on the general measure of source credibility and on the specific dimensions of competence and character. The results of the tests of simple effects revealed significant effects for women on source credibility, F (2, 158) = 10.85, $p < .05$; $\hat{\omega}^2 = .11$, on the dimensions of competence, F (2, 161) = 11.64, $p < .05$; $\hat{\omega}^2 = .11$, and on character, F (2, 159) = 11.52, $p < .05$; $\hat{\omega}^2 = .12$, for men on source credibility, F (2, 84) = 3.27, $p < .05$; $\hat{\omega}^2 = .06$, and on competence, F (2, 85) = 4.91, $p < .05$; $\hat{\omega}^2 = .08$.

Further examination of these means revealed a consistent pattern, such that among women receivers, only inoculation same pretreatments conferred more resistance to subsequent attack messages compared to the control condition. This effect was found on source credibility, t (1, 236) = 5.61, $p < .05$, two-tailed, and on the specific source credibility dimensions of competence, t (1, 240) = 5.32, $p < .05$, two-tailed, and character, t (1, 237) = 5.82, $p < .05$, two-tailed. Conversely, among male receivers, only the inoculation different pretreatments provided greater resistance compared to the control condition on the combined source credibility measure, t (1, 236) = 3.65, $p < .05$, two-tailed, and greater resistance than either the control condition, t (1, 240) = 4.74, $p < .05$, two-tailed, or inoculation same pretreatments on the source credibility dimension of competence, t (1, 240) = 3.55, $p < .05$, two-tailed.

Discussion. The 1988 investigation once again revealed that the effectiveness

Table 9.2

Summary of the Inoculation Condition Means for Females and Males on the General Configuration of Source Credibility and on the Source Credibility Dimensions of Character and Competence

Dependent Measure	Receiver Gender	
	Female	Male

Inoculation Same Pretreatments

Source Credibility: Character

	Female	Male
Mean	2.88	3.51
	(n=62)	(n=45)
SD	1.40	1.33

Source Credibility: Competence

	Female	Male
Mean	3.45	4.20
	(n=63)	(n=46)
SD	1.58	1.59

Source Credibility: Overall

	Female	Male
Mean	3.52	3.95
	(n=61)	(n=45)
SD	1.19	1.11

Inoculation Different Pretreatments

Source Credibility: Character

	Female	Male
Mean	3.51	3.22
	(n=36)	(n=17)
SD	1.36	1.58

Source Credibility: Competence

	Female	Male
Mean	3.66	3.10
	(n=36)	(n=17)
SD	1.66	1.21

Source Credibility: Overall

	Female	Male
Mean	3.89	3.52
	(n=36)	(n=17)
SD	1.17	0.95

Note: Ratings of the receivers' perceptions of the source credibility of the candidate supported in the attack message are based on seven-point scales. The higher the rating, the more persuasive the attack message.

of inoculation pretreatments varies somewhat on the basis of receiver gender, at least with regard to the source credibility of the candidate supported in the attack message. Again, given the importance of source credibility ratings in voter decision criteria, especially judgments of candidate character, this finding is important.

However, the results, while confirming the findings of the 1986 study, indicate a simpler configuration than two years earlier. The pattern of results of the 1986 study indicated that among women, inoculation same pretreatments are more effective in deflecting character attacks, while inoculation different messages are equally effective against both types of attack; whereas among men, inoculation different pretreatments are more effective in deflecting character attacks, while inoculation same messages are equally effective against both types of attack.

Thus, the 1988 results suggest a clearer pattern involving source credibility, while affirming the general patterns of the 1986 study. Among women, only inoculation same pretreatments confer resistance to attack messages, whereas among males, inoculation different messages provided more resistance to the influence of subsequent attack messages. These results are best explained in terms of the theoretical rationale offered above: that since women are more sensitive to "person concerns" (Eagly, 1978; Gilligan, 1982), it requires more specific information to alter their judgments about candidate credibility.

Confirmation of the 1986 pattern of results on the important competence and character dimensions of source credibility offers clearer direction for campaign professionals in the design and implementation of the inoculation strategy based on receiver gender.

INOCULATION AND RECEIVER AGE

Whereas receiver gender was examined in both the 1986 and 1988 investigations, receiver age and the effectiveness of the inoculation message strategy was explored for the first time in the 1988 study.

Receiver age and persuasibility has been examined in various studies during the past four decades. This research generally suggests the presence of a linear, inverse relationship between age and persuasibility, with greater persuasibility among younger receivers and the least among older receivers (Janis & Rife, 1959; Marple, 1933). As Littlejohn and Jabusch (1987, p. 82) put it, "the older you become, generally the less susceptible you become to change."

However, much of the age and persuasibility research has focused on suggestibility as opposed to persuasibility, and has covered the entire human life span (McGuire, 1969). Since the number of studies that concentrate specifically on age and persuasibility is more limited, Miller, Burgoon, and Burgoon (1984, p. 448) conclude that the "overall relationship between age and persuasibility is neither overwhelming nor terribly precise. . . . "

In the political science literature, strong emphasis is placed on low levels of interest, information, and participation by young adults due to their preoccupation "with *multiple role transitions*—completion of education, labor force entry, marriage and family formation—activities that take precedence over civil duties and public concerns" (Steckenrider & Cutler, 1989, p. 65). Further, the public opinion literature, consistent with the age and persuasibility findings noted above, suggests that people's opinions become more "fixed" over time (Jaros, 1973), tending toward increasing conservatism (Erikson, Luttbeg & Tedin, 1980; Nie, Verba & Petrocik, 1976; Sears, 1969).

Therefore, this investigation predicted that younger age cohorts are weaker targets for inoculation, and conversely, that older persons are stronger candidates for inoculation, especially since they are more likely to identify strongly with a political party (Miller, Miller & Schneider, 1980), which, as the results discussed in Chapter 8 indicate, enhances inoculation.

A 2 (attack message approach) × 3 (inoculation condition) × 3 (receiver age) factorial analysis of variance was computed to determine whether inoculation pretreatments vary in effectiveness among receivers who are younger (18–34 years), middle-aged (35–54 years), or older (55 or more years). The results of the 1988 investigation suggest a modest impact for age.

The factorial revealed a main effect for age on the primary dependent variable of attitude toward the candidate supported in the attack message, $F (2, 234) = 5.27$, $p < .05$; $\hat{\omega}^2 = .03$, in addition to a two-way interaction involving inoculation condition and age on the source credibility dimension of extroversion, $F (4, 235) = 3.78$, $p < .05$; $\hat{\omega}^2 = .04$.

A planned comparison was computed to further examine the main effect result. The comparison indicated that following inoculation, attack messages exerted more impact on younger receivers than middle-aged or older receivers, $F (1, 234) = 24.90$, $p < .05$; $\hat{\omega}^2 = .07$. The planned comparison revealed no further significant differences.

To probe the two-way interaction involving inoculation pretreatment and age on the source credibility dimension of extroversion, two steps were taken. First, a test of simple effects was computed on inoculation condition for young, middle-aged, and old receivers. The results indicated a significant effect for inoculation condition among both middle-aged, $F (2, 89) = 5.33$, $p < .05$; $\hat{\omega}^2 = .09$, and older receivers, $F (2, 78) = 3.42$, $p < .05$; $\hat{\omega}^2 = .07$.

Second, post-hoc tests were computed on these means. For middle-aged receivers, the results indicated that inoculation same pretreatments reduced the impact of the subsequent attack messages when compared to the control condition, $t (1, 235) = 3.32$, $p < .05$, two-tailed, and even more so compared to inoculation different pretreatments, $t (1, 235) = 4.52$, $p < .05$, two-tailed. For older receivers, inoculation same but not inoculation different pretreatments militated the impact of the attack messages compared to the control condition, $t (1, 235) = 3.62$, $p < .05$, two-tailed.

These results suggest that age plays a minor role in the process of inoculation. The main effect finding for age on the primary dependent variable of attitude toward candidate simply indicates that following inoculation, younger receivers are more susceptible to political attack messages than middle-aged or older receivers. This outcome provides further support for the finding in past research that there is an inverse relationship between age and persuasibility (Janis & Rife, 1959; Littlejohn & Jabusch, 1987; Marple, 1933).

The two-way interaction involving inoculation pretreatment and age on the source credibility dimension of extroversion is the more interesting and useful finding. The simple effects and post-hoc tests indicate that inoculation same pretreatments are more effective in conferring resistance to attack messages among both middle-aged and older receivers. The relative superiority of inoculation same pretreatments among middle-aged and older receivers carries potentially useful nuances for the design of inoculation pretreatment messages in political campaigns. However, since the effect was limited to a single dimension of source credibility, its credence is somewhat suspect. Thus, while these results point to a possible pattern, the relationship between inoculation and age should be further pinpointed in future investigations.

INOCULATION AND RECEIVER EDUCATION

Receiver ability is a function of intelligence, education level, and knowledge of a subject area. While there has been a long line of research that focused on the relationship between receiver intelligence and persuasibility, there has been limited research specifically directed at receiver education level and persuasibility.

The classic research studies produced what appeared to be contradictory results concerning the relationship between receiver ability and persuasibility. Hovland, Lumsdaine, and Sheffield (1949) reported that greater receiver education levels enhanced the attitudinal impact of *Why We Fight* indoctrination films during World War II. However, Hovland, Janis, and Kelley (1953) reported no significant relationship involving receiver intelligence and persuasibility.

McGuire subsequently posited an inverted U curve rationale concerning the relationship between receiver intelligence and persuasibility. McGuire (1969) maintained that the likelihood of yielding to persuasive communication is a function both of the capacity to process messages coupled with the tendency to yield. Greater intelligence enhances the former and retards the latter, such that moderately intelligent receivers are generally the most persuasible. Further, McGuire's explanation assumes that the complexity of the message plays a crucial role in determining overall persuasibility. He (McGuire, 1969, p. 249) posits that with simple material, expect a negative relationship between intelligence and yielding, but with more complex messages, the relationship is likely to be smaller, if negative, or shift to positive.

Still, the research suggests mixed results. Cronkhite's (1969, p. 138) syntheses of existing studies concluded that "there appears to be no evidence for any relationship between intelligence and general persuasibility." On the other hand, Whitehead (1971) reported that more intelligent receivers were affected more by a persuasive presentation, and, in application to the resistance domain, Ward and Wackman (1971) found that more intelligent receivers were more influenced by, or less resistant to, mass media persuasive appeals.

As a result of the lack of clarity in past research findings involving intelligence and persuasibility, the 1988 investigation focused on receiver education, not intelligence. Education is a more common focal point of the public opinion and voting behavior literature, which indicates that higher education levels are associated with increased citizen involvement in politics (Campbell, 1976; Conway, 1985; Stephens & Long, 1970; Wolfinger & Rosenstone, 1980).

Indeed, receiver education has emerged as one of the single best predictors of political involvement—better than occupation, income, or other socioeconomic variables. Conway (1985) argues that this is because of the strong relationship of education to political knowledge, political and bureaucratic skills, cognitive skills that facilitate political activity, the greater likelihood of following political events in the mass media, the greater likelihood of having opinions on a wide range of subjects, and higher scores on perceptions of government responsiveness to their interests and activities.

The 1988 study simply attempted to determine whether receiver education level made any difference in the effectiveness of inoculation pretreatments. The results indicate that it does.

A 2 (attack message approach) $\times$ 3 (inoculation condition) $\times$ 3 (education level) factorial analysis of variance was computed to examine the impact of education level in the effectiveness of inoculation in conferring resistance to the impact of political attack messages. Education level was trichotomized as low (no formal education beyond high school), moderate (attended college or college graduate with no formal education beyond the bachelor's degree) and high (formal education beyond the bachelor's degree).

The results of the omnibus ANOVA revealed that education level was an active variable in the process of inoculation. The factorial indicated significant main effects for education on the primary dependent variable of attitude toward the position taken by the candidate supported in the attack message, F (2, 234) $= 3.20$, $p < .05$ $\hat{\omega}^2 = .02$, and on the source credibility dimensions of composure, F (2, 234) $= 3.32$, $p < .05$; $\hat{\omega}^2 = .02$, and sociability, F (2, 233) $= 4.67$, $p < .05$; $\hat{\omega}^2 = .03$.

In addition, the factorial revealed a double interaction involving inoculation condition and receiver education level on the dependent measure of the likelihood of voting for the candidate supported in the attack message, F (4, 231) $= 3.09$, $p < .05$; $\hat{\omega}^2 = .03$, which approached statistical significance on the source credibility dimension of competence, F (4, 234) $= 2.25$, $p < .10$; $\hat{\omega}^2 = .02$, and which overrode the main effect finding on the source credibility dimension of sociability, F (4, 233) $= 2.55$, $p < .05$; $\hat{\omega}^2 = .02$.

Subsequent analyses of the main effect findings, for which no interaction effect was reported, indicated that inoculation pretreatments left high education-level receivers more resistant to subsequent attack messages than low education-level receivers. This effect was found on the dependent measures of attitude toward position, $t(1, 234) = 3.66$, $p < .05$, two-tailed, and composure, $t(1, 234) = 2.32$, $p < .05$, two-tailed. No significant differences were found for moderate education-level receivers.

However, the four two-way interactions involving inoculation condition and receiver education level suggested a more intricate relationship than reported above. To explore these interactions, a test of simple effects was computed on inoculation condition across each of the receiver education levels (low, moderate, and high) on each of the four dependent variables in lieu of post-hoc explorations.

The tests of simple effects indicated significant results for low and moderate education-level receivers. The one-way ANOVAs revealed significant effects for low, $F(2, 104) = 23.40$, $p < .05$; $\hat{\omega}^2 = .29$, and moderate educated, $F(2, 118) = 7.63$, $p < .05$; $\hat{\omega}^2 = .10$, on the measure of likelihood of voting for the candidate supported in the attack message; low, $F(2, 106) = 8.61$, $p < .05$; $\hat{\omega}^2 = .12$, and moderate educated, $F(2, 119) = 7.82$, $p < .05$; $\hat{\omega}^2 = .10$, on the source credibility dimension of competence; and low, $F(2, 105) = 8.11$, $p < .05$; $\hat{\omega}^2 = .12$, and moderate educated, $F(2, 119) = 8.58$, $p < .05$; $\hat{\omega}^2 = .11$, on the credibility dimension of sociability.

Subsequent post-hoc tests were computed on these means. On likelihood of voting for the candidate supported in the attack message, the pattern of results indicated that for low education-level receivers, both inoculation same, $t(1, 231) = 6.73$, $p < .05$, two-tailed, and inoculation different pretreatments, $t(1, 231) = 8.37$, $p < .05$, two-tailed, were effective in deflecting subsequent attacks when compared to the control condition; whereas for moderate education-level receivers, only inoculation same pretreatments were effective compared to the control condition, $t(1, 231) = 5.26$, $p < .05$, two-tailed.

On the credibility dimension of the competence of the candidate supported in the attack messages, for low education-level receivers, inoculation different pretreatments were more effective than the control condition, $t(1, 234) = 6.50$, $p < .05$, two-tailed, and also more effective than inoculation same pretreatments, $t(1, 234) = 3.85$, $p < .05$, two-tailed; whereas for moderate education-level receivers, both inoculation same, $t(1, 234) = 4.80$, $p < .05$, two-tailed, and inoculation different pretreatments, $t(1, 234) = 2.91$, $p < .05$, two-tailed, were more effective in deflecting the attack messages in comparison to the control condition.

Finally, on the credibility dimension of sociability, for low education-level receivers, both inoculation same, $t(1, 233) = 3.44$, $p < .05$, two-tailed, and inoculation different messages, $t(1, 233) = 5.78$, $p < .05$, two-tailed, were more effective in deflecting the attack messages compared to the control condition; whereas among moderate education-level receivers, only inoculation same pretreatments were more effective in conferring resistance compared to the control group, $t(1, 233) = 4.98$, $p < .05$, two-tailed.

The results of the 1988 study indicate two distinct findings involving the effectiveness of inoculation and receiver education level. First, the results re-

Table 9.3

Summary of the Inoculation Conditions Means for Low Education-Level and Moderate Education-Level Receivers on the Primary Dependent Measure of Likelihood of Voting for and the Source Credibility Dimensions of Competence and Sociability

Dependent Measure	Inoculation Pretreatment		
	Same	Different	Control
Low Education-Level Receivers			
Likelihood of Voting for			
Mean	15.66	7.67	48.42
	(n=50)	(n=21)	(n=36)
SD	21.26	13.56	33.95
Source Credibility: Competence			
Mean	4.15	3.06	4.90
	(n=51)	(n=21)	(n=37)
SD	1.70	1.74	1.34
Source Credibility: Sociability			
Mean	3.89	3.29	4.77
	(n=50)	(n=21)	(n=37)
SD	1.55	1.42	0.97
Moderate Education-Level Receivers			
Likelihood of Voting for			
Mean	12.09	22.46	35.04
	(n=46)	(n=28)	(n=47)
SD	21.34	28.62	33.64
Source Credibility: Competence			
Mean	3.41	3.89	4.63
	(n=46)	(n=28)	(n=48)
SD	1.67	1.63	1.41
Source Credibility: Sociability			
Mean	3.05	3.73	4.19
	(n=46)	(n=28)	(n=48)
SD	1.44	1.51	0.92

Note: Ratings of receivers' perceptions of the source credibility of the candidate supported in the attack message are based on seven-point scales. Assessment of the likelihood of voting for the candidate supported in the attack message is based on a 100-point probability scale. The higher the rating or assessment, the more persuasive the attack message.

vealed main effects, with subsequent analyses indicating that inoculation pretreatments rendered high education-level receivers more resistant to attack
messages than low education-level receivers, on the primary dependent measure
of attitude toward position and the secondary source credibility dimension of
composure. This pattern of results suggests the presence of an inverse relationship
between education level and persuasibility, contrary to the previous resistance
findings of Ward and Wackman (1971). The results revealed no significant
differences involving those receivers of moderate education levels, either in
comparison to receivers of low or high education levels.

Second, the results revealed four two-way interactions on primary and secondary measures involving inoculation pretreatment and receiver education level.
These results are more interesting because they suggest that receiver education
level influences the variant of inoculation pretreatment that will prove to be the
most effective.

The subsequent simple effects and post-hoc tests indicated that for receivers
with low education levels, although both inoculation same and different inoculation pretreatments confer resistance to attack messages, inoculation different
messages may be somewhat superior, given the findings involving competence
of candidate supported in the attack message. On the other hand, among receivers
with moderate education levels, only inoculation same pretreatments were generally effective, with the exception of the finding that both approaches were
equally effective on the source credibility dimension of competence.

Thus, the results indicate that, for optimal effectiveness, political professionals
must take into account receiver education levels in preparing inoculation messages for use in political campaigns, adapting inoculation pretreatment approach
for both receivers of low and moderate education.

Conclusion

You must aim at one of two objects—you must make yourself out a good man and him [your opponent] a bad one.

—Aristotle
(cited in Solmsen, ed., *The Rhetoric and Poetics of Aristotle*, p. 217)

There is no such thing as a fair-minded political campaign. Remember the literal meaning of campaign: a military operation carried out in pursuit of a specific objective.

—Jeff Greenfield, Media Analyst (Greenfield, 1980, p. 37)

Unless we understand ways of inducing resistance to change, a gullible populace may prove to be an easy mark for the unscrupulous persuasive huckster.

—Gerald R. Miller and Michael Burgoon,
Professors of Communication (Miller & Burgoon, 1973, p. 103)

Although the use of attack messages has been an intrinsic feature of American political campaigns since 1800 (Jamieson, 1988), there is no doubt that the attack strategy *seems to be* much more pervasive in recent campaigns (Guskind & Hagstrom, 1988; Nyhan, 1988; Schneider, 1988; Taylor, 1986a). This perception stems, at least in part, from the increased use of television advertising as the communication modality of choice for the delivery of candidates' attacks, which insures maximum possible penetration (Axelrod, 1988), and in part from a steady increase in the use of negatives during the 1980s (Taylor, 1986a; Young, 1987).

The actual increase in the use of attack politics during the past decade is the direct result of the growing perception among consultants, who wield increasing power over strategy and tactics in contemporary campaigns, that attack politics works, and works well (Armstrong, 1988; Ehrenhalt, 1985; Guskind & Hagstrom, 1988; Johnson-Cartee & Copeland, 1989; Louden, 1987; Mann & Ornstein, 1983; Martinez & DeLegal, 1988; May, 1988; Nugent, 1987; Pfau & Burgoon, 1989; Sabato, 1981; Schneider, 1988; Surlin & Gordon, 1977; Taylor, 1986a, 1989; Young, 1987). Attack messages are viewed as more compelling. As a result, they are processed more rapidly and remembered longer (Ehrenhalt, 1985; Kern, 1988; Taylor, 1986a). As Guskind and Hagstrom (1988, p. 2787) put it: "While positive ads require as much as 5 or even 10 viewings to make an impression on voters, the information in a negative commercial can sink in after only 1 or 2 viewings."

Although attack politics always carries a risk that more offensive messages will result in a voter backlash against sponsors, this risk is perceived as acceptable, given the fact that over time voters tend to forget the origins of political messages while retaining their content (Hagstrom & Guskind, 1986; Pfau, Kenski, Nitz & Sorenson, 1989b). As a result, the former conventional wisdom that acted to restrain the use of attack politics (that it works only for challengers and then only when they use third parties to deliver the message and once they have established a strong positive base) quite literally has been turned on its head. Attack politics is now employed by both challengers and incumbents, often uses the candidate to deliver the message, and sometimes is employed early in a campaign, even prior to the use of positive advertising (Guskind & Hagstrom, 1988). The bottom line is that attack politics has arrived, and as long as it is perceived to be effective, it will remain a staple in candidates' tactical arsenals.

This book detailed the use of attack politics in recent political campaigns and examined the inadequacy or limitation of existing defenses and proposed remedies to check the increased use and impact of well-conceived and executed attack messages. Given the inadequacy of legal remedies, the improbability of voluntary restraint, and the limitations of various post-hoc responses to political attacks, we noted the emergence of a new strategic genre, preemption, which made its first appearance as a candidate response option in campaigns from 1982 to 1988. This strategic approach anticipates specific attacks that might be initiated, and answers them via on-point messages delivered in advance of the attacks (Frantzich, 1989; Salmore & Salmore, 1985; Taylor, 1986a). We also noted, however, an important weakness of preemption: that it requires candidates and their consultants to anticipate all potential attacks and to prepare and implement specific messages covering all vulnerabilities, a difficult and costly undertaking.

Thus, we recommend a particular form of preemption, the inoculation message strategy. Inoculation seeks to strengthen the receiver's attitudes against change. It is a strategy designed to promote resistance against changes in attitudes and behaviors (Miller & Burgoon, 1973), thus minimizing the possibility that political attacks might influence a potential voter's attitudes.

The strategy, which is based on William J. McGuire's work on the inoculation construct nearly thirty years ago (McGuire, 1961a, 1961b, 1962; McGuire & Papageorgis, 1961, 1962; Papageorgis & McGuire, 1961), overcomes the major limitation of preemption. Inoculation employs threat, operationalized as a warning of an impending and potentially persuasive attack, to motivate receivers to bolster existing attitudes. The threat component is the integral element in inoculation (Anderson & McGuire, 1965; McGuire, 1962, 1964, 1970; Papageorgis & McGuire, 1961). Threat triggers an internal process, motivating receivers to defend against *any potential attack*. Thus, whereas preemption is effective in promoting resistance to very specific attacks, but leaving receivers defenseless against other attacks that might be encountered, inoculation employs an internal process to spread a blanket of protection over the receiver against a wide array of attacks. It is thus a cost-effective strategy to confer resistance to the influence of political attacks. Moreover, inoculation allows a candidate to act first in order to set the campaign agenda.

We investigated the potential of the inoculation message strategy to confer resistance to political attack messages in two large, experimental field studies. The results of the 1986 and 1988 studies clearly indicate that the inoculation message strategy promotes resistance to attitude change, deflecting the persuasiveness of subsequent political attack messages which might be launched by an opponent during a campaign, thus reducing the likelihood that political attacks will influence receiver attitudes. The results indicate that inoculation undermines the potential influence of the source of such attacks, and reduces the likelihood that the political attacks will influence receiver voting intention.

The breadth of the results suggests that inoculation is a viable construct. Although the results identified differences in the relative effectiveness of the inoculation pretreatments in specific circumstances, thus informing the use of this message strategy by practitioners, inoculation promoted resistance to each of the political attacks employed in the 1986 and 1988 studies, both refutational same and different; for each of the candidates in both studies; using both traditional and direct mail channels; and among all the receiver groups: strong and weak political party identifiers as well as nonidentifiers, Democrats and Republicans, women and men, low, moderate, and high education-level receivers, and young and old.

The 1988 investigation underscored the viability of direct mail as a communication channel for inoculation. Additional research on inoculation should explore the effectiveness of the inoculation message strategy employing additional communication modalities, particularly radio and television. Further research also is needed on the effectiveness of inoculation with diverse types of voters in a variety of political settings. The 1986 and 1988 results indicate that inoculation is most effective among strong party identifiers, making it best suited as a voter reinforcement strategy. Although the results also indicated that inoculation works with weak identifiers and nonidentifiers, these effects should be investigated further.

Another important factor in close campaigns involves the politics of addition or mobilization of new voters. The effectiveness of inoculation with new voters, and the message strategies that are the most salient for them, is also a fitting topic for future research on inoculation.

This book implies that means of persuasion, techniques used to alter receiver attitudes and behaviors, as well as resistance to persuasion, are both integral features of American political campaigns. Of course, the central role of persuasion in American political campaigns is not new. More than fifty years ago, Harold D. Lasswell, one of the "Founding Fathers" of contemporary political science (Schramm, 1983, p. 8), observed that "the study of politics is the study of influence" (Lasswell, 1936, p. 1). More recently, McBath and Fisher (1969, p. 17) posited that "campaigning is essentially a process of communication, a persuasive process." In this spirit, this book has focused on the growth and nature of attack politics in American political campaigns, a significant, though lamented, strategic approach to influence.

However, the central role of resistance to persuasion in American political campaigns is new. In syntheses of the extant research, Kraus and Davis (1976) and Dan Nimmo and Keith Sanders (1981) emphasized the dominance of conversion in studies of political campaign communication. This book adopts the view of Miller and Burgoon (1973, p. 16), who posit that "the former objective [conversion] has been extensively studied by students of persuasion; the latter [resistance to persuasion] has been relatively unexplored." Our research program indicates that inoculation, a resistance strategy, is a viable approach for candidates to deflect the persuasiveness of political attack messages.

References

Abramson, P. R. (1983). *Political attitudes in America*. San Francisco: W. H. Freeman.

Abramson, P. R., Aldrich, J. H. & Rohde, D. W. (1983). *Change and continuity in the 1980 elections* (rev. ed.). Washington, D.C.: Congressional Quarterly Press.

"Alabama" (1986). Congressional outlook. *Congressional Quarterly Weekly Report, 44* [Supplement, 41], 2400–2401.

Albert, J. A. (1986). The remedies available to candidates who are defamed by television or radio commercials of opponents. *Vermont Law Review, 11*, 33–73.

Alexander, H. E. & Haggerty, B. A. (1988). Misinformation on media money. *Public Opinion, 11*, 5–7 & 59.

Allen, J., Long, K. M., O'Mara, J. & Judd, B. (1987). Candidate image, voter values, and gender as determinants of voter preference in the 1984 presidential campaign. In L. B. Nadler, M. K. Nadler & W. R. Todd-Mancillas (eds.), *Advances in gender and communication research* (pp. 291–305). New York: University Press of America.

Alston, C. (1988). Litany of campaign-reform proposals . . . heads for new round of debates on hill. *Congressional Quarterly Weekly Report, 46*, 3526–3527.

Alston, C. & Hook, J. (1988). An election: Money can be dangerous. *Congressional Quarterly Weekly Report, 46*, 3366–3367.

Anatol, K. W. E. & Mandel, J. E. (1972). Strategies of resistance to persuasion: New subject matter for the teacher of speech communication. *Central States Speech Journal, 23*, 11–17.

Anderson, L. R. & McGuire, W. J. (1965). Prior reassurance of group consensus as a factor in producing resistance to persuasion. *Sociometry, 28*, 44–56.

Anderson, P. A. & Kibler, R. J. (1978). Candidate valence as a predictor of voter preference. *Human Communication Research, 5*, 4–14.

Aristotle Industries (1985). *The best campaign commercials of 1984* [A Videotape Documentary]. Washington, D.C.: Aristotle Industries.

Aristotle Industries (1988a). *1988 presidential campaign commercials round I* [A Videotape Documentary]. Washington, D.C.: Aristotle Industries.

Aristotle Industries (1988b). *1988 presidential campaign commercials round II* [A Video-tape Documentary]. Washington, D.C.: Aristotle Industries.

Aristotle Industries (1989). *The best of 1988 political campaign commercials* [A Videotape Documentary]. Washington, D.C.: Aristotle Industries.

Armstrong, R. (1988). *The next hurrah: The communication revolution in American politics.* New York: Beach Tree Books, William Morrow.

Asher, H. (1980). *Presidential elections and American politics: Voters, candidates, and campaigns since 1952* (rev. ed.). Homewood, Ill.: Dorsey Press.

Atkin, C. K. (1971). How imbalanced campaign coverage affects audience exposure patterns. *Journalism Quarterly, 48*, 235–244.

Attack and counterattack (1986). A "cheap" response. *Campaigns & Elections, 7*, no. 6, 63.

Axelrod, D. (1988, November 9). Broadcast views. *Advertising Age*, pp. 88–92.

Axelrod, R. (1972). Where the voters came from: An analysis of electoral coalitions, 1952–1968. *American Political Science Review, 66*, 11–20.

Axelrod, R. (1974). Communication. *American Political Science Review, 68*, 717–720.

Axelrod, R. (1978). Communication. *American Political Science Review, 72*, 622–624 & 1010–1011.

Axelrod, R. (1982). Communication. *American Political Science Review, 76*, 393–396.

Axelrod, R. (1986). Presidential election coalitions in 1984. *American Political Science Review, 80*, 281–285.

Baker, R. K. (1989). The congressional elections. In G. M. Pomper, R. K. Baker, W. D. Burnham, B. G. Farah, M. R. Hershey, E. Klein & W. C. McWilliams (eds.), *The election of 1988: Reports and interpretations* (pp. 153–176). Chatham, N. J.: Chatham House Publishers.

Balzar, J. & Love, K. (1986, November 1). Cranston, Zschau shift gears, opt for "going positive" as voting nears. *Los Angeles Times*, I, p. 34.

Barber, J. D. (1978). *Race for the presidency: The media and the nominating process.* Englewood Cliffs, N.J.: Prentice-Hall.

Bart, J. & Pfau, M. (1989, April). *Turning the tables as a campaign strategy: A study of the 1986 South Dakota senatorial race.* Paper presented at the annual meeting of the Central States Speech Association, Kansas City, Mo.

Beck, P. A. (1988). Incomplete realignment: The Reagan legacy for parties and elections. In C. O. Jones (ed.), *The Reagan legacy: Promise and performance* (pp. 145–171). Chatham, N.J.: Chatham House Publishers.

Becker, L. B. & McCombs, M. E. (1978). The role of the press in determining voter reaction to presidential primaries. *Human Communication Research, 4*, 301–307.

Becker, S. W., Bavelas, A. & Braden, M. (1961). An index to measure contingency of English sentences. *Language and Speech, 4*, 138–145.

Beiler, D. (1987). *The classics of political television advertising: Viewers guide.* Washington, D.C.: Campaigns & Elections.

Benenson, R. (1982). *Women and politics.* Washington, D.C.: Congressional Quarterly Press.

Bennett, W. L. (1988). *News: The politics of illusion.* New York: Longman.

Berke, R. L. (1986, August 27). Mud: There seems to be more of it this year. *New York Times*, p. A18.

Blumler, J. & Gurevitch, M. (1981). Politicians and the press: An essay on role relationships. In D. Nimmo & K. R. Sanders (eds.), *Handbook of political communication* (pp. 467–493). Beverly Hills: Sage Publications.

Blumler, J. & McQuail, D. (1969). *Television and politics: Its uses and influences.* Chicago: University of Chicago Press.

Bonafede, D. (1986, October 18). Midterm election puzzle. *National Journal, 18*, 2503–2506.

Boyarsky, B. (1986, October 26). Video wars: Why negative TV ads work in today's political campaigns. *Los Angeles Times*, 1, IV, p. 3.

Broder, D. (1989, January 19). Politicians, advisers agonize over campaigns' character. *Washington Post*, pp. A1 & A22.

Broder, D., Edsall, T. B., Ifill, G., Taylor, P., & Rhoney, C. T. (1988). The candidates nobody wants. *Washington Post National Weekly Edition, 5*, 9–10.

Brokaw, C. (1986, December 10). Abdnor–Daschle race sets new state spending record. *Sioux Falls Argus Leader*, p. 2.

Brownstein, R. (1986, November 8). The big sweep. *National Journal, 18*, 2712–2713 & 2716–2718.

Burgoon, J. K. (1975). Conflicting information, attitude, and measurement variables as predictors of learning and persuasion. *Human Communication Research, 1*, 133–144.

Burgoon, M., Burgoon, J. K., Riess, M., Butler, J., Montgomery, C. L., Stinnett, W. D., Miller, M., Long, M., Vaughn, D. & Caine, B. (1976). Propensity of persuasive attack and intensity of pretreatment messages as predictors of resistance to persuasion. *Journal of Psychology, 92*, 123–129.

Burgoon, M. & Chase, L. J. (1973). The effects of differential linguistic patterns in messages attempting to induce resistance to persuasion. *Speech Monographs, 40*, 1–7.

Burgoon, M., Cohen, M., Miller, M. D. & Montgomery, C. L. (1978). An empirical test of a model of resistance to persuasion. *Human Communication Research, 5*, 27–39.

Burgoon, M., Jones, S. B. & Stewart, D. (1975). Toward a message centered theory of persuasion: Three empirical investigations of language intensity. *Human Communication Research, 1*, 240–256.

Burgoon, M. & King, L. B (1974). The mediation of resistance to persuasion strategies by language variables and active–passive participation. *Human Communication Research, 1*, 30–41.

Burgoon, M. & Miller, G. R. (1971). Prior attitude and language intensity as predictors of message style and attitude change following counterattitudinal advocacy. *Journal of Personality and Social Psychology, 20*, 246–253.

Burgoon, M., Pfau, M., Birk, T. & Clark, J. E. (1985). [The persuasive impact of Mobil Oil advertorials]. Unpublished raw data.

Caddell, P. (1985, December 30). Baby boomers come of political age. *Wall Street Journal*, p. 12.

"California" (1986). Congressional outlook. *Congressional Quarterly Weekly Report, 44* [Supplement, 41], 2405–2409.

Campaigns & Elections (1986a). *The classics of political advertising: a videotape documentary* [Videotape]. Aurora, Colo.: Meyer Communication Corp.

Campaigns & Elections (1986b). *Political television advertising classics: A videotape documentary* [Videotape]. Washington, D.C.: Campaigns & Elections.

Campbell, A. (1976). The passive citizen. In E. C. Dreyer & W. A. Rosenbaum (eds.), *Political opinion and behavior: Essays and studies* (3d ed.). North Scituate, Mass.: Duxbury Press.

Campbell, A., Converse, P. E., Miller, W. E. & Stokes, D. E. (1960). *The American voter*. New York: John Wiley & Sons.

Campbell, A., Gurin, G. & Miller, W. E. (1954). *The voter decides*. Evanston: Row, Peterson and Co.

Campbell, J. E., Munro, M., Alford, J. R. & Campbell, B. A. (1986). Partisanship and voting. *Research in Micropolitics, 1*, 99–126.

Carlson, M. B. (1988, August 8). Shoot-out at gender gap: Why don't women take a liking to Bush? *Time*, pp. 13 & 15.

Carroll, S. J. (1989). Gender politics and the socializing impact of the women's movement. In R. S. Sigel (ed.), *Political learning in adulthood* (pp. 306–399). Chicago: University of Chicago Press.

Chaffee, S. H. & Choe, S. Y. (1980). Time of decision and media use during the Ford–Carter campaign. *Public Opinion Quarterly, 44*, 53–69.

Chaffee, S. & Hernandez-Ramos, P. F. (1987). Political communication. In G. L. Dahnke & C. F. Fernandez (eds.), *Human communication as social science: An intermediate survey* (in press). Belmont, Calif.: Wadsworth Publishing Company.

Chaiken, S. (1987). The heuristic model of persuasion. In M. P. Zanna, J. M. Olson & C. P. Herman (eds.), *Social influence: The Ontario symposium*, Vol. 5 (pp. 3–39). Hillsdale, N.J.: Lawrence Erlbaum.

Cohen, R. E. (1986a, October 11). Transition politics. *National Journal, 18*, 2423–2427.

Cohen, R. E. (1986b, November 8). Back in the saddle. *National Journal, 18*, 2676–2679, 2684 & 2690–2692.

Colford, S. W. (1988a, March 14). Politicos resort to "ambush" ads on TV. *Advertising Age*, p. 3.

Colford, S. W. (1988b, August 22). GOP's Quayle quandary. *Advertising Age*, pp. 1 & 20.

Colford, S. W. (1988c, October 31). Campaign flak flies. *Advertising Age*, Sec. 1, p. 4.

"Colorado" (1986). Congressional outlook. *Congressional Quarterly Weekly Report, 44* [Supplement, 41], 2410–2412.

Conway, M. M. (1985). *Political participation in the United States*. Washington, D.C.: Congressional Quarterly Press.

Cook, R. (1989). The nominating process. In M. Nelson (ed.), *The elections of 1988* (pp. 25–61). Washington, D.C.: Congressional Quarterly Press.

Cooper, H. M. (1979). Statistically combining independent studies: A meta-analysis of sex differences in conformity research. *Journal of Personality and Social Psychology, 37*, 131–146.

Copesky, J. (1989). The best and worst campaigns of 1988: The Mississippi Senate race. *Campaigns & Elections, 9*, No. 6, 23.

Cronkhite, G. (1969). *Persuasion: speech and behavioral change*. New York: Bobbs-Merrill Company.

Dean, R. B., Austin, J. A. & Watts, W. A. (1971). Forewarning effects in persuasion: Field and classroom experiments. *Journal of Personality and Social Psychology, 2*, 210–221.

DeVries, W. & Tarrance, V. L. (1972). *The ticket-splitter: A new force in American politics*. Grand Rapids: William B. Eerdmans Publishing Company.

Diamond, E. & Bates, S. (1988). *The spot: The rise of political advertising* (rev. ed.). Cambridge, Mass.: MIT Press.

Dillin, J. (1986, November 14). Negative political ads will be back in 1988, says GOP pollster. *Christian Science Monitor*, p. 5.

Dionne, E. J., Jr. (1988, February 5). Gephardt assails Simon over TV ads. *New York Times*, p. 9.

Dowd, M. (1984, December 30). Reassessing women's political role: The lasting impact of Geraldine Ferraro. *New York Times Magazine*, pp. 18–19, 32, 42 & 44.

Eagly, A. H. (1978). Sex differences in influenceability. *Psychological Bulletin, 85*, 86–116.

Eagly, A. H. & Carli, L. L. (1981). Sex of researchers and sex-typed communications as determinants of sex differences in influenceability: A meta-analysis of social influence studies. *Psychological Bulletin, 90*, 1–20.

Edsall, T. B. (1988). Though this be meanness, yet there is method in it. *Washington Post National Weekly Edition, 5*, 26–27.

Ehrenhalt, A. (1985). Technology, strategy bring new campaign era. *Congressional Quarterly Weekly Report, 43*, 2559–2565.

Ehrenhalt, A. (1986, November 8). Failed campaign costs Republicans the Senate. *Congressional Quarterly Weekly Report, 44*, 2803 & 2871.

Elshtain, J. B. (1989). Issues and themes in the 1988 campaign. In M. Nelson (ed.), *The elections of 1988* (pp. 111–126). Washington, D.C.: Congressional Quarterly Press.

Entman, R. M. (1989). *Democracy without citizens: Media and the decay of American politics*. New York: Oxford University Press.

Erikson, R. S., Luttbeg, N. R. & Tedin, K. L. (1980). *American public opinion: Its origins, content, and impact* (2d ed.). New York: John Wiley & Sons.

Farah, B. G. & Klein, E. (1989). Public opinion trends. In G. M. Pomper (ed.), *The election of 1988: Reports and interpretations* (pp. 103–128). Chatham, N.J.: Chatham House Publishers.

Farney, D. (1988, October 24). Indiana race for governor finds GOP stumped by Democrat with a fresh face, legendary name. *Wall Street Journal*, p. A16.

Fialka, J. L. (1986, November 13). Intense mudslinging in South Dakota Senate race provokes many to favor restricting political ads. *Wall Street Journal*, p. 6.

Flanigan, W. H. & Zingale, N. H. (1987). *Political behavior of the American electorate* (6th ed.). Boston: Allyn and Bacon.

"Florida" (1986). Congressional outlook. *Congressional Quarterly Weekly Report, 44* [Supplement, 41], 2415–2416.

Frankovic, K. A. (1982, Summer). Sex and politics—New alignments, old issues. *PS*, p. 439.

Frantzich, S. E. (1989). *Political parties in the technological age*. New York: Longman.

Freedman, J. L. & Steinbruner, J. D. (1964). Perceived choice and resistance to persuasion. *Journal of Abnormal and Social Psychology, 68*, 678–681.

Freund, C. P. (1988, October 30). What's new? Mudslinging is an American tradition. *Washington Post*, Outlook, pp. C1–C2.

Gans, C. (1989, February 12). How those negatives developed. *Washington Post*, p. C2.

Garramone, G. M. (1984). Voter responses to negative political ads. *Journalism Quarterly, 61*, 250–259.

Garramone, G. M. (1985). Effects of negative political advertising: The roles of sponsors and rebuttal. *Journal of Broadcasting & Electronic Media, 29*, 147–159.

Garramone, G. M. & Smith, S. J. (1984). Reactions to political advertising: Clarifying sponsor effects. *Journalism Quarterly, 61*, 771–775.

Gaunt, J. (1987). Senate calls for clean campaigns. *Congressional Quarterly Weekly Report, 45*, 2194.

"Georgia" (1986). Congressional outlook. *Congressional Quarterly Weekly Report, 44* [Supplement, 41], 2416–2418.

Germond, J. W. & Witcover, J. (1986, October 25). Inside politics. *National Journal, 18*, 2579.

Getlin, J. (1988, March 10). Wright urges Democrats to end use of negative campaign ads. *Los Angeles Times*, Part 1, p. 24.

Gigot, P. A. (1988, January 29). Primary battle: Thirty seconds over Manchester. *Wall Street Journal*, p. 14.

Gilligan, C. (1982). *In a different voice: Psychological theory and women's development*. Cambridge: Harvard University Press.

Ginsberg, B. & Shefter, M. (1985). A critical realignment? The new politics, the re-constituted right, and the 1984 election. In M. Nelson (ed.), *The elections of 1984* (pp. 1–25). Washington, D.C.: Congressional Quarterly Press.

Godwin, R. K. (1988). *One billion dollars of influence: The direct marketing of politics*. Chatham, N.J. Chatham House Publishers.

Goldman, P. (1988a, November 21). Battle of the Republicans. *Newsweek* [Election Special], pp. 84–111.

Goldman, P. (1988b, November 21). Race to the finish. *Newsweek* [Election Special], pp. 112–146.

Goodman, E. (1986, September 27). Study: Self-interest doesn't appeal to women voters. *Sioux Falls Argus Leader*, p. 8A.

GOP ads may signal high noon in America (1988, August 1). *Advertising Age*, p 50.

Gopoian, J. D. (1982). Issue preference and candidate choice in presidential primaries. *American Journal of Political Science, 26*, 524–546.

Graber, D. A. (1989). *Mass media and American politics* (3d ed.). Washington, D.C.: Congressional Quarterly Press.

Greenfield, J. (1980). *Playing to win: An insider's guide to politics*. New York: Simon and Schuster.

Greenfield, J. (1988, October 24). *Ad wars*. [Television Program]. New York: ABC "Nightline."

Grove, L. (1988, February 2). Attack ads: Undesirable but effective. *Washington Post*, p. A10.

Grove, L. (1989, January 18). How experts fueled a race with vitriol. *Washington Post*, pp. A1 & A14.

Guskind, R. & Hagstrom, J. (1988). In the gutter. *National Journal, 20*, 2782–2790.

Hagstrom, J. & Guskind, R. (1986, November 1). Selling the candidates. *National Journal, 18*, 2619–2629.

Hargrove, E. C. & Nelson, M. (1985). The presidency: Reagan and the cycle of politics and policy. In M. Nelson (ed.), *The elections of 1984* (pp. 198–213). Washington, D.C.: Congressional Quarterly Press.

Heller, D. J. (1987). Mail, money, and Machiavelli. *Campaigns & Elections, 8*, No. 4, 32–45.

Hellweg, S. A. (1979). An examination of voter conceptualizations of the ideal political candidate. *Southern Speech Communication Journal, 44*, 373–385.

Hellweg, S. A., King, S. W. & Williams, S. E. (1988). Comparative candidate evaluation as a function of election level and candidate incumbency. *Communication Reports, 1*, 76–83.

Hendrie, P. (1989). Requiem for a heavyweight. *Campaigns & Elections, 9*, No. 6, 7–8.

Hershey, M. R. (1984). *Running for office: The political education of campaigners.* Chatham, N.J.: Chatham House Publishers.

Hershey, M. R. (1989). The campaign and the media. In G. M. Pomper (ed.), *The election of 1988: Reports and Interpretations* (pp. 73–102) Chatham, N.J.: Chatham House Publishers.

Hess, S. (1981). *Washington reporters.* Washington, D.C: Brookings Institution.

Hickey, N. (1986, October 18). Smear commercials can work: It's high noon for political mudslingers—let the targets beware. *TV Guide*, pp. 4–6.

Householder, T. (1989). Evening the score. *Campaigns & Elections, 9*, No. 6, 5–6.

Houston, P. (1986, October 14). High-tech tactics play big role in political ads. *Los Angeles Times*, I, p. 17.

Hovland, C. I., Janis, I. L. & Kelley, H. H. (1953). *Communication and persuasion.* New Haven: Yale University Press.

Hovland, C. I., Lumsdaine, A. A. & Sheffield, F. D. (1949). *Experiments on mass communication.* Princeton N.J.: Princeton University Press.

Hunt, A. R. (1981). The campaign and the issues. In A. Ranney (ed.), *The American elections of 1980* (pp. 142–176). Washington, D.C.: American Enterprise Institute.

Hunt, A. R. (1983). National politics and the 1982 campaign. In T. E. Mann & N. Ornstein (eds.), *The American election of 1982* (pp. 1–43). Washington, D.C.: American Enterprise Institute.

"Idaho" (1986). Congressional outlook. *Congressional Quarterly Weekly Report, 44* [Supplement, 41], 2420–2421.

Infante, D. A. (1975). Effects of opinionated language on communicator image and in conferring resistance to persuasion. *Western Speech Communication, 39*, 112–119.

Insko, C. A. (1967). *Theories of attitude change.* New York: Appleton-Century Crofts.

Jacob, C. E. (1981). The congressional elections. In G. M. Pomper (ed.), *The election of 1980: Reports and interpretations* (pp. 119–141). Chatham, N.J.: Chatham House Publishers.

Jacob, C. E. (1985). The congressional elections. In G. M. Pomper (ed.), *The election of 1984: Reports and interpretations* (pp. 112–132). Chatham, N.J.: Chatham House Publishers.

Jacobson, G. C. (1985). Congress: Politics after a landslide without coattails. In M. Nelson (ed.), *The elections of 1984* (pp. 215–238). Washington, D.C.: Congressional Quarterly Press.

Jacobson, G. C. & Kernell, S. (1981). *Strategy and choice in congressional elections.* New Haven: Yale University Press.

Jamieson, K. H. (1984). *Packaging the presidency: A history and criticism of presidential campaign advertising.* New York: Oxford University Press.

Jamieson, K. H. (1988, October 30). For televised mendacity: This year is the worst ever. *Washington Post*, Outlook, pp. C1–C2.

Janis, I. L. & Rife, D. (1959). Personality and emotional disorder. In C. I. Hovland &

I. L. Janis (eds.), *Personality and persuasibility* (pp. 121–140). New Haven: Yale University Press.

Jaros, D. (1973). *Socialization to politics.* New York: Praeger Publishers.

Jeffries, L. W. (1986). *Mass media: Processes and effects.* Prospect Heights, Ill.: Waveland Press.

Johnson-Cartee, K. S. & Copeland, G. A. (1989, May). *Alabama voters and acceptance of negative political advertising in the 1986 elections: An historical anomaly.* Paper presented at the annual meeting of the International Communication Association, San Francisco.

Joslyn, R. A. (1986). Political advertising and the meaning of elections. In L. L. Kaid, D. Nimmo & K. R. Sanders (eds.), *New perspectives on political advertising* (pp. 139–183). Carbondale: Southern Illinois University Press.

Katz, E. & Lazarsfeld, P. F. (1955). *Personal influence: The part played by people in the flow of mass communications.* New York: Free Press.

Kennamer, J. D. & Chaffee, S. H. (1982). Communication of political information during early presidential primaries: Cognition, affect, and uncertainty. In M. Burgoon (ed.), *Communication yearbook 5* (pp. 627–650). New Brunswick, N.J.: Transaction Books.

Kenski, H. C. (1987). Campaigns and elections in the Mountain States, 1984. In P. F. Galderisi, M. S. Lyons, R. T. Simmons & J. G. Francis (eds.), *The politics of realignment: Party change in the Mountain West* (pp. 175–195). Boulder: Westview Press.

Kenski, H. C. (1988). The gender factor in a changing electorate. In C. M. Mueller (ed.), *The politics of the gender gap: The social construction of political influence* (Vol. 12 of Sage Yearbooks in Women's Policy Studies), pp. 38–60. Beverly Hills: Sage Publications.

Kenski, H. C. & Lockwood, W. (1988, September). *Party coalitions in the eighties.* Paper presented at the annual meeting of the American Political Science Association, Washington, D.C.

Keppel, G. (1982). *Design and analysis: A researcher's handbook* (2d ed.). Englewood Cliffs, N.J.: Prentice-Hall.

Kern, M. (1988, May). *Schools of media consulting: "Emotional," new informational and quick response thinking in the eighties.* Paper presented at the annual meeting of the International Communication Association, New Orleans.

King, M. (1977). Assimilation and contrast of presidential candidates' issue positions. *Public Opinion Quarterly, 41,* 515–522.

Kirk, R. E. (1982). *Experimental design: Procedures for the behavioral sciences* (2d ed.). Belmont, Calif.: Brooks/Cole Publishing Company.

Kirschten, D. (1986, November 8). Building bridges. *National Journal, 18,* 2701–2702.

Kotok, D. (1989). The best and worst campaigns of 1988: The Nebraska Senate race. *Campaigns & Elections, 9,* No. 6, 21–22.

Kraus, S. & Davis, D. (1976). *The effects of mass communication on political behavior.* University Park: Pennsylvania University Press.

Kostroski, W. L. (1973). Party and incumbency in postwar Senate elections: Trends, patterns, and models. *American Political Science Review, 68,* 1213–1234.

Lane, M. B. (1989). The best and worst campaigns of 1988: The Ohio Senate race. *Campaigns & Elections, 9,* No. 6, 22.

Lasswell, H. D. (1936). *Politics, who gets what, when, how*. New York: Whittlesey House.

Light, P. C. & Lake, C. (1985). The election: Candidates, strategies, and decisions. In M. Nelson (ed.), *The elections of 1984* (pp. 83–110). Washington D.C.: Congressional Quarterly Press.

Littlejohn, S. W. & Jabusch, D. M. (1987). *Persuasive transactions*. Glenview, Il.: Scott, Foresman and Company.

Louden, A. (1987, May). *Political advertising in the Hunt/Helms race: Pot shots and hot spots*. Paper presented at the annual meeting of the International Communication Association, Montreal, Canada.

"Louisiana" (1986). Congressional outlook. *Congressional Quarterly Weekly Report, 44* [Supplement, 41], 2434–2437.

Lowi, T. J. (1985). An aligning election, a presidential plebiscite. In M. Nelson (ed.), *The elections of 1984* (pp. 277–301). Washington, D.C.: Congressional Quarterly Press.

Lumsdaine, A. A. & Janis, I. L. (1953). Resistance to "counterpropaganda" produced by one-sided and two-sided "propaganda" presentations. *Public Opinion Quarterly, 17*, 311–318.

McAllister, B. (1988, November 10). Negative ads, visits by Bush help produce victory for Burns. *Washington Post*, p. A47.

McBath, J. H. & Fisher, W. R. (1969). Persuasion in presidential campaign communication. *Quarterly Journal of Speech, 55*, 17–25.

Maccoby, E. E. & Jacklin, C. N. (1974). *The psychology of sex differences*. Palo Alto, Calif.: Stanford University Press.

McCroskey, J. C. (1970). The effects of evidence as an inhibitor of counter-persuasion. *Speech Monographs, 37*, 188–194.

McCroskey, J. C., Holdridge, W. & Toomb, J. K. (1974). An instrument for measuring the source credibility of basic communication instructors. *Speech Teacher, 23*, 26–33.

McCroskey, J. C., Young, T. J. & Scott, M. D. (1972). The effects of message sidedness and evidence on inoculation against counterpersuasion in small group communication. *Speech Monographs, 34*, [Special Reports], 205–212.

McGinnis, J. (1969). *The selling of the president, 1968*. New York: Trident.

McGuire, W. J. (1961a). The effectiveness of supportive and refutational defenses in immunizing and restoring beliefs against persuasion. *Sociometry, 24*, 184–197.

McGuire, W. J. (1961b). Resistance to persuasion conferred by active and passive prior refutation of the same and alternative counterarguments. *Journal of Abnormal and Social Psychology, 63*, 326–332.

McGuire, W. J. (1962). Persistence of the resistance to persuasion induced by various types of prior belief defenses. *Journal of Abnormal and Social Psychology, 64*, 241–248.

McGuire, W. J. (1964). Inducing resistance to persuasion: Some contemporary approaches. In L. Berkowitz (ed.), *Advances in experimental social psychology* (Vol. 1, pp. 191–229). New York: Academic Press.

McGuire, W. J. (1969). The nature of attitudes and attitude change. In G. Lindzey & E. Aronson (eds.), *The handbook of social psychology*, Vol. 3: *The individual in a social context* (2d ed.) (pp. 136–314). Reading, Mass.: Addison-Wesley Publishing Company.

McGuire, W. J. (1970, February). A vaccine for brainwash. *Psychology Today, 3*, 36–39 & 63–64.

McGuire, W. J. & Papageorgis, D. (1961). The relative efficacy of various types of prior belief-defense in producing immunity against persuasion. *Journal of Abnormal and Social Psychology, 62*, 327–337.

McGuire, W. J. & Papageorgis, D. (1962). Effectiveness of forewarning in developing resistance to persuasion. *Public Opinion Quarterly, 26*, 24–34.

McWilliams, W. C. (1985). The meaning of the election. In G. M. Pomper, R. K. Baker, C. E. Jacob, S. Keeter, W. C. McWilliams & H. A. Plotkin (eds.), *The election of 1984: Reports and interpretations* (pp. 157–183). Chatham, N.J.: Chatham House Publishers.

Madison, C. (1986). Cranston may have bounced back. *National Journal, 18*, 2188.

Maisel, L. & Sacks, P. M. (eds.) (1975). *The future of political parties*. Beverly Hills: Sage Publications.

Mandel, R. B. (1982). How women vote: The new gender gap. *Working Woman, 7*, 128–131.

Mann, T. E. & Ornstein, N. J. (1981). The Republican surge in Congress. In A. Ranney (ed.), *The American elections of 1980* (pp. 263–302). Washington, D.C.: American Enterprise Institute.

Mann, T. E. & Ornstein, N. J. (1983). Sending a message: Voters and Congress in 1982. In T. E. Mann & N. J. Ornstein (eds.), *The American election of 1982* (pp. 133–152). Washington, D.C.: American Enterprise Institute.

Mann, T. E. & Wolfinger, R. E. (1984). Candidates and parties in congressional elections. In R. G. Niemi & H. F. Weisberg (eds.), *Controversies in voting behavior* (2d ed.) (pp. 269–291). Washington, D.C.: Congressional Quarterly Press.

Markus, G. B. & Converse, P. E. (1979). A dynamic simultaneous equation model of electoral choice. *American Political Science Review, 73*, 1055–1070.

Marple, C. (1933). The comparative susceptibility of three age levels to the suggestion of group versus expert opinion. *Journal of Personality and Social Psychology, 4*, 176–186.

Martinez, M. D. & DeLegal, T. (1988, April). *Negative ads and negative attitudes: Effects and non-effects on trust and efficacy.* Paper presented at the annual meeting of the Midwest Political Science Association, Chicago.

Maslach, C., Santee, R. T. & Wade, C. (1987). Individuation, gender role, and dissent: Personality mediators of situational forces. *Journal of Personality and Social Psychology, 53*, 1088–1093.

Mathews, T. (1988, November 21). The Democrats' quest. *Newsweek* [Election Special], pp. 42–83.

Matthews, C. (1988). *Hardball: How politics is played —Told by one who knows the game*. New York: Summit Books.

May, C. D. (1988, November 4). Political mud can yield gold, analysts agree. *New York Times*, p. A13.

Mayer, J. (1986, October 2). Nasty campaign tactics become central issue in normally reserved Vermont. *Wall Street Journal*, p. 68.

Melder, K. (1989a). Creating candidate imagery: The man on horseback. In L. J. Sabato (ed.), *Campaigns and elections: A reader in modern American politics* (pp. 5–11). Glenview, Ill.: Scott, Foresman and Company.

Melder, K. (1989b). The first media campaign. In L. J. Sabato (ed.), *Campaigns and elections: A reader in modern American politics* (pp. 229–236). Glenview, Ill.: Scott, Foresman and Company.

Merritt, S. (1984). Negative political advertising: Some empirical findings. *Journal of Advertising, 13*, 27–38.

Miller, A. H. (1988). Gender and the vote: 1984. In C. M. Mueller (ed.), *The politics of the gender gap: The social construction of political influence* (Vol. 12 of Sage Yearbooks in Women's Policy Studies) (pp. 258–282). Beverly Hills: Sage Publications.

Miller, G. R. & Burgoon, M. (1973). *New techniques of persuasion.* New York: Harper & Row.

Miller, G. R., Burgoon, M. & Burgoon, J. K. (1984). The functions of human communication in changing attitudes and gaining compliance. In C. A. Arnold & J. W. Bowers (eds.), *Handbook of rhetorical and communication theory* (pp. 400–474). Boston: Allyn and Bacon.

Miller, M. D. & Burgoon, M. (1979). The relationship between violations of expectations and the induction of resistance to persuasion. *Human Communication Research, 5*, 301–313.

Miller, W. E., Miller, A. H. & Schneider, E. J. (1980). *American national election studies data sourcebook, 1952–1978.* Cambridge, Mass.: Harvard University Press.

Moving right along? Campaign 1984, lessons for 1988. An interview with Peter Hart and Richard Wirthlin (1985). *Public Opinion, 7*, 8–11 & 59–63.

Moyers, B. (1984a). *The thirty second president* [Video]. New York: PBJ.

Moyers, B. (1984b). Press perspectives. In R. C. Jeffrey (ed.), *Election 84: Search for a new coalition* (pp. 24–40). Austin: University of Texas Press.

National Journal (1986, November 8). Of the 13 new faces in the Senate . . . nine are veterans of the House. *National Journal, 18*, 2682–2683.

Neale, T. H. (1987). *Negative campaigning in national politics: An overview.* Report no. 87–868 Gov. Washington, D.C.: Library of Congress, Congressional Research Service.

Nie, N. H., Verba, S. & Petrocik, J. R. (1976). *The changing American voter.* Cambridge: Harvard University Press.

Niemi, R. G. & Weisberg, H. F. (eds.) (1984). *Controversies in voting behavior* (2d ed.). Washington, D.C.: Congressional Quarterly Press.

Nimmo, D. D. & Sanders, K. R. (eds.) (1981). *Handbook of political communication.* Beverly Hills: Sage Publications.

Norpoth, H. (1987). Under way and here to stay: Party alignment in the 1980s? *Public Opinion Quarterly, 51*, 376–391.

Norpoth, H. & Rusk, J. G. (1982). Partisan dealignment in the American electorate: Itemizing the deductions since 1964. *American Political Science Review, 76*, 522–537.

"North Dakota" (1986). Congressional outlook. *Congressional Quarterly Weekly Report, 44* [Supplement, 41], 2649.

Nugent, J. F. (1987). Positively negative. *Campaigns & Elections, 7*, No. 6, 47–49.

Nyhan, D. (1988). *The Duke: The inside story of a political phenomenon.* New York: Warner Books.

Obermayer, A. (1989). A bad year for the polls. *Campaigns & Elections, 9*, No. 6, 47–49, and 62.

O'Keefe, G. J. (1975). Political campaigns and mass communication research. In S. H. Chaffee (ed.), *Political communication: Issues and strategies for research* (pp. 129–164). Beverly Hills: Sage Publications.

"Oklahoma" (1986). Congressional outlook. *Congressional Quarterly Weekly Report, 44* [Supplement, 41], 2473–2474.

Opinion roundup (1982, April/May). *Public Opinion, 5,* 21–32.

Opinion roundup (1984, April/May). Declarations of independents. *Public Opinion, 7,* 21–39.

Orren, G. R. (1985). The nomination process: Vicissitudes of candidate selection. In M. Nelson (ed.), *The elections of 1984* (pp. 27–82). Washington, D.C.: Congressional Quarterly Press.

Paddock, R. C. (1986, April 12). Governor calls Bradley ads "dirty." *Los Angeles Times,* I, p. 32.

Paletz, D. & Entman, R. (1981). *Media power politics.* New York: Free Press.

Paolantino, S. A. (1989). The best and worst campaigns of 1988: The New Jersey House race. *Campaigns & Elections, 9,* 23–24.

Papageorgis, D. & McGuire, W. J. (1961). The generality of immunity to persuasion produced by pre-exposure to weakened counterarguments. *Journal of Abnormal and Social Psychology, 62,* 475–481.

Partlow, B. (1989). What the spin doctors ordered. *Campaigns & Elections, 9,* No. 6, 4–5.

Patterson, T. E. & McClure, R. D. (1976). *The unseeing eye: The myth of television power in national elections.* New York: G. P. Putnam's Sons.

Perry, J. M. (1988, November 3). Close Senate race in Connecticut has a bear growling. *Wall Street Journal,* pp. A1 & A12.

Perry, J. M. & Langley, M. (1988, October 27). Bush thrives on one-a-day tv-message capsules prescribed by his skilled poli-tech image makers. *Wall Street Journal,* p. A24.

Peterson, B. (1988a, February 25). Gephardt toughens tone with personal attacks on Dukakis, Gore. *Washington Post,* p. A10.

Peterson, B. (1988b, September 25). A campaign of distortions, untruths. *Washington Post,* pp. A1 & A10.

Peterson, B. & Broder, D. S. (1988, February 26). Dukakis blasts "flip-flopper" Gephardt. *Washington Post,* p. A8.

Petrocik, J. R. (1980). Contextual sources of voting behavior: The changeable American voter. In J. C. Pierce & J. L. Sullivan (eds.), *The electorate reconsidered* (pp. 257–277). Beverly Hills, Calif.: Sage Publications.

Petrocik, J. R. (1981). *Party coalitions: Realignment, and the decline of the New Deal party system.* Chicago: University of Chicago Press.

Petrocik, J. R. (1987). Realignment: New party coalitions and the nationalization of the South. *Journal of Politics, 49,* 347–373.

Petty, R. E. (1977). The importance of cognitive responses in persuasion. *Advances in Consumer Research, 4,* 357–362.

Petty, R. E. & Cacioppo, J. T. (1979). Issue involvement can increase or decrease persuasion by enhancing message-relevant cognitive responses. *Journal of Personality and Social Psychology, 37,* 1915–1926.

Petty, R. E. & Cacioppo, J. T. (1981). *Attitudes and persuasion: Classic and contemporary approaches.* Dubuque, Iowa: Wm. C. Brown Company Publishers.

Petty, R. E. & Cacioppo, J. T. (1984). The effects of involvement in responses to argument quantity and quality: Central and peripheral routes to persuasion. *Journal of Personality and Social Psychology, 46*, 69–81.

Pfau, M. & Burgoon, M. (1988). Inoculation in political campaign communication. *Human Communication Research, 15*, 91–111.

Pfau, M. & Burgoon, M. (1989). The efficacy of issue and character attack message strategies in political campaign communication. *Communication Reports, 2*, 53–61.

Pfau, M., Kenski, H. C., Nitz, M. & Sorenson, J. (1989a, November). *The use of direct mail communication to promote resistance to the influence of political attack messages.* Paper presented at the annual meeting of the Speech Communication Association, San Francisco.

Pfau, M., Kenski, H., Nitz, M. & Sorenson, J. (1989b, November). *Use of the attack message strategy in political campaign communication.* Paper presented at the annual meeting of the Speech Communication Association, San Francisco.

Pomper, G. M. (1975). *Voter's choice: Varieties of American electoral behavior.* New York: Harper & Row.

Pomper, G. M. (1981). The presidential election. In G. M. Pomper (ed.), *The election of 1980: Reports and interpretations* (pp. 65–96). Chatham, N.J.: Chatham House Publishers.

Pomper, G. M. (1985). The presidential election. In G. M. Pomper (ed.), *The election of 1984: Reports and interpretations* (pp. 60–90). Chatham, N.J.: Chatham House Publishers.

Pomper, G. M. (1989a). The presidential nominations. In G. M. Pomper, R. K. Baker, W. D. Burnham, B. G. Farah, M. R. Hershey, E. Klein, & W. C. McWilliams (eds.), *The election of 1988: Reports and interpretations* (pp. 33–72). Chatham, N.J.: Chatham House Publishers.

Pomper, G. M. (1989b). The presidential election. In G. M. Pomper, R. K. Baker, W. D. Burnham, B. G. Farah, M. R. Hershey, E. Klein, & W. C. McWilliams (eds.), *The election of 1988: Reports and interpretations* (pp. 129–152). Chatham, N.J.: Chatham House Publishers.

Poole, K. T. & Ziegler, L. H. (1985). *Women, public opinion, and politics: The changing political attitudes of American women.* New York: Longman.

Post, D. J. (1983). *Candidate image and source valence: Predicting the outcome of a local primary election.* Unpublished master's thesis, West Virginia University.

Press, C. & Verburg, K. (1988). *American politicians and journalists.* Glenview, Il.: Scott, Foresman and Company.

Pryor, B. & Steinfatt, T. M. (1978). The effects of initial belief level on inoculation theory and its proposed mechanisms. *Human Communication Research, 4*, 217–230.

Quirk, P. J. (1989). The election. In M. Nelson (ed.), *The elections of 1988* (pp. 63–92). Washington, D.C.: Congressional Quarterly Press.

Raasch, C. (1989, July 20). Pressler to co-sponsor "clean campaign" bill. *Sioux Falls Argus Leader*, p. C1.

Rasky, S. F. (1988, January 18). Gephardt's campaign resurgent in Iowa. *New York Times*, p. 13.

Reinhold, R. (1988, October 30). Nevada Senator's hope is revived. *New York Times*, p. 19.

Reinsch, J. L. (1988). *Getting elected: From radio and Roosevelt to television and Reagan*. New York: Hippocrene Books.

Rheem, D. L. (1988, March 22). "Negative" to negative ads. *Christian Science Monitor*, pp. 1 & 6.

Roddy, B. L. & Garramone, G. M. (1988, June). *Negative political advertising: Appeals and strategies*. Paper presented at the annual meeting of the International Communication Association, New Orleans.

Robinson, M. J. (1981). The media in 1980: Was the message the message? In A. Ranney (ed.), *The American elections of 1980* (pp. 177–211). Washington, D.C.: American Enterprise Institute.

Rosenfeld, L. & Christie, V. (1974). Sex and persuasibility revisited. *Western Journal of Speech Communication, 38*, 224–253.

Rosenthal, A. (1988a, February 15). Candidates sharpen attacks in New Hampshire TV ads. *New York Times*, pp. 1 & 11.

Rosenthal, A. (1988b, February 26). Gephardt ads summon strong and proud U.S. *New York Times*, p. 8.

Rosenthal, R. (1984). *Meta-analytic procedures for social research*. Beverly Hills: Sage Publications.

Rosnow, R. & Robinson, E. (1967). *Experiments in persuasion*. New York: Academic Press.

Sabato, L. J. (1981). *The rise of political consultants: New ways of winning elections*. New York: Basic Books.

Sabato, L. J. (1983). Parties, PACS, and independent groups. In T. E. Mann and N. J. Ornstein (eds.), *The American election of 1982* (pp. 72–110). Washington, D.C.: American Enterprise Institute.

Salmore, S. A. & Salmore, B. G. (1985). *Candidates, parties, and campaigns: Electoral politics in America*. Washington, D.C.: Congressional Quarterly Press.

Scheidel, T. (1963). Sex and persuasibility. *Speech Monographs, 30*, 353–358.

Schneider, W. (1986, November 8). Return to normalcy. *National Journal, 18*, 2708–2710.

Schneider, W. (1988). Solidarity's not enough. *National Journal, 20*, 2853–2855.

Schramm, W. (1983). The unique perspective of communication: A retrospective view. *Journal of Communication, 33*, 6–17.

Schwartz, M. & Grove, L. (1988a, July 27). GOP airs $3 million ad campaign. *Washington Post*, p. A8.

Schwartz, M. & Grove, L. (1988b, September 1). Democrats' ads to stress economy, Dukakis' abilities. *Washington Post*, p. A16.

Schwartz, M., Kurtz, H. & Grove, L. (1988, May 1). Jackson's negative ad. *Washington Post*, p. A15.

Sears, D. O. (1969). Political behavior. In G. Lindzey & E. Aronson (eds.), *The handbook of social psychology* (Vol. 5): *Applied social psychology* (2d ed.) (pp. 315–458). Reading, Mass.: Addison-Wesley Publishing Company.

Secter, B. (1986, September 25). Zschau resorts to big lie in TV ads, Cranston charges. *Los Angeles Times*, I, p. 3.

Seglem, L. (1989). The best and worst campaigns of 1988: The New Jersey Senate race. *Campaigns & Elections, 9*, No. 6, 24–25.

Shapiro, M. A. & Rieger, R. H. (1989, May). *Comparing positive and negative political advertising*. Paper presented at the annual meeting of the International Communication Association, San Francisco.

Shapiro, M. J. (1969). Rational political man: A synthesis of economic and social-psychological perspectives. *American Political Science Review, 63*, 1106–1119.

Shapiro, R., Mahajan, H. & Veith, K. (1984, November). *Gender differences in policy choices: Trends from the 1950s to the 1980s*. Paper presented at the annual meeting of the Midwest Association for Public Opinion Research, Chicago.

Sherif, C. W. & Sherif, M. (1967). *Attitude, ego-involvement and change*. New York: Wiley.

Sherrod, D. (1971). Selection perceptions of political candidates. *Public Opinion Quarterly, 35*, 354–362.

Shively, W. P. (1980). The nature of party identification: A review of recent developments. In J. C. Pierce & J. L. Sullivan (eds.), *The electorate reconsidered* (pp. 219–236). Beverly Hills: Sage Publications.

Shribman, D. (1986, October 7). Cranston–Zschau race may offer a glimpse of future U.S. politics. *Wall Street Journal*, pp. 1 & 28.

Shribman, D. (1988, October 31). In Wisconsin, candidates for U.S. Senate engage in race out of keeping with state traditions. *Wall Street Journal*, p. A16.

Shribman, D. & Perry, J. M. (1988, November 8). Dukakis campaign was marred by a series of lost opportunities. *Wall Street Journal*, pp. A1 & A8.

Sigal, L. (1973). *Reporters and officials*. Lexington, Mass.: D. C. Heath.

Sistrunk, S. & McDavid, J. W. (1965). Achievement motivation, affiliation motivation, and task difficulty as determinants of social conformity. *Journal of Abnormal and Social Psychology, 66*, 41–50.

Sistrunk, S. & McDavid, J. W. (1971). Sex variable in conforming behavior. *Journal of Personality and Social Psychology, 17*, 200–207.

Sloan, L. R., Love, R. E. & Ostrom, T. M. (1974). Political heckling: Who really loses? *Journal of Personality and Social Psychology, 30*, 518–524.

Solmsen, F. (ed.) (1954). *The rhetoric and the poetics of Arisotle*. New York: Random House.

Solomon, B. (1986, October 25). Iowa's candidates are battling apathy. *National Journal, 18*, 2573.

Sorauf, F. J. & Beck, P. A. (1988). *Party politics in America* (6th ed.). Glenview, Ill.: Scott, Foresman/Little, Brown College Division.

"South Dakota" (1986). Congressional outlook. *Congressional Quarterly Weekly Report, 44* [Supplement, 41], 2486–2487.

Stanga, J. T. & Sheffield, J. T. (1987). The myth of zero partisanship: Attitudes toward American political parties, 1964–84. *American Journal of Political Science, 31*, 829–855.

Stanley, H. W., Bianco, W. T. & Niemi, R. G. (1986). Partisanship and group support over time: A multivariate analysis. *American Political Science Review, 80*, 969–976.

Steckenrider, J. S. & Cutler, N. E. (1989). Aging and adult political socialization: The importance of roles and role transitions. In R. S. Sigel (ed.), *Political learning in adulthood* (pp. 56–88). Chicago: University of Chicago Press.

Stengel, R. (1986, November 17). Of tall winners, big losers, frogs and a bird. *Time*, [Election Notebook] p. 53.

Stengel, R. (1988, November 21). Nine key moments. *Time*, pp. 48–56.

Stephens, W. N. & Long, C. S. (1970). Education and political behavior. In J. A. Robinson (ed.), *Political science annual: An international review* (Vol. 2) (pp. 3–33). Indianapolis: Bobbs-Merrill Company.

Stewart, C. J. (1975). Voter perceptions of mudslinging in political communication. *Central States Speech Journal, 26*, 279–286.

Stone, V. A. (1969). Individual differences and inoculation against persuasion. *Journalism Quarterly, 46*, 267–273.

Surlin, S. H. & Gordon, T. F. (1977). How values affect attitudes toward direct reference political advertising. *Journalism Quarterly, 54*, 89–98.

Tannenbaum, P. H., Macaulay, J. R. & Norris, E. L. (1966). Principle of congruity and reduction of persuasion. *Journal of Personality and Social Psychology, 2*, 233–238.

Tannenbaum, P. H. & Norris, E. L. (1965). Effects of combining congruity principle strategies for the reduction of persuasion. *Sociometry, 28*, 145–157.

Tarrance, V. L., Jr. (1980). *Negative campaigns and negative votes: The 1980 elections.* Washington, D.C.: Free Congress Research and Education Foundation.

Tate, E. & Miller, G. R. (1973, April). *Resistance to persuasion following counter-attitudinal advocacy: Some preliminary thoughts.* Paper presented at the annual meeting of the International Communication Association, Montreal, Canada.

Taylor, P. (1986a). Accentuating the negative: Forget issue; campaign ads this year are heavy on "air pollution." *Washington Post National Weekly Edition, 3*, 6–7.

Taylor, P. (1986b, October 24). Scranton drops ads and his mitts; opponent Casey keeps punching. *Washington Post*, p. A3.

Taylor, P. (1989, January 17). Consultants: Winning on the attack. *Washington Post*, pp. A1 & A14.

Taylor, P. & Broder, D. S. (1988). How the presidential campaign got stuck on the low road. *Washington Post National Weekly Edition, 6*, 14–15.

Television bashing (1986, October 26). *Los Angeles Times*, IV, p. 4.

Trent, J. S. & Friedenberg, R. V. (1983). *Political campaign communication: Principles and practices.* New York: Praeger Publishers.

Udall, M. K. (1988). *Too funny to be president.* New York: Henry Holt and Company.

Ullman, W. R. & Bodaken, E. M. (1975). Inducing resistance to persuasive attack: A test of two strategies of communication. *Western Speech Communication, 39*, 240–248.

United States Senate (84th Congress, 2nd Session, 1956). Committee on Government Operations, Permanent Subcommittee on Investigations. *Communist interrogation, indoctrination and exploitation of American military and political prisoners.* Washington. D.C.: United States Government Printing Office.

Van Gieson, J. (1989). The best and worst of 1988: The Florida Senate race. *Campaigns and Elections, 9*, No. 6, 26–27.

Ward, S. & Wackman, D. (1971). Family and media influence on adolescent consumer learning. *American Behavioral Scientist, 14*, 415–427.

Watson, T. (1984). Republicans pick up one governorship. *Congressional Quarterly Weekly Report, 42*, 2911–2913.

Wattenberg, M. P. (1986). *The decline of American political parties, 1952–1984.* Cambridge: Harvard University Press.

Weisberg, H. F. & Rusk, J. G. (1970). Dimensions of candidate evaluation. *American Political Science Review, 64*, 1167–1185.

Whitehead, J. (1971). Effects of authority-based assertion on attitude and credibility. *Speech Monographs, 38*, 311–315.

Whiteley, P. F. (1988). The causal relationships between issues, candidate evaluations, party identification, and vote choice—The view from "Rolling Thunder." *Journal of Politics, 50*, 961–984.

Wicker, T. (1986, October 24). The road not taken. *New York Times*, p. A35.

Williams, D. C., Weber, S. J., Haaland, G. A., Mueller, R. H. & Craig, R. E. (1976). Voter decisionmaking in a primary election: An evaluation of three models of choice. *American Journal of Political Science, 20*, 37–49.

Wolfinger, R. E. & Rosenstone, S. J. (1980). *Who votes?* New Haven: Yale University Press.

Yang, J. E. (1988a, September 7). Gorton emulating the phoenix, hope, new life in politics will spring from the ashes of defeat. *Wall Street Journal*, p. 54.

Yang, J. E. (1988b, October 25). New Jersey candidates for Senate make race one of the nastiest. *Wall Street Journal*, pp. A1 & A10.

Young, M. (1987). *American dictionary of campaigns and elections.* Lanham, Md.: Hamilton Press.

Author Index

Abramson, P., 126–27, 131
Albert, J. A., 62–63
Aldrich, J. H., 127, 131
Alexander, H. E., 61, 63–64, 84
Alford, J. R., 126, 131
Allen, J., 146
Alston, C., 56–57, 65
Anatol, K. W. E., 78
Anderson, L. R., 75, 78, 80, 85, 90–91, 121, 159
Anderson, P. A., 146
Aristotle Industries, 23–24, 26, 41, 43, 50, 52, 55, 70
Armstrong, R., 3, 86, 117, 158
Asher, H., 146
Atkin, C. K., 127, 130
Austin, J. A., 142, 146
Axelrod, D., 4, 7, 157
Axelrod, R., 126, 132–33

Baker, R. K., 51, 53, 56–57
Balzar, J., 31
Barber, J. D., 9
Bart, J., 27
Bates, S., 7
Bavelas, A., 91
Beck, P. A., 126–27
Becker, L. B., 105, 108

Becker, S. W., 91
Beiler, D., 7–9, 13, 15, 20–26, 70
Benenson, R., 142
Bennett, W. L., 69
Berke, R. L., 13
Bianco, W. T., 126
Birk, T., 89
Blumler, J. G., 69, 127, 130
Bodaken, E. M., 80, 105
Bonafede, D., 28
Boyarsky, B., 33
Braden, M., 91
Broder, D., 21, 39, 43, 45–46, 48–50, 64–66, 68–70, 84
Brokaw, C., 85
Brownstein, R., 37
Burgoon, J. K., 134, 150
Burgoon, M., 2–3, 73–75, 78, 81–83, 88–89, 91, 96, 99, 105, 140, 150, 157–60

Cacioppo, J. T., 120, 140–41
Caddell, P., 132, 134
Campaigns and Elections (video documentary), 7, 15, 26–28, 35
Campbell, A., 126, 153
Campbell, B. A., 126, 131
Campbell, J. E., 126, 131

Carli, L. L., 141, 146
Carlson, M. B., 142
Carroll, S. J., 142
Chaffee, S. H., 9, 108, 127, 130
Chaiken, S., 120
Choe, S. Y., 127, 130
Christie, V., 140
Clark, J. E., 89
Chase, L. J., 78, 81, 105
Cohen, M., 81, 88–89, 91, 96, 105
Cohen, R. E., 28–29, 33
Colford, S. W., 41, 46, 70
Congressional Quarterly Weekly Report,
    29–31, 34–37
Converse, P. E., 126
Conway, M. M., 153
Cook, R., 44
Cooper, H. M., 141
Copeland, G. A., 3, 158
Copesky, J., 52
Craig, R. E., 108
Cronkhite, G., 140, 146, 152
Cutler, N. E., 151

Davis, D., 83, 160
Dean, R. B., 142, 146
DeLegal, T., 158
DeVries, W., 146
Diamond, E., 7
Dillin, J., 37–38
Dionne, E. J., Jr., 42
Dowd, M., 142

Eagly, A. H., 141, 146–47, 150
Edsall, T. B., 45–46
Ehrenhalt, A., 3, 28, 83–84, 158
Elshtain, J. B., 49
Entman, R., 69
Erikson, R. S., 151

Farah, B. G., 47, 50, 86, 142
Farney, D., 56
Fialka, J. L., 36, 85, 97, 108
Fisher, W. R., 83, 160
Flanigan, W. H., 125
Frankovic, K. A., 140, 142
Frantzich, S. E., 84, 158
Freedman, J. L., 81, 105

Freund, C. P., 1, 5–6
Friedenberg, R. V., 108

Gans, C., 64
Garramone, G. M., 3, 45
Gaunt, J., 67
Germond, J. W., 35
Getlin, J., 67
Gigot, P. A., 40
Gilligan, C., 139, 142, 147, 150
Ginsberg, B., 132, 134
Godwin, R. K., 117
Goldman, P., 40–41, 45–46, 48
Goodman, E., 142
Gopoian, J. D., 108
Gordon, T. F., 3, 158
Graber, D. A., 146
Greenfield, J., 6, 157
Grove, L., 39, 41, 43–44, 51
Gurevitch, M., 69
Gurin, G., 126
Guskind, R., 3, 28, 31, 33–34, 36–37,
    50–60, 83–86, 99, 157–58

Haaland, G. A., 108
Haggerty, B. A., 61, 63–64, 84
Hagstrom, J., 3, 28, 31, 33–34, 36–37,
    50–60, 83–86, 99, 157–58
Hargrove, E. C., 132, 134
Heller, D. J., 86, 117
Hellweg, S. A., 146–47
Hendrie, P., 58–59
Hernandez-Ramos, P. F., 9
Hershey, M. R., 13, 15–16, 18, 44–48,
    70, 83, 122
Hess, S., 69
Hickey, N., 3
Holdridge, W., 89
Hook, J., 56–57
Householder, T., 56
Houston, P., 30
Hovland, C. I., 152
Hunt, A. R., 14–15, 20

Ifill, G., 46
Infante, D. A., 81
Insko, C. A., 80

Jabusch, D. M., 140, 150, 152
Jacob, C. E., 17, 24

Jacklin, C. N., 141
Jacobson, G. C., 4, 23
Jamieson, K. H., 1, 9, 22–23, 61–62, 70, 157
Janis, I. L., 73, 78, 81, 140, 150, 152
Jaros, D., 151
Jeffries, L. W., 105
Johnson-Cartee, K. S., 3, 158
Jones, S. B., 140
Joslyn, R. A., 3
Judd, B., 146

Katz, E., 74
Kelley, H. H., 152
Kennamer, J. D., 108
Kenski, H. C., 4, 24–25, 82, 84, 127, 131, 142, 158
Keppel, G., 87
Kern, M., 158
Kernell, S., 4
Kibler, R. J., 146
King, L. B., 81, 105, 130
King, M., 127
King, S. W., 146–147
Kirk, R. E., 87
Kirschten, D., 30
Klein, E., 47, 50, 86, 142
Kostroski, W. L., 131
Kotok, D., 59
Kraus, S., 83, 160
Kurtz, H., 44

Lake, C., 23
Lane, M. B., 53
Langley, M., 46, 49
Lasswell, H. D., 160
Lazarsfeld, P. F., 74
Light, P. C., 23
Littlejohn, S. W., 140, 150, 152
Lockwood, W., 127, 131
Long, C. S., 153
Long, K. M., 146
Los Angeles Times, 34
Louden, A., 3, 158
Love, K., 31
Love, R. E., 141
Lowi, T. J., 132, 134

Lumsdaine, A. A., 73, 78, 81, 152
Luttbeg, N. R., 151

McAllister, B., 58
Macaulay, J. R., 78–80, 111, 120–21
McBath, J. H., 83, 160
McClure, R. D., 9
Maccoby, E. E., 141
McCombs, M. E., 105, 108
McCroskey, J. C., 81, 89, 105
McDavid, J. W., 146
McGinnis, J., 9
McGuire, W. J., 74–81, 85, 90–91, 96, 102, 105, 108, 120–21, 139–40, 146, 150, 152, 159
McQuail, D., 127, 130
McWilliams, W. C., 132, 134
Madison, C., 31
Mahajan, H., 142
Maisel, L., 125
Mandel, J. E., 78
Mandel, R. B., 142
Mann, T. E., 3, 19, 116–17, 126, 158
Markus, G. B., 126
Marple, C., 150, 152
Martinez, M. D., 158
Maslach, C., 141, 146
Mathews, T., 42–43
Matthews, C., 1, 10–11
May, C. D., 1, 4, 158
Mayer, J., 29
Melder, K., 5
Merritt, S., 3, 45
Miller, A. H., 126, 142, 151
Miller, G. R., 73–75, 81–83, 88, 96, 99, 105, 150, 157, 159–60
Miller, M., 81, 88–89, 91, 96, 105
Miller, W. E., 126, 151
Montgomery, C. L., 81, 88–89, 91, 96
Moyers, B., 3, 7–8
Mueller, R. H., 108
Munro, M., 126, 131

National Journal, 32–33
Neale, T. H., 63–64, 67, 84
Nelson, M., 132, 134
Nie, N. H., 151
Niemi, R. G., 126–127

Nimmo, D. D., 160
Nitz, M., 82, 84, 158
Norpoth, H., 126, 132, 133
Norris, E. L., 78–80, 111, 120–21
Nugent, J. F., 3, 158
Nyhan, D., 40–43, 157

Obermayer, A., 40–41
O'Keefe, G. J., 146
O'Mara, J., 146
Opinion Roundup, 126, 142
Ornstein, N. J., 3, 16–17, 19, 158
Orren, G. R., 22
Ostrom, T. M., 141

Paddock, R. C., 33
Paletz, D., 69
Paolantino, S. A., 57
Papageorgis, D., 74–75, 78–79, 85, 90, 105, 121, 159
Partlow, B., 52
Patterson, T. E., 9
Perry, J. M., 46, 49, 58
Peterson, B., 3, 43
Petrocik, J. R., 126, 151
Petty, R. E., 120, 140–41
Pfau, M., 2, 27, 82, 84, 89, 158
Pomper, G. M., 14, 23, 40, 43–44, 47–48, 132, 146
Poole, K. T., 142
Post, D. J., 146
Press, C., 69
Pryor, B., 80–81, 102, 105, 108
Public Opinion, 126–27, 142

Quirk, P. J., 49–50

Raasch, C., 64–65
Rasky, S. F., 42
Reinsch, J. L., 6
Rheem, D. L., 67
Rhoney, C. T., 46
Rieger, R. H., 45
Rife, D., 140, 150
Robinson, E., 134
Robinson, M. J., 14–16, 18, 40
Roddy, B. L., 45
Rohde, D. W., 127, 131
Rosenfeld, L., 140

Rosenstone, S. J., 153
Rosenthal, A., 41–42
Rosenthal, R., 42, 141
Rosnow, R., 134
Rusk, J. G., 127, 130–132, 133

Sabato, L. J., 3, 5, 7–12, 19–20, 22, 66, 69–70, 84, 117, 158
Sacks, P. M., 125
Salmore, B. G., 2, 11, 21, 24, 26, 32, 84, 158
Salmore, S. A., 2, 11, 21, 24, 26, 32, 84, 158
Sanders, K. R., 160
Santee, R. T., 141, 146
Scheidel, T., 140
Schneider, E. J., 126, 151
Schneider, W., 3, 31, 157–58
Schramm, W., 160
Schwartz, M., 44, 51
Scott, M. D., 81, 105
Sears, D. O., 151
Secter, B., 31
Seglem, L., 54
Shapiro, M. A., 45
Shapiro, M. J., 146
Shapiro, R., 142
Sheffield, F. D., 152
Sheffield, J. T., 126–27, 131, 152
Shefter, M., 132, 134
Sherif, C. W., 134
Sherif, M., 134
Sherrod, D., 127, 130
Shively, W. P., 127, 130, 131, 132, 134
Shribman, D., 31, 49, 53
Sigal, L., 69
Sistrunk, S., 141, 146
Sloan, L. R., 141
Smith, S. J., 3
Solmsen, F., 73, 157
Solomon, B., 30
Sorauf, F. J., 127
Sorenson, J., 82, 84, 158
Stanga, J. T., 126–27, 131
Stanley, H. W., 126
Steckenrider, J. S., 151
Steinbruner, J. D., 81, 105
Steinfatt, T. M., 80–81, 102, 105, 108
Stengel, R., 44, 86

Stephens, W. N., 153
Stewart, C. J., 3, 45
Stewart, D., 140
Stokes, D. E., 126
Stone, V. A., 142, 146–47
Surlin, S. H., 3, 158

Tannenbaum, P. H., 78–80, 111, 120–21
Tarrance, V. L., 3, 146
Tate, E., 81, 105
Taylor, P., 2–4, 27, 33–34, 37–39, 45–46, 48–50, 157–58
Tedin, K. L., 151
Toomb, J. K., 89
Trent, J. S., 108

Udall, M. K., 13
Ullman, W. R., 80–81, 105
United States Senate, 74

Van Gieson, J. V., 56
Veith, K., 142
Verba, S., 151
Verburg, K., 69

Wackman, D., 153, 156
Wade, C., 141, 146
Ward, S., 153, 156
Watson, T., 23
Wattenberg, M. P., 126
Watts, W. A., 146
Weber, S. J., 108
Weisberg, H. F., 127, 130
Whitehead, J., 152
Whiteley, P. F., 126–27, 131
Wicker, T., 34
Williams, D. C., 108
Williams, S. E., 146–47
Witcover, J., 35
Wolfinger, R. E., 126, 153

Yang, J. E., 51, 55
Young, M., 2–4, 7, 157–58
Young, T. J., 81, 105

Ziegler, L. H., 142
Zingale, N. H., 125

Subject Index

Abdnor, James, 29, 32, 35–36, 70, 83, 85–86, 90, 97, 100, 133, 137
Adams, Brock, 32, 51–52
Adams, John Quincy, 5
age and inoculation, 150–51, 159; in South Dakota 1988 Field Study findings, 151–52
Agnew, Spiro, 9
Ailes, Roger, 25, 36, 40, 123
American Association of Political Consultants, 66
Americans for Bush, 122
Andrews, Mark, 29, 32, 37
Aristotle, 73, 157
Ashley, Lud, 17
attack messages, 2–4; backlash effect against, 11–12, 14–15, 158; character-oriented type, 17, 24, 32–34, 57, 89–90; constitutional protection of, 62–65; effectiveness and reason for use, 2–4, 24, 28, 158; importance of credible attack, 20, 54–55; increased use in 1980s, 1, 3–4, 27–28, 84–85, 108–9; issue-oriented type, 16–17, 24–25, 32–34, 55–57; legal remedies against, 62–63; legislative remedy proposals, 63–65; media as referee of, 68–70; multiple issue type, 73; as necessary supple-

ment to positive messages, 20–21, 41; necessity of quick response to, 11, 21, 28, 41, 58; in 1988 presidential campaign, 90; responses to, 10–11, 17–18, 21–22, 25–26, 34–38; retention, 158; role in nomination process, 40–44; in South Dakota, 90; scope, 287–88; use before the New Deal, 5–6; use between 1932 and 1979, 6–12; use by incumbents, 25, 30–32, 50, 54–55; use by independent groups, 13, 15–17, 23–24, 28 voluntary restraint on, 66–68. *See also* inadequacy of defenses against attack messages
Atwater, Lee, 40, 45, 47
AuCoin, Les, 29–30
Awkward, George, 60
Azzolina, Joseph, 57

Baab, Sky, 123
Babbitt, Bruce, 43
Bailey, Douglas, 66
Bailey/Deardorff, 12
Baucus, Max, 26
Bauman, Robert, 17
Bayh, Birch, 16, 18, 70
Bayh, Evan, 56
Beard, Robin, 20

Beckel, Bob, 32
Bernstein, Carl, 69
Bird, Rose, 31, 33, 55
Black, Charlie, 84
Blanchard, Jim, 30
Bond, Kit, 32
Boren, David, 65
Brademas, John, 17
Bradley, Tom, 33
Brandstad, Terry, 30
Breaux, John, 32, 34–35
Brock, Bill, 13
Brown, Jerry, 20
Broyhill, James T., 32
Bryan, Richard, 56
Burdick, Quentin, 52–53
Burlison, Bill, 17
Burns, Conrad, 58
Bush, George, 40–41, 44–50, 86, 90, 108, 120, 122; attack strategy in election, 45–46; public image, 45–47; reluctance to use attack mes,sages, 45; standing in polls, 45, 47
Byrd, Robert, 65

Caddell, Pat, 14
campaign advertising, impact on vote: before 1980, 9; in 1980 presidential election, 14; in 1984 presidential nomination process, 22; in 1988 presidential election, 44–50; in 1988 presidential nomination, 40–44
campaign "spots": "America is Back," 27; "Bear," 23; "Belgian Endive?," 49; "Boston Harbor," 45, 49; "The Butler," 24; "Chauffeur Response," 60; "Cone of Strontium 90," 7–8; "Convention Litter," 8; "Daisy," 7–8; "Dixie," 20; "Doonesbury," 40; "Eisenhower Press Conference," 7; "Going to Work," 51; "He's Like Mike," 56; "Hound Dogs," 25; "Hyundai," 42; "I Remember You," 51; "List," 43; "Little Girl," 51; "Mama," 25–26; "Merely Another Weapon?," 8; "Mildred Ingram," 26; "Morning Again," 22–23; "Morning in America," 27; "Packaging of Bush," 49; "Pinocchio," 25; "Pledge of Allegiance," 45; "Post Office," 12; "Ride With Us, Wyoming," 12; "Sawed-Off Seaboard," 8; "Shame On You," 59; "Social Security," 20; "Straddle," 40; "Talking Cows," 22; "The Two McNultys," 24; "The Wallop Senate Drive," 12
campaign strategies, options, 84
Caperton, Gary, 54
Carey, Hugh, 12
Carter, Jimmy, 9, 14–15, 51
Casey, Bob, 33–34, 37, 68
Center for the Study of Communication, 91
Chappell, Bill, 57
Chavez, Linda, 33
Church, Frank, 16, 18, 70
Citizens for an Informed Electorate, 90, 92
Clark, Dick, 13
Clements, Bill, 33
Cleveland, Grover, 6
Cohen, William, 27
comparative messages, 2, 14, 24, 31, 42, 44, 55
concept spots, 22
congressional elections before 1980, 10–12
congressional elections of 1980, 14–18; in Missouri, 16; in South Dakota, 16
congressional elections of 1982, 19–22; in California, 20; in Missouri, 21; in Montana, 21–22; in New York, 21; in Tennessee, 20
congressional elections of 1984, 23–27; in Arizona, 24–25; in California, 26; in Iowa, 24; in Kentucky, 25; in Maine, 27; in Michigan, 25; in Montana, 26; in New Hampshire, 26; in Texas, 24–26
congressional elections of 1986, 3, 27–38; in Alabama, 37–38; in Arizona, 34; in California, 30–32, 36–37; in Colorado, 30; in Florida, 32, 34; in Georgia, 32; in Idaho, 30; in Louisiana, 34–35, in Maryland, 32–33; in Missouri, 33, in Nevada, 29, 33; in

North Carolina, 32; in North Dakota, 29, 32, 37; in Oregon, 29–30; in Pennsylvania, 29; in South Dakota, 29, 35–36; in Vermont, 35; in Washington, 32; in Wisconsin, 35–36

congressional elections of 1988, 50–51; in California, 52, 55–56, 59 in Connecticut, 56–59; in Delaware, 57–58; in Florida, 56; in Indiana, 56; in Minnesota, 59; in Mississippi, 52, 59–60; in Montana, 58; in Nebraska, 59; in Ne,vada, 52, 56; in New Jersey, 54–55, 57; in New York, 57; in North Dakota, 52–53; in Ohio, 53–54, 59; in Washington, 51–53, in West Virginia, 54; in Wisconsin, 53–54

congruity theory, 78

Conrad, Kent, 32, 37

Corman, Jim, 17

Cranston, Alan, 30–31, 36–37, 54, 84

cultural truisms, 75–76, 80

Culver, John, 16, 18

DMI (Decision Making Information), 10

D'Amato, Alphonse, 17

D'Amours, Norman, 26

Danforth, John, 21, 64

Daschle, Tom, 28–29, 32, 35–36, 43, 83, 85–86, 90, 97, 100, 133, 137

Dawkins, Peter, 54–55, 68

Democratic Congressional Campaign Committee, 18, 28

Democratic Senatorial Campaign Committee, 67

Denton, Jeremiah, 32, 37–38

Deukmejian, George, 33

Dewey, Thomas E., 10

Diamond, Edwin, 14

DioGuardi, Joseph, 57,

direct mail, 84, 86, 99, 159

Doggett, Lloyd, 24–25

Dolan, John T. "Terry," 21

Dole, Robert, 40–41

Douglas, Helen Gahagan, 11

Dowdy, Wayne, 53, 60

Doyle-Dane-Bernbach, 8–9

Dukakis, Michael, 42–50, 83, 86, 90, 108, 120, 122; attacks on Gephardt, 43; failure to respond quickly to attacks, 48–49; lack of clear image, 46–47; reluctance to use attack messages, 42, 44; standing in polls, 45–46

Durenberger, Dave, 59

Duryea, Perry, 12

Eagleton, Tom, 16, 18

education: inoculation and education, 152–53, 159; South Dakota 1988 Field Study findings, 153–56

educational messages, 27

Eisenhower, Dwight D., 6–7, 21

Engeleiter, Susan, 53–54

Evans, Daniel, 51–52

Fair Campaign Practices Commission: operation from 1956 to 1976, 65; revival proposed, 65

Fala speech, 10

Falwell, Jerry, 23

Federal Communication Commission, 63

Federal Trade Commission, 63

Felknor, Bruce, 65

Feltus, Will, 3, 38

Flaherty, Peter, 12

"flip-flop" ads, 9, 31, 43

focus groups, use in campaigns, 45–46

Fonda, Jane, 36, 59, 85

Ford, Gerald R., 9–10

Fowler, Wyche, 32, 37

Gallen, Hugh, 21

Gannett Center Journal, 69

Gans, Curtis, 63–64

Garin, Geoffrey, 66

Garvey, Ed, 35

gender: inoculation and gender, 140–43, 159; South Dakota 1986 Field Study findings, 143–47; South Dakota 1988 Field Study findings, 147–50

generic advertising by political parties: first use, 13; in 1980, 15; in 1982, 19; in 1984, 23; in 1986, 28; in 1988, 51

Gephardt, Richard, 41–44

Glenn, John, 59

Goldwater, Barry, 7–8

Goodman, Bob, 12, 28, 99
Gore, Albert, 43–44
Gorton, Slade, 17, 32, 51–52
Graham, Robert, 32, 34
Gramm, Phil, 24–27, 34, 70
Gravel, Mike, 17
Greeley, Horace, 5
Greenberg, Stanley, 48, 66,
Grove, Lloyd, 68
gubernatorial elections of 1982: Connecti-
　cut, 20–21; New Hampshire, 21
gubernatorial elections of 1984, 23
gubernatorial elections of 1986, 30, 33–
　35, 37; in California, 33; in Colorado,
　35; in Iowa, 30; in Michigan, 30; in
　Pennsylvania, 33–34, 37; in Texas, 33
gubernatorial elections of 1988, 50–51; in
　Indiana, 56; in North Carolina, 55; in
　West Virginia, 51, 54
Guggenheim, Charles, 64

Hance, Kent, 24
Harkin, Tom, 24
Harrison, William H., 5
Hart, Gary, 22, 43
Hart, Peter, 127
Haskell, Floyd, 13
Hawkins, Paula, 32, 34
Hecht, Chic, 52, 56
Helms, Jesse, 24
Heston, Charles, 59
Horton, Willie, 48
Howard, James, 57
Huddleston, Walter Dee, 24, 34
Humphrey, Gordon, 26, 70
Humphrey, Hubert H., 9, 59
Humphrey, Skip, 59
Hunt, James, 24

image transference, 8
inadequacy of attack defenses, 61–62;
　candidate defenses, 70–71; Fair Cam-
　paign Practices Commission, 65; legal
　remedies, 62–63; media as referee, 68–
　70; participant interest, 68–70; profes-
　sional code of ethics, 66; proposed leg-
　islative responses, 63–65; voluntary

agreements by parties and/or candi-
　dates, 67–68
independent spending, 28
Index of Contingency, 91
Innocenzi, Jim, 83–84
inoculation message strategy: biological
　analogy, 74–75, 81; combined ap-
　proach and resistance, 78, 84–85; defi-
　nition and description, 74–75, 158–59;
　early research findings, 76–77; efficacy
　of, 83, 86, 159–60; extending the do-
　main, 80–82; future research needs,
　160; individual differences, 139–40;
　other findings, 79–80; political attack
　message application, 82–97; postrefuta-
　tion, 79; preemptive refutation, 75,
　83–84; prerefutation, 79, 84; pretreat-
　ment decay, 79–80; refutation differ-
　ent, 78–79, 90–91; refutation the same,
　78–79, 90–91; reinforcement, 78–80,
　91; role of bolstering, 75–76, 84; role
　of motivation, 75–76, 84; role of
　threat, 75–76, 84, 90–91; South Da-
　kota 1986 Field Study findings, 108–
　23; South Dakota 1988 Field Study
　findings, 100–108; superiority of refu-
　tational as opposed to supportive ap-
　proach, 78, 81. *See also* age;
　education; gender; party identification
Inouye, Daniel, 64
issues in campaigns: age, 52–53; Agnew,
　Spiro, 9; attendance at congressional
　votes, 25, 34–35, 37; Baker, Bobby,
　8; Boston Harbor, 45–46, big business,
　7, 24; Bird, Rose, 31, 33, 55; cam-
　paign contributions, 33; corruption, 55,
　56; cost of living adjustments, 52;
　crime, 30, 47, 56; death penalty, 31,
　45–46, 55; defense, 7, 9, 14, 46; dis-
　tance from constituents, 16, 24–25, 31,
　33–34, 36–37; economic vulnerability,
　47, 52; economy, 15, 19–10, 27, 34–
　35, 43–44, 52; energy shortages, 15;
　environment, 33, 51–52, 55, 57–58;
　Estes, Billy Sol, 8; farm policy, 7, 28–
　29, 35–36, 43; Fonda, Jane, 36, 59,
　85; foreign trade, 42; government

spending, 12, 26, 29, 35, 56, 60; homeless, 52; Horton, Willie, 48; INF Treaty, 42; Iran, 41; Iran-Contra, 49; liberalism, 4, 11, 17, 24–25, 32–33, 52; Marcos, Ferdinand, 49; morality, 8; Nixon, Richard M., 7, 9; Noriega, Manuel, 49; nuclear weapons, 7–8, 27, 31; Panama Canal Treaty, 17; personal conduct, 9, 17, 33–34, 35, 52; personal effectiveness, 30, 33–34, 37, 41, 43; personality, 53, 58; Pledge of Allegiance, 45–46; prison furlough program, 45–46; race, 14; Reagan, Ronald, 25, 29; Social Security, 19–20, 25–26, 32, 36–37, 52; taxes, 30, 33, 35, 43, 46; terrorism, 31; toxic wastes, 31, 33; wealth, 53; welfare, 9

Jackson, Andrew, 5
Jackson, Jesse, 43–44, 47
Javits, Jacob, 17
Jefferson, Thomas, 5
Jenrette, John, 17
Jepsen, Roger, 24
Johnson, Harold "Bizz," 17
Johnson, Lyndon B., 7–8
Jordan, Bob, 55

Karnes, David, 59
Kasten, Robert, 35
Kefauver, Estes, 7
Kemp, Jack, 40
Kennedy, John F., 7
Kerrey, Robert, 59
Kimball, Richard, 33
Kirk, Paul, 67
Koch, Ed, 44
Kohl, Herbert, 53–54
Kolbe, Jim, 24
Korean War study, 74
Kramer, Ken, 30, 32

Lautenberg, Frank R., 1, 4, 54–55, 68, 84
Leach, "Buddy," 17
Leahy, Pat, 29, 35
Levin, Carl, 25
Lieberman, Joseph I., 56–59

Lincoln, Abraham, 6
Longworth, Alice Roosevelt, 1
Lott, Trent, 52, 60
Lousma, Jack, 25
Lowry, Mike, 51–52
Lucas, William, 30

McCain, John, 33, 64–65
McCarthy, Leo, 55–56, 59
McConnell, Mitch, 24, 34, 64
McGee, Gale, 12
McGovern, George, 9, 16, 18, 70, 85
McIntyre, Tom, 13
Mack, Connie, 56
McKay, Buddy, 56
McMillan, Bob, 57
McNulty, Jim, 24–25
Magnuson, Warren, 16–17
Mahe, Eddie, 4
Manion, Daniel, nomination of, 32
Marcantonio, Vito, 11
Market Opinion Research, 3, 38
Martin, Jim, 55
Maslin, Paul, 4, 42
mass media influence, limited effects view, 9, 74
Mattingly, Mack, 17, 32, 37
Melcher, John, 21–22, 58, 70
Mellman, Mark, 3, 54
messenger strategies, types of: one-sided, 73; two-sided, 73–74, 81
Metzenbaum, Howard, 53–54, 59, 69
Mikulski, Barbara, 32–33, 36
Moe, Richard, 39, 49
Mondale, Walter, 14, 22–23
Moore, Arch, 51, 54
Moore, Henson, 34–35
Moral Majority, 23
Moyers, Bill, 6–7
Moynihan, Daniel P., 21, 57
Murphy, John, 17
Mutz, John, 56

National Conservative PAC, 15–16, 18, 23–24, 28, 38
National Republican Congressional Committee, 13

National Republican Senatorial Commit-
tee, 67
negative spot, first use on television, 7
Nelson, Gaylord, 16
Nickles, Don, 29
Nixon, Richard M., 7, 9–11

O'Leary, Bradley, 66
O'Neill, Thomas P. "Tip," 16, 27
O'Neill, William, 20–21

Pallone, Frank, 57
Panetta, Leon, 26
party identification: influence on the vote,
125–27, 132; inoculation and party
identification, 127–28, 159; operationalization of, 128; South Dakota 1986
Field Study findings, 128–130, 132–
35; South Dakota 1988 Field Study
findings, 130–32, 134–37
Pepper, Claude, 11
persuasion: as facilitator of change, 73–
74; importance in political campaigns,
160; objects of, 83–84; resistance to,
73–74, 157, 160 political messages,
types of, 2 polls: ABC News/Washing-
ton Post exit polls, 117, 118, 123,
133, 137n; Gallup, 45; Los Angeles
Times California Exit Poll, 31; New
York Times/CBS News, 47, 132
preemption messages, 19, 26–27, 29–30,
51–54, 71, 75, 83–84, 158–59
presidential elections before 1980, 6–10
presidential election of 1980, 14–15
presidential election of 1984, 22–23
presidential election of 1988: electoral
campaign, 44–50; issue definition by
Bush campaign, 46; nomination process, 40–44

Reagan, Ronald, 10, 14, 23
Reeves, Rosser, 6–7
refutation, post-hoc, 84
Reid, Harry, 29–33
Republican National Committee, 15
response messages, 2, 10, 17–18, 21–22,
25–26, 41, 57–60; limits on, 70
Robertson, Pat, 40–41

Rome, Lewis, 20
Romer, Ray, 35
Roosevelt, Franklin D., 10
Roth, William, 57
Rudman, Warren, 64

St. Germain, Fernand, 57
Sanford, Terry, 32
Santini, Jim, 33
Sasser, Jim, 20
Schneiders, Greg, 14
Schwartz, Tony, 7, 9
Scranton, William, III, 33–34, 37, 59, 68
selective exposure, 75, 80
semantic differential items, 88–89
Shelby, Richard, 32, 37
Simon, Paul, 42–43
Sipple, Don, 68
Smathers, George A., 11
Smith, Al, 6
Snelling, Dick, 35
source credibility, 89
South Dakota Field Study, 1986: dependent variables, 88–89; description of,
85–86, 99; design and data analysis,
86–87; findings, 95–97, 100–108; in-
dependent variables, 87–88; message
construction, 89–91; procedure, 91–94;
and viability of inoculation, 100–108
South Dakota Field Study, 1988: descrip-
tion of, 85–86, 99; dependent varia-
bles, 88–89; design and data analysis,
86–87; findings, 97, 109–23; indepen-
dent variables, 87–88; message con-
struction, 89–91; procedure, 93–94;
and viability of inoculation, 108–23
Specter, Arlen, 29
Squier, Robert, 13, 68–69
Stevenson, Adlai, 7, 21
Stone, Richard, 17
Stone, Roger, 46
Strickland, Ted, 35
Strinder, Earl, 53
Struble, Karl, 28
Sununu, John, 21, 40
Swindall, Pat, 57
Symms, Steve, 30

Talmadge, Herman, 16–17
Teeter, Robert, 15, 37, 59
Thompson, Frank, 17
Thornburgh, Richard L., 12
Threlkeld, Richard, 68
total word counts, 91

Udall, Morris K., 13
Ullman, Al, 17

Van Buren, Martin, 5
Voinovich, George V., 54, 59, 69

Wallop, Malcolm, 12
Washington, George, 5

Weicker, Lowell, 56–59
White, Kevin, 26
White, Mark, 33
Wicker, Tom, 34
Wilson, Pete, 20, 52, 55–56, 59
Wirth, Tim, 30, 32
Wirthlin, Richard, 10, 39–40, 49–50, 68
Wolff, Lester, 17
Woo, S. B., 58
Woods, Harriet, 21
Woodward, Bob, 69
Wright, Jim, 67

Zschau, Ed, 31, 36–37

ABOUT THE AUTHORS

MICHAEL PFAU is Professor and Chair of the Department of Speech Communication at Augustana College, Sioux Falls, S. Dak. His academic interests focus on argument and on the broad area of social influence, with particular emphasis on political communication. He earned a B.A. and M.A. from the University of New Hampshire and a Ph.D. from the University of Arizona, where he studied social influence under the direction of Michael Burgoon. He has been actively involved in research on political argument and persuasion for nearly a decade. He has published more than thirty chapters and articles, appearing in such journals as: *Argumentation and Advocacy, Communication Education, Communication Monographs, Communication Reports, Communication Research, Health Communication, Human Communication Research, Journal of Broadcasting & Electronic Media, The Western Political Quarterly*, and others. He authored, along with David Thomas and Walter Ulrich, *Debate and Argument: A Systems Approach to Advocacy* (1987).

HENRY C. KENSKI is an Associate Professor holding joint appointments in the Communication and Political Science Departments at the University of Arizona. He earned a B.A. at the University of Arizona and a Ph.D. at Georgetown University. A former American Political Science Association Congressional Fellow (1975–1976), he is the author of *Saving the Hidden Treasure: The Evolution of Groundwater Policy*, as well as various articles and book chapters on public opinion, campaigns and elections, Congress, the presidency, natural resources policy, and economic policy. His work has been published in the *Journal of Politics, American Politics Quarterly, Public Opinion Quarterly, Social Science*

Quarterly, as well as in various other journals and books. A former member of the editorial board of the *American Political Science Review* (1976–1981), he has also served as book review editor of the *Western Political Quarterly* (1983–1988), and is currently a member of the editorial board of *Teaching Political Science* (1983–present). His current research interests focus on political communication, particularly campaigns and elections, as well as political leadership and communication. In the applied realm, he has been a partner with his wife, Margaret Corgan Kenski, in their research firm, Arizona Opinion and Political Research. They have been involved in more than 100 political campaigns since 1979, including work as campaign polling consultants for U.S. Representatives Morris K. Udall, Jim Kolbe, and Jon Kyl of Arizona.

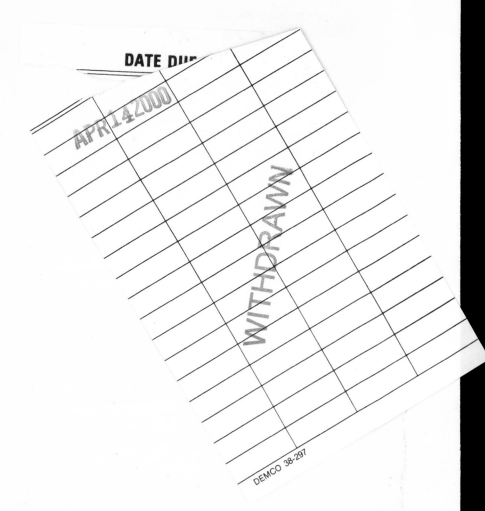

DATE DUE

APR 14 2000

WITHDRAWN